Re-Envisioning Past Musical Cultures

Chicago Studies in Ethnomusicology
Edited by Philip V. Bohlman and Bruno Nettl

Re-Envisioning Past Musical Cultures

Ethnomusicology in the Study of Gregorian Chant

Peter Jeffery

The University of Chicago Press
Chicago and London

Peter Jeffery is associate professor of music at the University of Delaware in Newark. On leave with a John D. and Catherine T. MacArthur Fellowship, he is currently a visiting scholar at the Center for Literary and Cultural Studies at Harvard University.

THE UNIVERSITY OF CHICAGO PRESS, CHICAGO 60637
THE UNIVERSITY OF CHICAGO PRESS, LTD., LONDON

Printed in Mexico
00 99 98 97 96 95 94 93 92   5 4 3 2 1
ISBN (cloth): 0-226-39579-0

Library of Congress Cataloging-in-Publication Data
Jeffery, Peter.
Re-envisioning past musical cultures : ethnomusicology in the study of Gregorian chant / Peter Jeffery.
p.   cm.—(Chicago studies in ethnomusicology)
Includes bibliographical references (p.   ) and index.
1. Chants (Plain, Gregorian, etc.)—History and criticism.
2. Ethnomusicology. I. Title. II. Series.
ML3082.J34   1992   91-34137
782.32′22—dc20   CIP
MN

This publication has been supported by a grant from the Andrew W. Mellon Foundation.

à MICHEL HUGLO
en témoignage d'amitié

"Unde oro, [bone amice,] quicquid in eo, temeritate mea faciente ac stulta praesumptione, inrationabiliter scriptum est, per vestram prudentiam correptionem habere mereatur, et nos indulgentiam apud omnes doctores. Scripsi enim quidquid mihi videbatur iustum et honestum. . . . Scripsi, ut nostis, quos illos arbitrabar imitari qui in choro stant, et cantant intrante episcopo in ecclesiam, ut postea in sequenti opere demonstrabitur . . . ."

Amalarius (Hanssens 1948–50/1 : 230)

Contents

Acknowledgments

Some of the material in this book was presented previously in two papers: "Ethnomusicological Issues in Research on Gregorian Chant," read at the Annual Meeting of the Society for Ethnomusicology in Vancouver (1985), and "What Do We Mean by Oral Transmission?" read at the Special Colloquium on Transmission in Medieval Chant organized by Helmut Hucke at Rutgers University (1986). All of us who read papers at the Rutgers University meeting agreed to dedicate the resulting publications to Professor Michel Huglo, and this I have gladly done.

Special thanks are due to the many people who read early versions of this book for me and offered their advice, and to the John D. and Catherine T. MacArthur Foundation, without whose generous support it might never have been finished. I appreciate the interest that Bruno Nettl showed in this essay from early on.

After the manuscript of this book was essentially completed, the international community of musicologists was saddened by the news that Professor Hucke had experienced a serious decline in health. I join his many other colleagues in extending to him and his family my most sincere hopes and prayers.

Introduction

Gregorian chant, the best known of the many medieval dialects of Christian liturgical monophony, has often been depicted as a kind of crossroads, where ethnomusicology and the history of European art music may "meet." To many musicians trained in the Western classical tradition, the chant appears to represent all that is oldest, most primitive and elemental in music—closely resembling the popular conception of "folk music" as the age-old, ingenuous song of unlettered simple folk, springing spontaneously from the common heart of the human race.[1] Writers of a more scholarly bent have sometimes appealed to Gregorian chant to support their own broad theories about the history of music,[2] and many have found in the chant a convenient source of terms and concepts that can be used metaphorically to describe musical phenomena of other cultures. Thus countless descriptions of non-Western and Western folk scales have borrowed terminology from Gregorian modal theory (Powers 1980a:418–47, 448–50). Medieval methods of chanting the psalms have supplied such terms as "antiphony" and "responsorial," as well as models for describing the interrelations of texts and melodies.[3] The notation of at least one Asian

1. A typical expression of this view is the very uninformed book of G. B. Chambers (1956). The introductory tirade by Ralph Vaughan Williams (p. v) complains that "bat-eyed musicologists . . . cannot altogether ignore the connection between plain song and folk song, but they have put the cart before the horse and imagine that the music of the people is the debased descendant of that of the church. In their opinion the written word was impeccable and oral tradition fallible. But in truth the clerk may make errors in his copying while the memory of the unlettered countryman is sure."

2. For example Brăiloiu 1984:252: "It is in the relationship between Gregorian chant and Protestant chorale that one may best follow the road of the pentatonic towards the heptatonic, by the progressive insertion of the *pyens*." See also Sachs 1962:70, 88.

3. Sachs 1962:70, 126–9; Kaufman 1975:8; Chen 1983; Porter 1985:613–4.

musical tradition (Tibetan Buddhist chant) has been described as consisting of "neumes."[4]

But the assumptions underlying the making of such parallels need to be subjected to more critical examination. Even aside from the issue of whether or when the music of one culture can ever be described in the technical language of another, the analogies made to chant are often especially questionable for other reasons. Frequently they reflect an inadequate or outdated understanding of the chant—one that chant historians would find discomfiting. Sometimes they assume historical relationships between Gregorian chant and the musical traditions of the Synagogue and the Eastern Christian churches that are in fact very problematic (Jeffery 1986a, 1987, 1989a, forthcoming; Jeffery and Fassler forthcoming). But more than this, such cross-cultural analogies have been hampered by the absence of ethnomusicological perspectives from medieval chant scholarship. Any attempt to liken some feature of Asian or African music to Gregorian chant is likely to draw a merely superficial parallel, because the social, cultural, and anthropological contexts of the chant are so poorly understood.

It is of course understandable that the critical study of medieval chant has been left to historical musicologists, because highly specialized skills are needed to investigate the ancient manuscripts and notations, the complex history of ancient Latin and Greek theoretical concepts, and the intricacies of the liturgy and its theological rationale. But because ethnomusicologists have shied away from chant research, many very basic questions that they routinely raise about every musical tradition have gone virtually unasked. As a result, entire areas of chant study that ethnomusicologists would find especially interesting and useful are very poorly researched.

Ethnomusicological studies of medieval chant are needed, then, not only because they would put on a sounder footing the use of the chant in

4. Kaufman 1967:360–3. Kaufman's view that the Tibetan neumes may be historically derived from the notations of the chant used by Nestorian Christians is quite unlikely, for these Christians (whose liturgical tradition is more commonly designated East Syrian or Chaldean) are not known to have used such neumes. Their chant is transmitted orally today (Ross 1979), but it is possible that some of their medieval punctuation systems (Segal 1953:18–118) may have helped to serve the cantillation of the texts. Plates CLXXI–CLXXII in Hatch 1946 depict an East Syrian manuscript with large round dots over certain letters that have no known grammatical meaning; thus they may perhaps have had a musical purpose, but they do not resemble the neumes of Tibetan chant. The theory that Tibetan neumes derive from Nestorian notation also appears unlikely from the perspective of the Tibetan sources themselves, according to Ellingson 1986. On the activity of medieval Nestorian missionaries in Tibet, see Dauvillier 1983.

cross-cultural comparisons, but because they would reveal much that has been overlooked about this important and very old musical tradition—a musical tradition that, moreover, has been studied and performed throughout much of the world, in modern times on every inhabited continent. Investigation of medieval chant would also help ethnomusicology as a whole to develop its own historical methodologies, something that increasing numbers of ethnomusicologists have been calling for.[5]

Of course, the development of ethnomusicological perspectives on medieval chant would be of great benefit to historical musicology also. The most obvious indicator of this is the fact that, for the past two decades, one of the most debated subjects in chant study has been the problem of oral and written transmission, a subject that was once regarded as the peculiar province of ethnomusicology. The fact that most historical musicologists lack experience and training in this subject is a major reason that the debate remains unresolved, and it is no wonder that several of them have appealed to ethnomusicologists to get involved in the discussion (Treitler 1984b: 159, 1988: 575; Kenneth Levy quoted in Jeffery 1988a: 132). But chant scholars have sometimes conceived much too narrowly their need for ethnomusicological assistance, as if they believe that the transmission issue is the only area of their field to which ethnomusicologists could contribute. In fact a truly ethnomusicological investigation of medieval chant would cover every aspect of the subject, from the broadest cultural context to the narrowest melodic analysis, with the same thoroughness that ethnomusicologists apply to any other musical tradition. For the problem of oral and written transmission is not a narrow topic that can be split off from the rest of a musical tradition and studied independently; by its very nature it touches on virtually every other aspect of the subject.

Thus an ethnomusicological investigation of medieval chant would be an enormous boon to both fields of musical scholarship, quite apart from the specific contribution it would make to our understanding of the chant. It would help each discipline come to terms with problems it has largely ignored in the past, enriching both in ways that cannot now be entirely foreseen. The purpose of the present essay is to identify some of the major areas of chant study where greater cooperation between historians and ethnomusicologists is badly needed, to suggest some of the ways

5. See, for instance, Suppan and Mauerhofer 1978; "Symposium I: Geschichtlichkeit in aussereuropäischer und europäischer Musik," in Mahling and Wiesmann, eds. 1984: 1–75; Elschek 1985; Cavanagh 1987; Rice et al. 1987; Shelemay and Jeffery forthcoming.

that joint approaches might be formulated, and to hint at the benefits of such cooperation that may be expected to accrue to both.

Some of those who read this manuscript before it was published found my suggestions unsettling, even disturbing. Clearly, what I am proposing would force the study of chant to grow well outside of its present boundaries as a subcategory of medieval musicology, into a much wider field that will interact increasingly with other disciplines: not only with ethnomusicology, but with modern liturgiology, with medieval and ecclesiastical history, and with the study of musical cognition. But I see no alternative, and I take comfort in the fact that my views are not really new: the adoption of ethnomusicological perspectives in medieval musicology has been advocated for at least thirty years,[6] and such perspectives have consistently been a regular feature of Eastern European scholarship, where folk and classical music have always been regarded as equally worthy of study.[7] In general medieval studies, also, it is now possible to say that "after a divorce lasting more than two centuries, historians and ethnologists are showing signs of converging once again . . . . Looking at the societies he studies with the eyes of an ethnologist, the historian better understands what may be called the 'liturgical' aspect of historical society. . . . Here, more than ever, collaboration between the two attitudes, historical and ethnological, is needed."[8]

There is nothing wrong with the traditional methods of chant study—on the contrary, they are all essential and must continue. But in the past they have been pursued at times in overly narrow ways that caused us to overlook far too much, both in the area of transmission and in many other areas. "The parameters of musical transmission extend to phenomena physiological and psychological, acoustical and anthropological, as well as to matters musical that we conventionally consider." It is necessary "to interrelate [the] seminal contributions of various disciplines to the study of transmission, with the aim of broadening what has been, up to now, a too often culturally-biased perspective upon a topic too narrowly defined" (Kleeman 1985–6:22). In short, the transmission issue is only a catalyst; were it pursued aggressively, using the full range of available

6. Sachs 1960; Harrison 1972:327. But see also the caveats in Reckow 1984.

7. See, for instance, Bardos 1975; Dobszay 1971, 1988, 1990; Dobszay and Szendrei, eds. 1988; Kartsovnik, ed. 1988, 1989; Kouyumdjieva and Todorov, eds. 1989; and the many writings of Rajeczky.

8. Le Goff 1980:227–8. See also Jennings 1987; Sahlins 1981.

approaches from both historical musicology and ethnomusicology, most of the other areas within our field of chant studies would begin to take on a new and very different mien.

In what follows, I will look first at the transmission problem itself, and at some of the most important hypotheses that chant scholars have proposed for solving it. Then, expanding outward, I will look at what could happen if some typical ethnomusicological concerns were broadly applied to chant studies. Finally, I will call attention to some well-known characteristics of medieval chant that I think may be closely linked with processes of oral transmission, and that therefore need to be re-examined from new ethnomusicological perspectives. Rather than drawing firm conclusions, I will sum up by saying that the way to develop an ethnomusicological approach to music history is to learn to see the past less as a precursor of our own period and more as a distinct culture, existing of itself and intelligible on its own terms.

The Problem

At one time, as the late antique world was turning into the early medieval one, the Christian communities of Europe, north Africa, and the Middle East worshipped using a great variety of liturgical chant dialects. Between about the fourth and the eighth centuries A.D., each major city or region seems to have developed its own local repertory of texts and melodies, although some common material circulated widely (with variations), and a few texts were known almost everywhere. Gradually, internal and external pressures provoked movements toward uniformity, and the traditions of the more influential centers began to replace or merge with some of the weaker ones. In the Greek-speaking East, the increasing centralization of the Byzantine Empire around its capital at Constantinople was strengthened by the fall of the other Greek centers (Alexandria, Antioch, Jerusalem) to Islamic conquerors, and by missionary expansion into the Slavic world. What gradually developed as a result was the Byzantine rite as we know it today, a compromise mainly between the formerly local usages of Constantinople and of the Greek-speaking monasteries in Palestine.[1] In the process the chant texts were written down, and collected into books that were repeatedly revised; the liturgical regulations of important churches were assembled into rule books (*typika*) and widely adopted by churches elsewhere; a notation was developed to record the melodies; theoretical concepts—notably the system of the eight church modes—were devised with the help of terminology from the writings of classical antiquity, and a new literature of music theory began to be written for the purpose of training singers. Oriental Christian communities that used languages other than Greek (Syriac, Armenian, Georgian, Coptic, Nubian, Ethiopic) experienced similar movements toward standardization within their own

1. A brief account of the process is Arranz 1976. See also Jeffery forthcoming.

linguistic areas, but usually at a slower pace and on a smaller scale, and with continuing tension between the authority of their own centers and the strong gravitational pulls of Constantinople and Rome (Triacca, ed. 1976; Vellian, ed. 1975). While all of them eventually collected their chants and liturgical regulations into written books, most did not develop music notation, and only some adopted the theory of the eight Byzantine modes.

In the Latin-speaking West, the great cities and monasteries of Northwest Africa, Italy, Dalmatia (Yugoslavia), Gaul (France), Ireland, and Spain all were home to flourishing local chant traditions.[2] But by about the eighth century they had begun to lose ground to the more prestigious liturgy and chant associated with the city of Rome. The central importance of Rome increased as missionaries pressed the boundaries of the Latin world outward into the lands of the Anglo-Saxons, the Germans and the Scandinavians, the Balts and the West Slavs, and the Finns and the Magyars, establishing Roman-derived liturgies among each of these peoples. As in the East, the increasingly irresistible processes of standardization and centralization led to, and were furthered by, the emergence of written collections of chant texts, the rise of liturgical rule books (*ordines* or *ordinalia*), the invention of music notation, and the (at least partial) adoption of Greek music theory and the Greek modal system.[3]

2. The Christians who celebrated the African liturgy, concentrated around ancient Carthage (modern Libya and Tunisia) were overwhelmed by Islam, and their chant tradition did not survive long enough to be written down with notation, though a few textual fragments are extant. There are other traditions for which notated manuscripts survive and are known to chant scholars: In northern Italy, Ambrosian chant was used in Milan, and there are also traces of local traditions at Ravenna and Aquileia-Grado. The local tradition of the city of Rome is usually called Old Roman chant, though some scholars are compelled by their theories of chant origins to give it other names. Southern Italy was the home of Beneventan chant, also used in Dalmatia, and there are traces of a Naples-Capua tradition also. Gallican chant is the catch-all term for what was once a broad variety of local traditions in France, all of which are only poorly preserved. Gallican chant cannot be fully distinguished from what has been called Celtic chant, preserved in a few unnotated manuscripts from Irish monasteries founded on the continent. The Mozarabic chant of Spain was, like Gallican chant, a network of interrelated local traditions, but it is much better preserved than its French counterpart. In general, the longer or the more successfully a local tradition resisted assimilation into the Roman rite with its Gregorian chant, the better preserved it is today. A recent book on Beneventan chant (Kelly 1989) can serve as an introduction to the study of the non-Gregorian Latin chant traditions. The historical interrelationships of all these traditions will be considered at length in my book in progress, working title *Prophecy Mixed with Melody: From Early Christian Psalmody to Gregorian Chant,* which investigates the processes by which the medieval chant repertory was formed.

3. The historical witnesses to this process are described in detail in Vogel 1986. See also Jeffery 1988b, forthcoming.

It was because of its alleged Roman provenance that the new international Latin chant repertory, called "Gregorian chant" after Pope Gregory the Great (reigned 590–604), was almost universally adopted in the West. But the state of the surviving historical sources makes it impossible for scholars to accept its reputed Roman origin without reservation. The melodies seem not to have been written down in musical notation before the tenth century, or perhaps the ninth.[4] How closely, then, could they have been connected with the activity of the historical Gregory two or three centuries earlier, particularly when his authentic literary writings reveal little concern for music? And these earliest notated manuscripts come from the Frankish Kingdom or Carolingian Empire north of the Alps, while the earliest notated manuscripts from Rome itself (which date from the eleventh through thirteenth centuries) contain a somehow related but superficially very different corpus of melodies, attached to what is almost the same repertory of texts. In what way, therefore, could the "Gregorian" melodies be said to represent the tradition of Rome? These and related questions have for a long time formed one of the most fiercely debated areas of medieval musicology; they seem to take us right to the heart of the issue of chant origins.[5] The inability to agree on a quick and simple answer has forced chant scholars to delve more deeply into the entire complex of processes by which the loosely related local traditions—oral, varied, provincial—were replaced by the one ecumenical repertory in the West—written, relatively uniform, and "catholic" or universal because it was considered "Roman." For it was at this historical turning point, amid the interaction of so many powerful historical forces, that Gregorian chant as we know it began.

For many chant scholars, then, there could be no more urgent or interesting problem than the attempt to reconstruct fully what happened at the time of this historic watershed. What were the melodies of the old local repertories like, and how were they created, taught, and performed? How were the texts and melodies collected and organized into the great annual cycle of the liturgical year? How were the principles of performance practice worked out and codified? How did the eight-mode system origi-

4. For recent opinions on the date, see Levy 1987a, 1987b, 1988; Treitler 1984b, 1988; Hucke 1988a:326–30; McKinnon 1990:94–6, 99–100.

5. Two summaries of the debate through the 1970s are Hucke 1980a; Hughes 1980:89–94, 276–7. For some recent views on Gregory's personal role, see H. Schmidt 1980; Cusack 1983:164–5; Fontaine et al., eds. 1986:637–9; Jeffery forthcoming.

nate and become so widely adopted? How did the neumatic notation come to be invented and what were the earliest meanings of its signs?

Unfortunately, these and other such questions will not be answered easily. Our very sources of information—liturgical books, ordinals, notation—were themselves products of the move toward uniformity and standardization, and most of them date from the period after this historic corner had already been turned. The melodies preserved in our earliest sources are already melodies that have begun to be expressed by means of written notation; they are no longer quite the purely oral melodies that prevailed at an earlier time. Those repertories that adopted the eight modes have already done so in our earliest sources, so that we no longer have any melodies in a "pure" state from the period before the adoption. And the earliest chant books and rule books we have are already completed works, not primitive or transitional collections drawn up during the period when the contents were still fluid. As a result, almost every attempt to divine what actually happened at this historic watershed is fraught with extraordinary methodological problems. How can we possibly look "beneath" or "behind" our earliest written documents, to envision hypothetically what the state of affairs was before they were written? The difficulties were aptly summed up by Oliver Strunk, who wrestled with them repeatedly throughout his career, and whose many published discussions of the problem are models of cautious restraint and sound judgment. "[This is,] in short, . . . the recurrent central problem of early Christian music. How can we control the evidence of our earliest manuscripts? To what extent does their melodic tradition reflect that of earlier times? . . . Throughout the early Christian world an impenetrable barrier of oral tradition lies between all but the latest melodies and the earliest attempts to reduce them to writing" (1955:85; 1977:60–1).

If this "impenetrable barrier" is ever to be breached, it will only be possible to do it hypothetically, for there is no way to recover melodies that were never recorded because they circulated before there was musical writing. The hypothesis would have to include detailed theories about the nature of the oral tradition, the ways it operated to shape the melodies up to the time they began to be written down, and the interaction of oral and written processes during the period (however long it was) that the tradition metamorphosed from an exclusively oral to a predominantly written one, leaving behind the notated manuscripts that are now our chief source of information.

Forming such a hypothesis would not be difficult—if oral tradition were a relatively simple phenomenon that musical scholars had studied for a long time and knew a great deal about. If that were so, one could determine the role of oral tradition in the earliest period of chant history simply by turning to the extensive body of available data about the ways oral traditions function, and then applying whichever facts seemed relevant to the interpretation of the earliest written chant melodies. But of course there is no such body of accumulated, indisputable facts about oral tradition. Oral tradition is something that most literate Westerners know scarcely anything about, and that historical scholars in all disciplines have begun only relatively recently to give serious attention to. The many careless and contradictory ways in which expressions like "oral tradition" have been used in modern writing should be warning enough that we are not yet working with an agreed-upon theoretical model, with all the details pinned down by empirical research. In practice, the phrase "oral tradition" is often used as a catchall term for all sorts of phenomena, which have manifested themselves in countless ways across the entire spectrum of human history and culture. Almost every variety of memorization, improvisation, variation, recomposition, teaching, learning, performance without written notation, adaptation of pre-existent material, use of general-purpose models, persistence of features deemed to be ancient—all these and more have at some time or other been called "oral tradition" by one author or another: and each of them will be again in the future. How are we to know which of these many alleged varieties of oral tradition were really active in early medieval Europe, and what influence each would have had on the written melodies that actually survive?

The most serious and extensive attempt to develop a responsible hypothesis regarding oral transmission in medieval chant has been the work of Leo Treitler and Helmut Hucke, who deserve much credit for bringing the matter to the forefront of our attention and for insisting on its importance. Consideration of their views is therefore essential to any discussion of the problem. This will be the subject of the next two chapters.

2

The New Historical View of Chant Transmission

A. The Theories of Treitler and Hucke

Though it has been recognized for a long time that oral transmission processes must have had some role in the formation of the chant repertories, the credit for initiating the contemporary scholarly debate belongs to Leo Treitler, followed by Helmut Hucke, whose proposals one of them has called "a New Historical View of Gregorian Chant" (Hucke 1980d), and the other has likened to a "scientific revolution" (Treitler 1982a:46).[1] The two chant scholars ask their colleagues to give "serious attention . . . to the fact that the Gregorian Chant tradition was, in its early centuries, an oral performance practice" (Treitler 1982b:237). This oral performance practice, they maintain, formed the melodies in particular ways that would have been different had they been created through exclusively non-oral processes. As a result, the oral practice can be said to have "left its mark" on the melodies that survive, so that they still reveal traces of their oral origin even though they are preserved only in written form. "The generative systems of the oral tradition . . . informed the music that was produced," and therefore "the oral origin [of the melodies] is visible through the written surfaces that are its progeny. . . ." Even after the widespread acceptance of writing, some of the processes of oral tradition continued to be active, so that it was "never completely out of the picture as a factor in musical practice" (Treitler 1988:575, 574, 575). Thus the key to understanding the chant melodies is the recognition that "the way the music has turned out is a consequence of the special constraints of an oral tradition,

1. It is, of course, an oversimplification to imply that these two scholars hold identical views. Nevertheless each has affirmed broad agreement with the other (Treitler 1981b:474 n. 5; Hucke 1980d:450). Thus it is not entirely inappropriate to use the phrase "New Historical View" as a convenient label for the ideas that both of them share. I use this label in the hope that it will serve as a constant reminder that my remarks are addressed *non ad homines, sed ad quaestionem.*

hence . . . learning to understand the music and learning to understand how it was transmitted is a single task" (Treitler 1974: 334).

The reluctance of some scholars to embrace the "New Historical View" has been interpreted by Treitler as "striking . . . resistance to a serious confrontation with the reality that at some time in history, no matter how far back one wants to push it, the Western musical heritage goes back to an oral tradition" (1988: 575). But in fact this reality is accepted by almost everyone. The singing that went on in Christian churches before the invention of notation could not have been anything but an oral tradition. The real question is not whether this oral tradition once existed (it did), but how the melodies that survive in written sources are related to it, and therefore how much they can still reveal to us about what it was like. Are the written melodies straightforward transcriptions of the oral melodies? If so, do they record a single performance by one particular individual, or something more complex? Or have the melodies suffered revisions, adaptations, or other changes, so that they now survive in a form that never existed during the period of pure oral transmission? If this latter possibility is the correct one, at what stage(s) during the process of writing down (whenever that took place) were these changes made, and for what reasons? Unfortunately, attempts to resolve this question are impeded by numerous methodological issues that must be resolved first. How do we determine whether or not any particular melodic feature is a vestige of the oral tradition? How are such features to be (first) recognized and (then) interpreted? And how do we confirm that our interpretations are correct, or at least more plausible and appropriate for the historical period than any other hypotheses? Merely acknowledging that the chant repertories began as oral traditions cannot in itself commit anyone to accept any particular opinion about the ways these oral processes may have operated, or the roles these processes may have played in shaping the melodies we actually have. There are, after all, very good reasons to be initially skeptical of every scholarly attempt to describe an oral tradition that was at its height a millennium ago, and that has scarcely existed for centuries.

The real challenge of Treitler's and Hucke's writings, then, is not that they proclaim the oral origin of the chant melodies, but that they ask us to accept a particular hypothetical reconstruction of what the oral tradition was like, and of how it was gradually transformed into a written tradition. In my opinion their hypotheses deserve more careful dissection and discussion than they have so far received, and this would be true even if their views did not amount to the most broadly conceived and internally consistent model in the current musicological docket. It is therefore very important to give Treitler's and Hucke's proposals the "serious attention" they have requested, to be sure that one has understood exactly what they are saying. What follows is my own attempt to describe the processes of chant transmission as envisioned in Treitler's and Hucke's published writings.

B. Oral and Written Transmission as Conceived in the New Historical View

In his first publication on the subject, entitled "Homer and Gregory" (1974), Treitler invoked the pioneering research of Milman Parry and his student Albert B. Lord on the oral transmission of epic poetry. Parry and Lord, seeking to reconstruct the processes by which Homeric poetry was created, looked for help to a modern culture that seemed to have some of the same essential characteristics as that of Homer. They turned to the tradition of epic poetry in the Serbo-Croatian language, carried on in Yugoslavia by the type of performer described in Lord's 1960 book, *The Singer of Tales*. The key to the Parry-Lord theory is the idea of the formula, which Parry defined as "a group of words which is regularly employed under the same metrical conditions to express a given essential idea" (Parry 1971: 272; Lord 1960: 30; Treitler 1974: 355–6). Parry and Lord concluded that the frequent use of such formulas in both the Homeric poems and the Serbo-Croatian epics resulted from the fact that both the Greek and the Slavic poets used similar procedures of orally reconstituting their material at each performance. Thus they were confident that, when large numbers of such formulas could be identified in a poem, this formulaic character was sufficient by itself to "indicate that the [text] as we have it . . . is an oral composition" (Lord 1960: 202–3). Followers of Parry and Lord have done much to expand and refine their ideas, especially by applying formulaic analysis to new languages and literatures.[2]

2. See especially J. Foley, ed. 1981, which includes a bibliography of Lord's writings (pp. 22–26), a history of the field by the editor (pp. 27–122) and, of course, many articles by scholars of this school. A briefer history of the field is Ong 1982: 16–30. A wide-ranging bibliography is Foley 1985. Other recent studies include Bakker 1988; Edwards 1983; Finnegan 1980; J. Foley, ed. 1987; Friedman 1983; Riedinger 1985. New studies continue

What Treitler suggested was that the use of stereotyped melodic passages in Gregorian chant—what has often been called "centonization"—should be seen as a musical counterpart of Parry's and Lord's formulaic composition, and therefore evidence of the oral processes by which the melodies were formed:

> In place of the paradigm in which one presumes an act of composition that produces a piece which, in the absence of writing, is submitted to memory and then repeatedly *reproduced* in performance, we might think of a repeated process of performance-composition—something between the reproduction of a fixed, memorized melody and the extempore invention of a new one. I would call it a *reconstruction*; the performer had to think how the piece was to go and then actively reconstruct it according to what he remembered. In order to do that he would have proceeded from fixed beginnings and sung toward fixed goals, following paths about which he needed only a general, configurational sense, being successively reinforced as he went along and recognized the places he had sung correctly. Different places in the melody would have been fixed in different degrees in his mind; there would have been some places where it would have been most helpful to him to have a note-for-note sense of exactly how it went and others where he could go by this way or that, making certain only that he passed through particular pitches or pitch-groups of importance and that eventually he arrived at the goal that he had before his mind's ear, so to speak. But there was always a tendency for paths to be worn smoother the more he sang the melody. . . . It may well be that [the melodic formulas] became stereotyped through precisely such a tradition as the one I have just set forth. The positions of the formulas within the melodies, that is, played a crucial role in the process of the oral reconstruction of chants, one that brought about their classification as formulas. (Treitler 1975 : 11, italics original)

But Treitler's proposal is not by any means a simplistic or mechanical adaptation of the Parry-Lord theory to Gregorian chant. It is in fact informed by much of the more recent scholarly literature written by Parry's and

to appear in the journal *Oral Tradition* (1986–), published in Columbus, Ohio, by Slavica Publishers. There are, of course, other approaches to the study of oral tradition and oral literature than that pioneered by Parry and Lord. A classic example is Vansina 1965; see also Wiseman 1989.

Lord's followers, and Treitler himself has more than once disagreed with Parry and Lord when modern research in literature or psychology seemed to offer better information (e.g., 1981b:476, 480–1). Therefore it is possible, indeed preferable, to engage Treitler's and Hucke's opinions directly, without simultaneously opening a debate on the Parry-Lord theory itself.

Of all the writers who have attempted to expand and develop the Parry-Lord theory, Treitler acknowledges being most attracted to those who have tried to combine this theory with the principles of transformational or generative grammar (1984a:118 n. 6), a theory of linguistics associated particularly with the name of Noam Chomsky.[3] Thus the central concept of Treitler's view of oral transmission seems not to be the "formula" (as it was for Parry) but what he calls the "generative system." A generative system is apparently a set of conventions that (Treitler believes) a trained performer would have used to generate a particular chant afresh at each performance, or each time he wrote it down. Treitler seems to envision a distinct generative system for each specific chant genre and mode (or subgroup within a mode). "Given a text, a knowledge of the principles [of the generative system] should be sufficient for the making of . . . a chant" (Treitler 1981b:480, 1984c:150). In his opinion it does not matter whether the generation is an actual aural performance (an example of oral transmission) or a mental recreation made during the act of writing the melody down in music notation (an example of written transmission). The two processes are not "fundamentally different" (1981b:480) from each other, but they are both to be clearly distinguished from performing or writing that relies directly on previously written prescriptive notation. When it is a notated manuscript, rather than a "generative system," that determines the details of a performance or a writing out, then Treitler would speak of "literate transmission" (1981b), the kind that (I understand him to believe) musicologists trained in the literate tradition of Western art music sometimes presuppose unwittingly whenever they work with medieval chant manuscripts (it is called "the Modern Paradigm" in Treitler 1981a). Even after "written transmission" had become common alongside

3. For a brief introduction to Chomsky's thought see Allen and Van Buren, eds. 1971. Examples of more recent work in this area of linguistics include Jacobsen 1986, Carr 1990, Gawron and Peters 1990. Transformational grammar is of course only one of a wide range of modern theories of linguistics; examples of how a variety of perspectives can be applied to the description of one particular language are Barbour and Stevenson 1990, Fox 1990. For further bibliography on generative reformulations of the Parry-Lord theory, see J. Foley, ed. 1981: 72–4, 113.

oral transmission, it took many centuries to complete the shift to "literate transmission" (1981b:481–2; 1985a).[4] For instance, Treitler perceives some basic differences in transmission between the regular chant repertory, which was once purely oral but later became increasingly literate, and the repertories of tropes (literary and poetic compositions inserted as prefaces or interpolations into the older psalmodic repertory), because he believes that "the transmission of tropes entailed the use of notation in some way from the very beginning" (Treitler 1982a:50).

A more concrete picture of the process Treitler envisions is offered by Hucke, who sought to answer the question of how the cantors (i.e., the soloists), the schola cantorum or choir, and the scribes (who wrote the manuscripts) may have acted and interacted:

> . . . in performing a gradual verse a cantor had a general pattern to follow, and certain rules to observe with respect to the text. But there were opportunities for him to demonstrate his artistry in the way that he accommodated each individual text to the general pattern. The more the text was understood by the cantor as deflecting from the normal pattern, the more he was to make decisions of his own about how to sing it. . . . When the performance practice was written down, a fluid tradition had to be frozen into a fixed melodic form. The notator could not write down the rules for singing the melodies, he had to exemplify them by following one cantor or one authority. . . . The notation of the solo parts of Gregorian chant gives an impression of patterns and rules; it reflects decisions made by the notator, but at the same time suggests that different decisions would have been possible. It gives an idea of how nota-

4. The trichotomy "oral, written, literate" somewhat resembles the more nuanced view of Brian Stock (1983), who distinguished "orality, textuality, and literacy" (p. 6). "Before the year 1000 . . . there existed both oral and written traditions in medieval culture. But throughout the eleventh and twelfth centuries . . . a new type of interdependence . . . arose between the two. In other words, oral discourse effectively began to function within a universe of communications governed by texts" (p. 3). This constituted a "rebirth of literacy" (p. 59), which brought about the rise of "textual communities" within medieval society (pp. 88–240). It is important to note that Stock distinguishes two types of oral tradition: "pure orality, that is, verbal discourse uninfluenced by the written mode" and "verbal discourse which exists in interdependence with texts," which is of course "the type of orality for which the Middle Ages furnishes the most abundant evidence" (p. 8). In chant study, too, we have direct evidence only for the second type, and indeed only for the written half of the interaction. It is only on this uncertain basis that we can make any surmises at all about the "pure" type.

> tors may have written down the same piece in different ways, and how one notator would have possibly written down the melody if he had followed another authority, or if his authority had changed his mind. (Hucke 1980d:460, 453–4, 460)

Thus, whether a singer was teaching orally, performing, or writing down, it was "not . . . the whole, finished melody as such [that] was transmitted, but the knowledge how to make such a melody" (Treitler 1981a:208). The material actually being communicated was the "generative system" that an informed musician could use to make melodies. Of course the purpose of the generative system was not to support improvisation and originality. Its "object and effect [was] to preserve traditions, not play fast and loose with them" (Treitler 1974:346). And by the time the melodies were beginning to be written down, "the tradition of oral composition had declined." The performance practice was becoming less a matter of applying and reapplying the "rules" of a "generative system"; it was moving in the direction of more nearly fixed melodies joined to specific texts: ". . . by the time of writing the melodies were being transmitted as *individual* melodies, not as concrete instances of melodic types . . . the model for each performance was a particular plainchant, not the principles of a melodic type—something more nearly like the ordinary notion of memorization than oral composition . . ." (Treitler 1974:367–8). Nevertheless the "residuals" of oral tradition (Treitler 1981b:481; 1985a)—vestiges of oral procedures such as the continued presence of melodic formulas—remained in the melodies as clues to their ultimately oral origin, so that "even if we regard [the written transmission] exclusively as a product of copying faithfully from one source to another, it is transparent to the oral tradition that was its ultimate source" (Treitler 1988:574–5).

The "generative system" envisaged would govern what might be called the "grammar" of the chant melody, which is to be clearly distinguished from its "rhetoric."

> Like verbal language, the melody of tropes conforms to a grammar—generally the grammar of the chant tradition. The grammar can be described in terms of principles that determine what will constitute a correct, or well-formed, melodic expression. Such principles may apply at different levels of melodic flow and structure: from the shortest note-groups (neumes), through phrases and phrase-groups, to entire melodies. These principles would be concerned mainly with modal coherence and contrast

> (ranges, intervals, formulas) and melodic syntax (phrase sequences and associations, cadence hierarchies, proprieties of formula-placement). Such principles determine both the resources and the constraints that define particular melodic domains—the domains of mode or melodic family. . . . But in itself the grammar is not sufficient. . . . A melody embodies choices made from among the correct things that the grammar makes available. The musician must choose *where* to place a caesura or a cadence, *when* to pose a modal contrast, *how* to open a phrase (with what intervals or formulas) and *how* to close it, and *when* to make associations between and among phrases [italics original]. We might say that these things have to do with the rhetoric of the melody. The grammar of a trope melody is a matter of musical tradition. Its rhetoric arises from the text as that text has been interpreted by the maker of the melody, who must attend to all the formal matters that have been enumerated above. (Treitler 1984a:110)

Treitler has expressed confidence that the principles of such a grammar can be reconstructed from inductive study of the surviving melodies. We are assured that "the knowledge that served as the basis of the transmission [i.e., the generative system] can be abstracted by us on the basis of an analysis in terms of the structural and syntactic principles that all the versions [of a given melody] jointly exemplify, and the optional features that individual versions [of the same melody] manifest" (1981a:208).[5]

But so far Treitler has not actually published a complete analysis of this kind, either from a perspective of generative grammar or from any other.[6] Even one of his more extended explorations of melodic "grammar"

5. Elsewhere Treitler expresses a similar agenda with greater detail: "We require a taxonomic approach to the tropes that takes in all 'variants' and that is based not on the impression of surface resemblance but on the analysis of the co-variant options presented by the musical idiom in general, by the stylization principles exhibited by particular collections, by the chants with which the tropes are associated, and by the structures that define the identities of individual tropes through their several exemplifications in different sources" (1982a:58).

6. An example of what a generative grammar of Gregorian chant might look like can be seen in Chen 1983, an attempt by a specialist in Chinese linguistics to describe a "grammar of singing" based on the Gregorian and Dominican psalm tones. Unfortunately Chen relied on the performance practice rules published in chant books of the early twentieth century. He seems unaware that these rules are considerably more rigid than the less fully regulated practice of the Middle Ages, and that they reflect some anachronistic concerns of post-medieval origin. Compare Bailey 1976, 1977, 1978; Hucke 1975, 1980b.

(1982a:12–46) was prefaced with the caution, "At this stage it is not my intention to develop a systematic theory about the transmission of tropes." But this discussion seems to show that a fully developed Treitlerian grammar would focus on the "underlying structures" common to related melodies, particularly at the level of the individual phrase (1982a:28–9, 39–40).

A more sustained attempt to describe a melodic grammar for plainchant is the "Syntactical Analysis" proposed by Treitler's and Hucke's student Edward Nowacki at the end of his dissertation (1980:297–342, summarized in Nowacki 1981), and praised by Treitler (1981a:208). Nowacki went further than Treitler by actually positing a series of generative rules. However, his grammar seems to focus particularly on the progression from pitch to pitch (described mostly in terms of the "upper neighbor" or "lower neighbor" relationship). Syntactical Analysis as described so far has not been expanded to deal fully with Treitler's other "levels of melodic flow and structure": "note-groups (neumes)," "phrases and phrase-groups," and "entire melodies" (1984a:110), though Nowacki gave more attention to these "levels" in the earlier part of his dissertation, prior to his exposition of Syntactical Analysis.

Treitler's own discussions of the musical illustrations in his articles often seem to focus more on their "rhetoric" than on their "grammar" (1981b, 1985a, 1985b, Jonsson and Treitler 1983), illustrating his view that "a chant melody records a reading of its text; . . . melody plays a role similar to that of punctuation" (Jonsson and Treitler 1983:22).[7] This idea, in turn, is one of the starting points for his explorations of the semiotics of neumatic notation, which he would derive historically from punctuation signs, reflecting the continuity he sees between "Reading and Singing" (the title of 1984b, see also 1982b).

Hucke's approach has been somewhat different. He has not used the expression "generative system," but has preferred to speak of "patterns and rules" or "rules and principles" (1980d:460, 454). However, Hucke's rules also seem to have more to do with what Treitler would call "rhetoric" than with "grammar." Though Hucke has not formulated specific rules himself in the way that Nowacki attempted, he has stated that "the basic principle of composition in Gregorian chant is the division of the text into units defined by sense; the melodic phrases correspond to these sense

7. See my own remarks in Jeffery 1989a:24, 29.

units" (1980d:452). His discussions of actual musical examples visualize a medieval singer deliberately weighing alternative ways of dividing a text, so as to decide where to place "certain formulas, especially cadential figures, . . . and some melismas" (1980d:453).

On one important question, Hucke has had more to say than Treitler. This is the question about the ways that the "rules" may have helped to govern the interactions among different groups of performers, and between performers and scribes. "The cantor [being a soloist] could command a more complex system of rules and performance procedures than could the schola [or choir]" (1980d:454). "In the solo-pieces and cantor-pieces, the cantor may have felt more strongly bound by the tradition and rules of his method of oral transmission than [he felt] in the pieces for the Schola Cantorum. Here [in the chants for the choir], he strove in the role of a preceptor to formulate examples" (1981 : 184) that would serve as the basis of the choral performance. "Thus the [notated] record of the Gregorian choir-pieces probably does not follow upon the performance of a choir; underlying the record is the setting of one authority, or of individual authorities, individual cantors" (1981 : 183).[8]

> When the performance practice was written down, a fluid tradition had to be frozen into a fixed melodic form. The notator could not write down the rules for singing the melodies, he had to exemplify them by following one cantor or one authority. . . . The cantor could command a more complex system of rules and performance procedures than could the schola. In writing down the melodies of the cantor, the notator was far more constrained by the rules than he would have been in writing down the melodies of the schola. . . . For the melodies of the schola he would have given examples of how they could artfully be sung. The appearance of the repertories in the manuscripts is deceptive. With the notated melodies of the cantor we are probably closer to what was sung because the notator was more closely guided by rules and principles. The breadth in the

8. "Das könnte man so erklären, dass der Kantor sich bei den Solostücken und Kantorenstücken durch die Tradition und die Regeln seiner mündlichen Überlieferungsweise stärker gebunden fühlte als bei den Stücken der Schola cantorum, dass er hier in der Rolle eines Praeceptors sich bemühte, exempla zu formulieren" (Hucke 1981 : 184). "Die Aufzeichnung der gregorianischen Chorstücke ist doch wohl nicht nach dem Vortrag eines Chors erfolgt; der Aufzeichnung liegt die Fassung eines Gewährsmanns bzw. einzelner Gewährsleute, einzelner Kantoren zugrunde" (Hucke 1981 : 183).

repertory for the schola reflects not so much a richness in its practice as the play of the notator's fancy under lesser constraints. (Hucke 1980d:453–4)

Clearly the proposal for a New Historical View is still preliminary and unfinished. Much more close work needs to be done to build up methodologies for extrapolating specific "rules" and organizing them into a complete reconstructed "grammar" and "rhetoric" of Gregorian melody. But if it really were possible to construct a sophisticated and historically reliable "grammar" for medieval chant melody, it seems to me that this would make possible the first truly systematic and exhaustive scrutiny of the Gregorian and other medieval chant repertories. As the first step toward developing such a grammar, I would select a chant genre and mode, and then roughly divide up all the extant chants of this group into their "generative systems" (or "melodic families"?). Then I would go over the same ground again but more carefully, proceeding to catalogue all the individual chants that wholly or partially belong to each "generative system." Next I would carefully select one such system, on the basis of manageable size and the relatively high frequency of interesting pieces. Finally I would try to fully reconstruct and spell out all the "rules" of this selected "generative system," through painstakingly detailed analyses of all the individual melodies that belong to it. This first such study of one "generative system" would then serve as a model for future studies.[9] Only after many "generative systems" had been investigated in this way would it then be possible to begin drawing up generalizations about the nature and historical development of the chant repertory as a whole. The total effort would take at least a generation, but, if it could be done, in the end it would be possible as never before to make authoritative statements about the ways chant melodies behave and the reasons they are the way they are.

9. Many studies of particular melodic or modal groups already exist, of course. Recent examples include Amargianakis 1977; Claire 1981; Hage 1967, 1972; Klöckner 1988; Kuckertz 1969; Madrignac 1986; Ribay 1988. But a study of this nature that was based on the concepts of the New Historical View would do much, both to refine the View itself and to demonstrate (or not) its basic validity.

3

Some Reflections on the New Historical View

I wrote earlier that Treitler's and Hucke's views demand much more of a response than they have so far received. My reflections here are meant as part of that response, and are intended to be entirely constructive. There are many aspects of the New Historical View that deserve more extensive comment and discussion than I will be giving here. But in what follows I will offer my own personal reflections in three of the areas that seem to me especially important. At least one area of obvious importance, Treitler's and Hucke's views on the origins of neumatic notation, will get little attention in this essay. This is partly because it has already received some attention from other scholars, but mainly because I intend to focus the present essay on the oral side of chant transmission, leaving the written side perhaps for another occasion.

My remarks will be grouped under three headings, bearing on the issues of "grammar" and "rhetoric," of historical confirmation, and of the consequences for the criticism and editing of the melodies.

A. The "Rules" of "Grammar" and "Rhetoric": Deciphering the "Language" of Formulaic Chant

It may well be true that the formulaic character of medieval chant readily submits to being described according to generative "grammatical" rules. If Treitler and Hucke would demonstrate this by actually spelling out the rules of a select group of chants, the results would doubtless be extremely interesting. However, there is a danger that even this demonstration would prove less than Treitler and Hucke hope about the oral and written processes of chant transmission. The reason for this, to put it simply, is that neither formulaicism nor generative grammar is necessarily connected with orality.

Critics of Parry's and Lord's work have more than once called attention to the fact that high concentrations of verbal formulas can be found even in poems that are known beyond question to have been composed in writing by literate authors.[1] They have argued from this that the mere presence of heavily formulaic language is no proof that the text originated orally. Some have gone even further, raising doubts that Parry's and Lord's theory is even applicable to medieval European literature (Green 1990: 269–73). As one student of medieval Greek poetry put it, after finding the Parry-Lord approach inadequate to his own material, "'orality' perhaps needs to be redefined" (Beaton 1981:27). Such challenges have forced disciples of Parry and Lord to attempt to refine their concept of the formula, to preserve its intimate connection with oral processes at least in some cases, under some circumstances.[2] Treitler of course is aware of the challenges, but I think he has dismissed them too lightly: "It strikes me that the wrong question has been asked of the evidence. Formulaic style . . . is . . . a 'residual' of oral tradition . . . , understandable in the light of a continuity from oral to written practice" (1981b:481). But it is not clear that this need always be so. Even if it were, a literate poet who writes a formulaic poem is not doing the same thing as a singer of tales, even if the literate poet is working within a tradition that is historically indebted to an older oral-formulaic practice.

For our purposes it is of course better to shift to the realm of musical evidence. Such phenomena as the clichés of late Baroque recitative, or the recurring motives in the first movement of Beethoven's Fifth Symphony, could easily be described as "formulaic," keeping well within the usual denotative field of this word in ordinary, non-technical English. But it would be difficult to argue from this that these examples of "formulaicism" were "residuals" of an earlier oral tradition. If formulaicism in music has any intrinsic connection with orality, this connection needs to be defined much more sharply, so that truly oral and residually oral formulas can be clearly recognized and distinguished from what are merely repeated motives or conventional musical figures. But there are reasons to doubt that such a definition is possible, or that any type of musical formulaicism can be considered exclusively the product of oral composition processes.

1. One that attracted particular attention is Benson 1966, dealing with Anglo-Saxon poetry. Spraycar 1977 offers a different interpretation of some of the same literature Parry and Lord were working with; see also Spraycar and Dunlap 1982.

2. See, for instance, the articles in J. Foley, ed. 1981:60–79, 262–81, 394–415; Treitler 1981b:480–1.

> Professor Finnegan (1980) has already argued that there is no special and distinct oral poetic style; oral and written symbolism overlap greatly in variety such that forms of repetition, parallelism, prosody, and formulae cannot be simultaneously a consequence of orality yet so widely distributed in oral, literate, and merged/merging traditions. Surely the same must be said for music: it is impossible to come up with a list of formal traits that *only* characterize musics of oral tradition. . . . What is important, ultimately, is not the musical traits, but the socio-historical processes through which they have become meaningful. (Feld 1986:25)

Even if the medieval chant melodies are demonstrably formulaic, therefore, this does not in itself prove that they originated in an oral milieu. Or even though we know that the chant melodies in the earliest manuscripts are somehow descended from an oral tradition, we cannot merely assume without question that their formulaic character is strictly a vestige of this oral practice: the relationship of the extant written melodies to the earlier oral tradition is precisely the question at issue. If possible (and in the case of medieval chant it may not be possible), the nature of the connection between formulaicism and orality in medieval chant must first be determined, perhaps by investigating "the socio-historical processes through which they have become meaningful" (Feld 1986:25).

A similar problem is inherent in the analogy to generative grammar. As developed by linguists, the theory of generative grammar is not intended to distinguish oral from written language, but to describe systematically the thought processes underlying all language. Analytical approaches that are inspired by and related to generative grammar have been applied to many musical compositions that originated in the last few centuries.[3] Thus even if a generative theory of formulaicism in Gregorian chant could be developed, it might prove nothing more than that music, like language, is a type of discourse (cf. Brown and Yule 1983; van Dijk and Kintsch 1983; Macdowell 1986). Wherever possible, other kinds of evidence must be employed to show just how this generative formulaicism was related to the oral processes of chant transmission.

3. There is an extensive literature on the applicability of generative grammar concepts to music, but one can begin with Powers 1980b:28–37; Baroni and Callegari 1984; Bevil 1984; Keiler 1978; Kippen 1987; Kōsaki 1982, 1985; Lerdahl and Jackendoff 1983; Sloboda 1985:11–7; West et al. 1985.

The conclusion that analyses based on generative grammar cannot in themselves distinguish melodies of oral origin from those that were composed in writing has already been reached by Nowacki, who wrote that with Syntactical Analysis "it is possible to transcend the controversy over . . . written or oral tradition . . . since written composition, no less than oral, must be the manifestation of mental structures shared by all practitioners of the art" (1980 : 342). This fact raises a caveat about Treitler's belief that oral and written processes are essentially similar to each other, but both dissimilar from literate processes. This belief may be true, but it would probably look that way to Treitler even if it were not, because, from his chosen vantage point of generative grammar, the oral and the written are at best difficult to distinguish. In other words, a true generative grammar of chant formulaicism, if it were developed, would describe a deep structure that is below the level(s) on which differences between oral and written transmission might be expected to appear. It thus might be powerless by itself to identify such differences, leaving open the whole question of how the musical formulaicism was related to orality.

Even apart from questions of grammar and formulaicism, moreover, the attempt to identify and distinguish vestiges of oral or written processes in written medieval melodies is a notoriously perilous one. How tricky it can be will be evident from example 1, a chant Treitler published in three articles in order to describe the basic features of its generative system.[4] It is an Old Roman offertory, transcribed from a late eleventh- or early twelfth-century manuscript thought to be from the church of St. John Lateran in Rome (Codex Vaticanus latinus 5319). This offertory apparently consists of a refrain (with the text "Factus est dominus firmamentum meum et salvum . . . hoderunt me" on the first four staves, marked ℟) and three verses (marked $℣_1$, $℣_2$, $℣_3$). One would normally expect that in performance each of the three verses would be followed by the last line of the refrain, i.e., the words "et ab his qui hoderunt me" (fourth staff, marked with an arrow). But in the manuscript from which this example was taken, only the second verse ("Persequar . . . deficiant" on the ninth through eleventh staves) is followed by a cue indicating this (the word "Et" with a

4. Treitler 1981b : 476–80; 1984c : 168–9; 1986 : 40–4. There are some disagreements among the examples, particularly in the labeling of the several variants of the formula *D*. After checking the example against the original manuscript and correcting some omissions, I have changed the labeling again to identify accurately the seven variants of *D*. See the remarks in Treitler 1984c : 149.

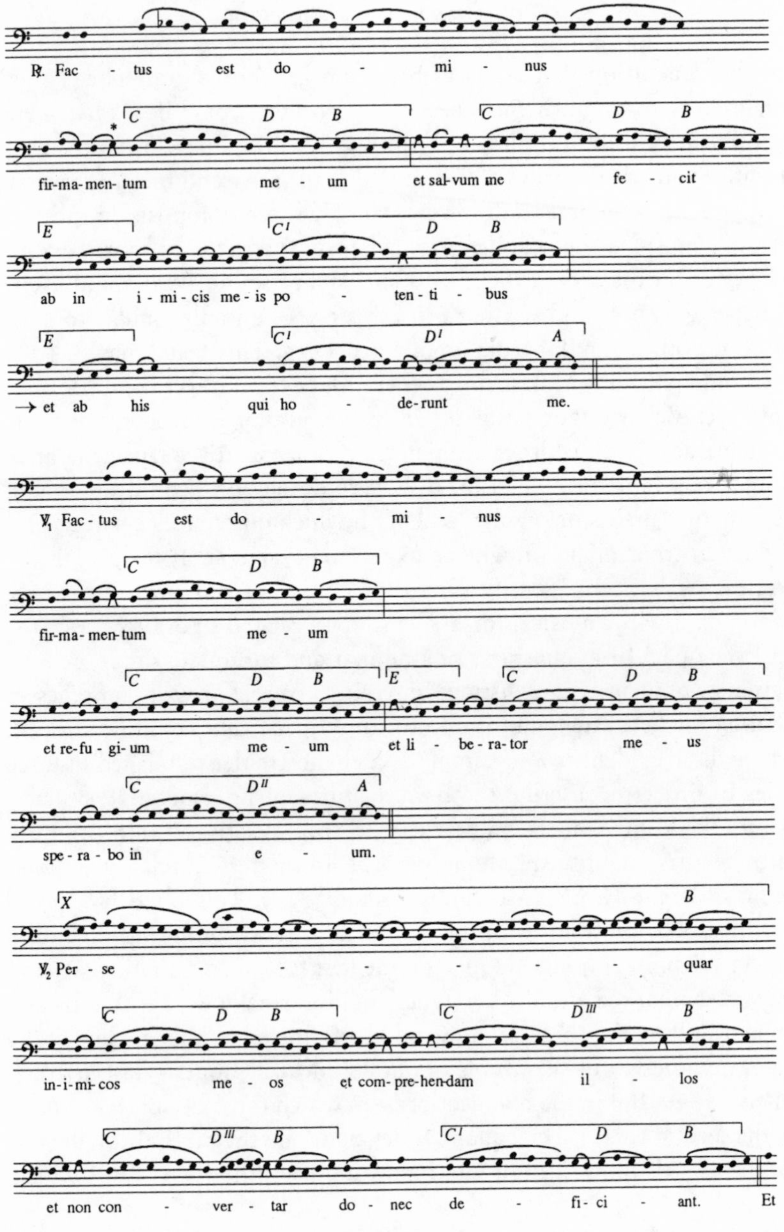

EXAMPLE 1. Treitler 1981b:478–9, with corrections. Compare Treitler 1984c:168–9, 1986:41–2.

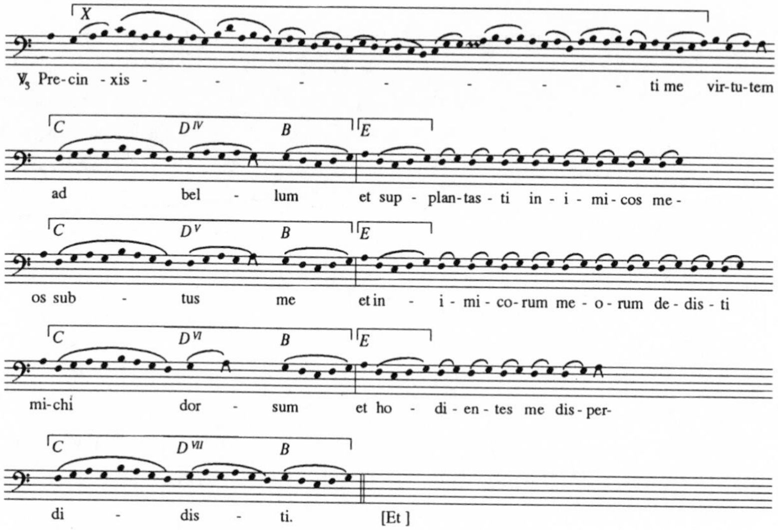

* The figure ∧ represents a liquescent neume in the original.

EXAMPLE 1, continued.

single note above it, at the end of the eleventh staff). This Old Roman offertory has an odd relationship to its Gregorian counterpart: the Gregorian offertory lacks the refrain "Factus est dominus firmamentum meum et salvum . . . hoderunt me." Instead the text of the Old Roman first verse ("Factus est dominus firmamentum meum et refugium . . . eum," fifth through eighth staves) serves as the Gregorian refrain; it is followed by the remaining two verses ("Persequar . . . deficiant" and "Praecinxisti . . . disperdidisti" on the twelfth through sixteenth staves). Following an analysis published by Hucke (1980c), Treitler begins with the arguable premise that "the Roman version is an adaptation of a Frankish [i.e., Gregorian] model" (Treitler 1981b:476). Because of this, "written process entered into the transmission" and somewhat disturbed "the realization of the Roman offertory out of its generative system," which was essentially "an oral process." That is to say, because the Old Roman scribe was trying both to follow a written Gregorian model and to realize an oral generative system at the same time, the Gregorian model "seems to have interfered with the Roman adaptor's correct application of the principles of his own tradition" (Treitler 1981b:482). As the result of this interference, the scribe violated the alleged rules of the generative system, by ending the melody of the first verse (over the syllable "-um" of "eum" in the eighth staff) with the melodic material that should have been reserved for the end of the refrain—

the two-note formula Treitler dubbed *A*, consisting of the pitches G–F.[5] In Treitler's opinion this formula, which amounts to a cadence or clausula on the modal final (or "tonic") "is reserved for the full close" at the end of the refrain; that is why it appears (this time correctly) at the end of the Old Roman refrain in this example (i.e, over the syllable "me" in the fourth staff). In this particular generative system (as Treitler sees it) verses were supposed to end with the formula labeled *B* (the pitches G–F–E–F–G), which, instead of cadencing on the "tonic," leads into the repetition of the end of the refrain, "et ab his qui hoderunt me" (on the fourth staff). This ending *B* is the one we actually find in the second and third verses (in the eleventh and sixteenth staves). But the Old Roman scribe, confused by the Gregorian source in which the Old Roman first verse served as the refrain, committed an "error" by ending the melody of this verse with "the wrong clausula": formula *A* (the refrain ending) instead of formula *B* (the verse ending). This arrival at the modal final eliminated the need to repeat the last line of the refrain, and therefore the scribe wrote no cue at this point. Instead he wrote the cue only after the second verse (the word "Et" at the end of the eleventh staff), violating the convention that required the refrain to be performed after every verse (Treitler 1981b:479).

Since Treitler wrote, however, another manuscript of the same Old Roman melody has become available (Lütolf 1987, wherein this chant will be found at ff. 62v–63r), after a long period during which it was inaccessible to most scholars. It was copied for use at the church of St. Cecilia in Transtiber or Trastevere (i.e., across the Tiber from the center of Rome) in the year 1071. The fact that the St. Cecilia manuscript contains essentially the same melody as the Lateran manuscript forces some modifications in Treitler's analysis. First, because the "error" of ending the first verse with formula *A* occurs in both manuscripts, the question arises of just who the erring scribe was. Some chant scholars would say that it could not have been the copyist who wrote either of the extant manuscripts—it must have been someone who wrote out an earlier manuscript, now lost, which was an ancestor of the two manuscripts we have. One or both of the two extant manuscripts may have been copied directly from the lost manuscript (in which case the lost manuscript would be called the "exemplar"), but it is more likely that they are descended more distantly from it through an

5. Pitches are cited according to their familiar letter names in the Guidonian gamut: Γ, A–G, a–g, aa–ee, in which c = modern middle C. See Hoppin 1978:63–4, especially example III-2.

unknown number of intermediary copies (in which case the lost manuscript would be known as the "archetype"). Treitler, however, might argue that it is equally plausible to imagine his scenario happening twice, as the scribes of our two extant manuscripts made the same error independently. This, of course, raises many questions, such as how likely it would be for such a mistake to have occurred more than once, and whether both scribes were working from the identical (written?) form of the Gregorian melody. The imaginable complexities multiply rapidly.

Our newly available manuscript, however, contains new information that raises further questions about the entire affair. After the second and third verses, it contains the cue "Et li," an abbreviation of the refrain line to be repeated: "et liberator meus sperabo in eum." However, this is the last line not of the Old Roman refrain ("Factus est dominus firmamentum meum et salvum . . . hoderunt me"), but of the Old Roman first verse and the Gregorian refrain ("Factus est dominus firmamentum meum et refugium . . . eum"). It is as if this scribe regarded the first verse as no verse at all, but rather as the second of two refrains, a possibility rendered more plausible by the fact that, in the Gregorian transmission, the same text supplies the only refrain. An offertory with two refrains would certainly be an anomaly, but this piece is an anomaly in any case, by Treitler's reckoning. If indeed the Old Roman scribes believed they were copying two refrains, it would have been entirely logical to end both of them with same formula *A*, which Treitler has identified as the correct refrain ending. Further, though the St. Cecilia manuscript clearly specifies that the last line of the second refrain is the one to be repeated after the verses, the Lateran manuscript Treitler used is more ambiguous: its one-word cue "Et" could refer to the last line of either of the two refrains (which set this word to the same pitch), as if the choice were being left to the performer. If that were the intention of the Lateran scribe, the use of formula *A* to end both refrains was not a mistake at all, but simply allowed the singer using the manuscript to choose which refrain to perform.

All this in turn suggests other possible explanations of the historical relationship between the Gregorian and Old Roman recensions of this offertory. Perhaps there was a time when both refrains were in circulation in the oral tradition (they are after all textually and melodically similar). When the Old Roman tradition was committed to writing both were preserved by being copied one right after the other—the second one was labeled with a ℣ for "verse" but could still be treated in performance as a refrain. The Gregorian tradition, on the other hand, did not preserve the first refrain at all, but only the one that occurs second in Old Roman sources. This explanation at least has the merit of being much simpler than that of Treitler and Hucke.

The St. Cecilia manuscript was not generally available to scholars at the time Treitler was writing, so he can hardly be faulted for not consulting it. But now that it is available, comparing it with Treitler's example shows how easy it is to cast doubt on any attempt to assign oral or written origins to the features of a particular melody; such a theory can readily be weakened by even a small amount of new information from even one additional manuscript. The idea of an offertory with two refrains may be unprecedented—it is in any case so unusual that Treitler could not responsibly have hypothesized it to explain this chant. Yet that is clearly how this chant was regarded in the tradition embodied in the St. Cecilia manuscript, and it makes possible a simpler explanation of the melody than the theory that the scribe was adapting the Gregorian recension in a partly oral, partly written act of realizing an Old Roman generative system.

The one major melodic difference between the two Old Roman manuscripts may indeed reflect differences between the two scribes, and suggest something about their ways of working. But there is room for differing opinions about what in fact it tells us. This difference has to do with the formula labeled *X*, which begins the two verses ("Persequar" in the ninth staff, "Precinxisti" in the twelfth). Treitler reported that, in eighteen occurrences throughout the melodic group, this formula "is at the same pitch level as in the second verse here ['Persequar']. And almost always the melisma exits to figure *B* as here." But "both the pitch level [i.e., one step higher than usual] and the liquidation of the melisma in the third verse ['Praecinxisti me . . .'] are unique," which Treitler explains as "the result of a writing error. . . . To account for the unorthodox continuation at the end of the melisma one has only to imagine that the notator saw that he had ended too high and could not conclude with figure *B*, so he had to make up something else" (1981b:480). The notion of a scribe making good on a mistake in this way is not necessarily inconsistent with traditional ideas of written transmission, and thus it need not be considered evidence that the scribe made use of an oral generative system. This case in particular could hardly have taxed the scribe's creativity, for the "unique liquidation of the melisma in the third verse" is the same as figure *B* except in two respects: it is transposed up a step, and it is applied to two syllables ("-ti me") rather than one. In the newly available St. Cecilia manuscript even the transposition is gone, for all the music over the words "Precinxisti me virtutem" (the twelfth staff in example 1) is notated at the customary pitch, one step lower than in Treitler's example, with scarcely any other differences. In both manuscripts, then, formula *X* actually does "conclude with figure *B*" (the pitches G–F–E–F–G in the St. Cecilia manuscript, transposed to a–G–F–G–a in the manuscript Treitler used), modified only slightly by being applied to two syllables instead of the usual one. All that happened in the Lateran manuscript used for example 1, then, is that a portion of the melody was written one step too high. This is readily explained in the traditional way as a simple copying error. No more elaborate concept of transmission is needed to account for it.

The reason for rehearsing these examples in such detail is to show how difficult it is for anyone to determine, in specific cases, the exact roles of oral, written, or literate processes in shaping a written melody that has come down to us in a medieval manuscript. Even in the rare instances when one is able to assemble all the physical evidence by consulting every surviving manuscript, much of the interpretation still depends on the implicit presuppositions and explicit opinions that determine one's basic viewpoint.

How then, can we possibly develop objective procedures for identifying and distinguishing whatever traces of oral or written procedures may still be discoverable in the medieval manuscripts? In attempting to sort individual chant melodies into related groups, how do we determine the limits of membership, even tentatively? How do we recognize a "formula," and distinguish mere variants from the more distantly related or only superficially similar "formulas?" How do we isolate abstract "grammatical rules" from the concrete actual melodies, and how are the exceptions to each "rule" accounted for? And, as always, how do we then confirm that our interpretations, reconstructions, generative grammars, or other theories of chant transmission are truly consistent with the musical culture of the early medieval period? How do we make sure they are not simply modern constructions, based on anachronistic premises, forced on the medieval melodies in a Procrustean manner? These questions all have to do with the issue of proof or confirmation; thus they lead to the second group of reflections.

B. Problems of Proof and Plausibility: The Need for Empirical Confirmation

If our methods are still so unrefined, this is due, in my opinion, to the fact that we control so little empirical data about musical transmission in general—the kind of data that ought to be an essential prerequisite to realistic speculation about oral and written traditions of the past. One unfortunate result of this is that we do not yet have comprehensive definitions of many of the key concepts that typically are bandied about in discussions of oral tradition. Such terms as "formula," "melodic group" (or "family," or "type"), "rule," even "oral" and "written," are used by almost everyone with as little precision as the term "oral tradition" itself. As long as we lack careful definitions of exactly what these and other terms ought to denote, it is no wonder we still argue about which melodic characteristics should be attributed to oral and which to written factors. The analysis—the mere description—even of individual chant melodies is still a very subjective and impressionistic undertaking for all of us.

In their many writings, Treitler and Hucke have made a number of assertions that cannot yet be confirmed. These have to do with how the oral and written processes of long ago should be envisioned, and how this vision should be used to interpret the written evidence that is all we actually have to work with today. A convenient example emerges in one of Treitler's most recent publications (1988), in which he disagreed with another scholar (Levy 1987a) for his "automatic and unquestioning" reliance on "the law that detailed agreement among the written sources of a text points to a common textual archetype," thus regarding "claimed agreement of neumation as a sign of a neumated archetype" (Treitler 1988: 568). Objecting to this "a priori idea" that "parallel neumations" (i.e., nearly identical written versions of the same melody in two or more manuscripts) are to be explained by "the inference of a common archetype for all sources," Treitler asserted that "it can also be explained on the hypothesis that the scribes understood the sense of the contents in the same way and [independently] translated their understanding into [notated versions] that are more or less identical" (Treitler 1988: 569). Does this mean that the "generative system" was by that time so rigid (or had so deteriorated in the direction of rote memory), that hundreds of early medieval singers, writing out chant manuscripts from memory by means of the customary "rules," could theoretically have produced—independently of each other and of written models—the hundreds of surviving manuscripts that contain the very uniform standard recension of Gregorian chant (D. G. Hughes 1987)? It may be so, but how is one to know? Is it humanly possible for an oral tradition to transmit so many melodies with so few variants but with no assistance from "literate" transmission? How do we prove that it is or is not? And if it is indeed possible, should we consider it likely, when the alternative is the easily believable possibility that the uniformity results from simple copying, ultimately from one or a few related written exemplars? Treitler cannot claim that his view on this question is self-evident, or that it is a conclusion that inevitably proceeds from his more basic premises, for even some prominent specialists in oral transmission have not accepted it. Lord's opinion is that "variation, sometimes not great, sometimes quite considerable, is the rule in oral composition. When there is exact line-for-line, formula-for-formula correspondence between manuscripts, we can be sure that we are dealing with a written tradition involving copied manuscripts or with some circumstance of collecting in which a fixed text has been memorized" (1960:203). Hucke, too, seems to assume that detailed agreement between two written melodies points in the direction of a written relationship between their sources. On this basis he has felt able to conclude that, in one instance, two differing melodies set to the same text "are both records of a way of performing." In a third source, containing a melody nearly identical to one of the first two, it is "no longer [that] another realization of the way of performing has been written down," but rather that a "written formulation has been copied." In another case "the Beneventan tradition, on the other hand, appears to be a written redaction of the melodic setting put forward in the Aquitainian manuscripts . . . , but one that varies within the framework of a way of performing."[6] Thus Treitler's claim that identical written formulations can arise independently may not be taken for granted; its reasonability must first be established.

For support, Treitler appealed to a textual analogy, namely the medieval system of punctuating *per cola et commata*. In this system punctu-

6. "Beide Melodiefassungen sind Aufzeichnungen einer Vortragsweise. In der Handschrift 1871 ist nicht mehr eine andere Realisation der Vortragsweise niedergeschrieben, sondern die auch in Handschrift 1120 vorliegende schriftliche Formulierung kopiert worden." "Die beneventanische Überlieferung dagegen erscheint als eine schriftliche, aber im Rahmen der Vortragsweise verändernde Redaktion der in den aquitanischen Handschriften Paris 1120 und 1871 vorliegenden Melodiefassung." Hucke 1985:112, 123.

ation marks are not used. Instead the text is broken up into rhetorical units or "sense lines" (Berger 1893:318)—the scribe begins a new line after each clause or other textual segment, where a modern writer would put a punctuation mark. In the Middle Ages this system was used most often in manuscripts of the Latin Vulgate Bible, probably because it could assist those who read aloud or intoned the text by showing them where to pause at, or musically mark, the syntactical divisions of the text.[7] However it is also sometimes used in modern critical editions of other Latin texts (notably Jonsson et al. 1975–) because it simplifies editorial decisions; the editor can mark the main divisions in the text clearly without having to decide whether a comma, period, or other mark is the most appropriate one. "Let us imagine," Treitler asked,

> a number of sources for an early medieval Latin text, all identical in lexical content, and all written out in a manner that was called *per cola et commata* (phrases comprising sense units are written in separate text lines, as a way of guiding the reading-out of the text, exactly in parallel with the purpose of punctuation at the time). And let us imagine that the lineation in all sources is more or less identical. That can be explained by the inference of a common archetype for all sources, but it can also be explained on the hypothesis that the scribes understood the sense of the contents in the same way and translated their understanding into lineations that are more or less identical. And, last-not-least, it can be explained by any number of combinations of these two models.
>
> The neumation of a melody has this in common with the lineation of a language text: both correspond to immanent properties of the thing denoted that would be projected in a performance of it and of which the scribe or notator *might* take cognizance while writing, and by the same token two scribes or notators might take cognizance of those properties independently of one another. (1988:569, italics original)

But this is very questionable. First, the analogy may not be appropri-

7. In the preface to his translation of the book of Isaiah, St. Jerome (ca. 342–420) claims to have introduced it himself "for its usefulness to readers [*utilitati legentium*]." See Monachi Abbatiae Sancti Hieronymi 1926–/13:3; Arns 1953:114–5. In the sixth century, Cassiodorus Senator recommended that this type of punctuation be used only for Bibles, see Courcelle 1969:368, R. Weber 1955. For more general information see Bischoff 1989:29, 169.

ate, because this punctuation system is a very simple one, which marks only the most important pauses in the text, and marks them all the same way (i.e., with a line break). The complex and ornamental melodies of medieval chant might be compared more readily to a more complex punctuation system, like the one used in Hebrew Bibles. The Hebrew system, which is certainly used to support public declamation of the text, indicates very fine distinctions among different kinds of semantic divisions, clearly marking the relative importance both of different kinds of pauses and of different kinds of non-pauses. It is unlikely that two scribes would independently utilize such a complex system in an identical way, and in fact Jewish tradition has developed an elaborate system of safeguards (known as the Masorah) to ensure uniformity of copying (see Leiman, ed. 1974; Yeivin 1980). But a more basic objection can be made to Treitler's analogy, and that is that his hypothetical case does not actually happen. The punctuation of the Latin Vulgate text differs greatly from one manuscript to another—to such a degree that the critical edition (Monachi 1926–) devotes an entire critical apparatus (one of three) just to recording punctuation variants. Thus when the punctuation of two Vulgate manuscripts is very similar, the likelihood is that they are somehow related in origin, not that they were produced through coincidence by two scribes working independently. Indeed, it is difficult to imagine a lengthy text that is so devoid of ambiguity it could only be understood and punctuated one way.

Of course, Treitler acknowledged that his analogy was intended as an abstraction. He does not really conceive the problem as one of either/or—either a written "common archetype" or an oral "taking cognizance independently." In actual historic situations he is inclined to believe it more likely that we are dealing with some complex of "combinations of these two models," that some mixture of copying from both written and oral sources took place. The question then becomes the following: is there any way to tell, with any particular melody in any particular manuscript, which type of copying the scribe was engaged in at any particular point, or which melodic features are to be attributed to one type or the other? In one attempt to answer this question, Treitler once again turned to a textual analogy, averring that "characteristic flatness, repetitiveness, less differentiated and less subordinating form . . . are all characteristics of the products of an oral tradition," while "larger, integrated designs" show that "the technology of writing . . . has worked an effect on the compositional style" (1985a:183). But how do we know that "larger, integrated designs" are less likely in musical oral traditions? How do we define "characteristic flatness?" And how do we know what would have seemed "flat" to a medieval singer? Treitler was relying here on an opinion of Walter Ong (1982), who of course was writing about the oral transmission of texts, not music. Treitler reproduced Ong's example of two English translations of the Bible (Genesis 1:1–5): the Douai version published in 1609, which Ong believed displayed more oral features ("flatness," "repetitiveness," etc.), and the New American Bible of 1970, in which Ong saw more literate features ("larger, integrated designs") (Ong 1982:37). But Ong's interpretation of these two passages is doubtful at best. He seems to forget that both are translations, and that more than anything else their differences reflect different philosophies of translating. The alleged oral characteristics of the 1609 version are translated word for word from the Hebrew original (by way of the Latin Vulgate, not the Greek as Ong says; see R. Brown et al., eds. 1990:1112), following what modern biblical translators call the method of "formal correspondence." The twentieth-century version, on the other hand, departs from the repetitious Hebrew word order according to the modern method of translating known as "dynamic" or "functional equivalence," which aims at communicating the underlying sense in fully idiomatic modern language, without necessarily preserving the more superficial linguistic characteristics of the original.[8] Thus the two different translations are actually the products of two different literate processes, and whatever "oral residues" they may contain belong mainly to the original Hebrew text (cf. Whallon 1979). Indeed the latest trend among English-speaking Bible translators is back in the direction of "formal correspondence" (Walsh 1989, 1990; Omanson 1990), in other words toward translations that would appear to Ong to contain too much "oral residue" for the twentieth century.[9]

8. See Nida and Taber 1969; Waard and Nida 1986. Other recent works on the theory of Bible translation (and the Bible has been translated more times than any other text in history) include Buzzetti 1973, Margot 1979. Two journals that deal with the issue of Bible translation are: *Notes on Translation* (irregular until vol. 2– [1988–]), published by the Summer Institute of Linguistics in Dallas, Texas, and *The Bible Translator* (1950–) published in New York by the United Bible Societies. There are, of course, many other writings on the theory of translation apart from biblical studies. One attempt to outline a more broadly based discipline of "translatology" is Snell-Hornby 1988; while Shaw 1988 looks at "transculturation: the cultural factor in translation." See also Biguenet and Schulte 1989, and the journal *Multilingua* (1981–), published in Berlin by Walter de Gruyter.

9. In spite of this, I do not intend to impugn Ong 1982 in general or to deny its potential interest to chant scholars and other musicologists. Indeed I would like to see more

In discussing an example he has used often (1984a:111–7, 1984c: 174, 1985a:174–6, 1985b) Treitler has attempted to utilize Ong's views to compare differing versions of the "same" trope from two different manuscripts (see ex. 2). He has found one of them (from Apt MS 17) "flatter" and more reminiscent of oral transmission, because it begins three phrases with the same upward leap of a fifth (on "Ecclesiae," "baptismatis," and "quem") while the other version (from Paris, Bibliothèque Nationale MS latin 909) is more expressive or "artful" because it has "reserved" this figure for use as a "special effect" to set the name "Ihesus" (Jesus), which name does not occur in the text of the Apt version. Hence he judges the Paris 909 version more distant from the conventions of oral transmission. Confirmation for this interpretation is sought in the well-known fact that medieval religious thought experienced a shift toward a more "personal" spirituality beginning in the eleventh century.

But there are reasons to demur.[10] It is debatable whether an upward leap of a fifth at the beginning of a musical phrase could have been considered a "special effect" in the Middle Ages. In some modes it was such a common melodic opening that it could plausibly be described as an oral formula—in fact Hucke has more recently attempted to formulate rules governing its use as such (1988a:309–17). If we are to imagine that the scribe of Paris 909 was deliberately choosing to use one traditional oral formula instead of another available one, this brings us very close to the concept of centonization that Treitler rejects (1975). But actually it might be better to treat the entire musical setting over the words "[Ihesus] quem reges gentium" as the formula, rather than just the opening fifth leap, because the descent from and return to the pitch a is one conventional way of continuing a melody that has begun D–a. If the phrase rather than the leap is the real formula, it occurs at the same place in both versions, but nowhere else in either, for the two earlier phrases that begin D–a in Apt

musicological discussion of Ong's nine "characteristics of orally based thought and expression" (1982:36–57).

10. In particular, I disagree with Treitler's transcriptions at a number of places. Most significantly I believe that, in Apt 17, the music over the first syllables of "Ecclesiae" and "baptismatis" is actually D–G rather than D–a. However, there is room for doubt because the dry-point lines (staff lines scratched in the parchment without ink) are often incompletely visible in the microfilms. Therefore, rather than attempt to revise the transcription, I have reprinted it essentially as Treitler published it, and my reply to his discussion of it assumes that this transcription is correct.

17 are continued differently. This suggests that there are other ways of interpreting the difference between the two melodies. Perhaps the scribe of Paris 909 inherited a tradition that used this formula at this point, and he achieved his special effect not by manipulating the music, but by inserting the word "Ihesus" into the text. Or perhaps both versions are simple transcriptions from two (not entirely unrelated) oral traditions. These traditions agree on having versions of this musical formula at the words "[Ihesus] quem reges gentium," but earlier, at the words "Ecclesiae sponsus" and "baptismatis sacrator," they agree only on the general melodic direction, so that Apt begins with open fifth leaps and Paris 909 does not.

Treitler's attempt to interpret the melody and text in light of the history of medieval thought is laudable in intention, but in fact superficial and thus difficult to sustain. The devotional shift he referred to certainly took place, but if the accepted date of Paris MS latin 909 (ca. 1000–1034) is correct, the manuscript was probably copied too early to have been influenced by it, for it antedates the activity of Anselm of Canterbury (ca. 1033–1109) and others who were responsible for this change of emphasis in medieval spirituality.[11] Nor were Anselm and the others closely connected with the place where Paris MS 909 originated, St. Martial in Limoges. All this demonstrates how important it is for medieval musicology to be thoroughly informed by the history of medieval philosophy and theology. As is the case with any other culture or historical period, the surviving music will be understood most fully only if we enter as fully as possible into the mental world of the people who created and used it.

Clearly Treitler's views of chant transmission rely heavily on analogies to textual transmission. They are at least questionable because of the problems inherent in all linguistic analogies to music (Feld 1974; Powers 1980b); some of them also involve questionable interpretations of the textual material to which the analogy is being made. It is true of course that textual criticism, the discipline that studies the written transmission of ancient and medieval texts, is a hoary field from which musicologists have learned much. But to what degree and in what ways should we be willing to formulate or entertain analogies between textual and musical transmission? This issue comes to a head when we get involved in the actual tran-

11. See, for instance, McGinn et al. 1985: 196–228, 256–8, 323–8, 422–5. While there have been few discussions of trope texts by theologians, see Rasmussen 1983.

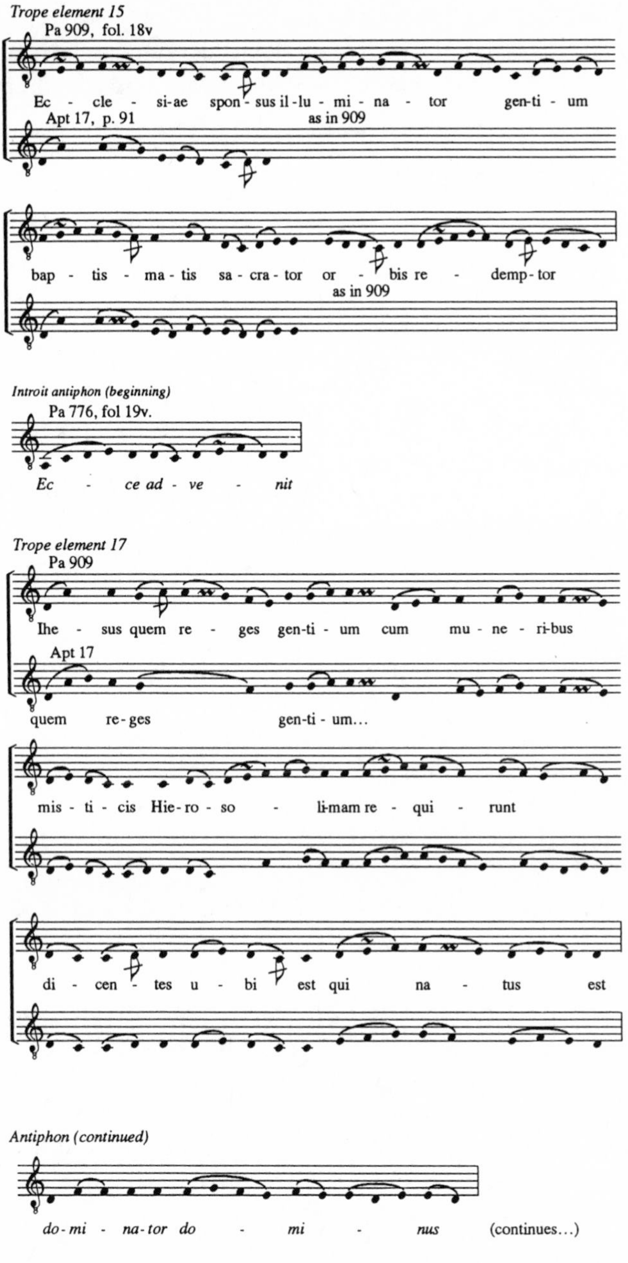

EXAMPLE 2. Excerpt from Treitler 1984a:111–2, with some corrections based on collation with other publications (compare 1984c:174, 1985a:173, 1985b:129).

scription, editing, and analysis of the medieval melodies—those activities, in other words, that most closely resemble the practice of textual criticism.

C. Implications and Applications: Toward Methodologies for Melodic Criticism and Editing

"It is both intuitively and evidentially clear that writing down, especially in the early times that we are talking about here, can have been a mix of copying and putting down what was in the scribe's head" (Treitler 1988: 569). To provide a more concrete picture, Treitler once offered the analogy of his own compositional process: "I usually keep a record of my thoughts in handwritten notes and sketches, and eventually I prepare a manuscript copy of a text. Finally I transcribe from that text onto a typewriter. . . . As I transcribe I may copy passages of the text word-for-word from the manuscript. But at other times I may treat the manuscript as just one concretization of the ideas I want to express. In that case the manuscript serves only to re-present those ideas to me, and I may give them quite different expression." Similarly, a notated melody in a medieval manuscript "may be thought of as a representation of the melody as a whole object. But the melody has a variety of possible expressions," and a performer or copyist who is consulting the manuscript may choose to perform or write down a different one. In this instance, what the manuscript actually transmitted to the performer or copyist was an "underlying structure," which he realized as he saw fit within the constraints of what the tradition permitted (1982a: 53–4, cf. 39).

One can debate whether this is an accurate picture of the medieval scribe or performer at work, and also whether it should be considered an example of "written" or "literate" transmission. But I will ask only about its methodological implications. It appears to lead to the conclusion that a twentieth-century analyst, editor, or performer can never fully accept what is actually written in a manuscript, but must always defer to the unwritten "rules" of the "generative system" within which the scribe was operating. It was the "generative system" that the scribe intended his manuscript to communicate, and the written tune is merely an example of it for illustrative purposes, not a completed musical composition. "It is as though the notator, in writing down the piece, were saying 'look, this is how it goes,' just as a performer might say that before performing the piece" (Treitler 1982a:49). Therefore, in commenting on the ten different versions of a trope melody found in ten Aquitainian manuscripts (1981a:205–7), Treitler asserted that

> We cannot establish a genealogy of the sources, and therefore we cannot establish an original or archetypical version. If we want to give an authoritative presentation of this verse in print, we must publish all the versions of it. . . . For . . . we cannot tell . . . whether the differences reflect scribal error, an imprecise notation, or compositional intention . . . . we cannot be certain that *any* score provided exact specifications for a performance . . . . we cannot guarantee that any given score represents even one fixed version of the work. . . . the near identity in the notations of [two of the manuscripts] may be no more than an artifact of the notation, a convention of representation. (1981a:207, italics original)

Even when the notation of a melody is virtually identical in a large number of manuscripts, we cannot conclude that "all performances . . . were identical in the level of detail covered by the notation, . . . for there is no guarantee that the notational uniformity is not again a case of stereotyping in the system of [written] signs itself" (1982a:57, cf. 55).

Treitler's list of all the things we cannot do seems at first to exclude just about every traditional approach to medieval manuscript study. The written melodies, he seems to say, are only examples of the "real" fact of transmission, the "generative systems," which should be the chief focus of scholarly study. All the more reason, then, why it should be an urgent priority to develop the critical tools for identifying and analyzing "generative systems," and determining their melodic "grammars." It is almost as if little other research can even be undertaken until that task is accomplished.

But I wonder if this impasse seems more formidable than it actually is. It strikes me as somewhat artificial, born of attempts to emphasize the newness of the New Historical View by creating too sharp an opposition between it and an alleged "older" view, which Treitler has dubbed "the Modern Paradigm." "Research in music history has been guided by this paradigm," he has written.

> The importance of writing for the Modern Paradigm is not to be underestimated. . . . The written score, as symbol of the work, is the vehicle of transmission. . . . Copying is assumed to be an entirely passive act. . . . Differences between scores for the same work are to be explained on the grounds of revision,

and if they are not they are attributed to error. (Treitler 1981a:202)

This seems to describe the most conservative method of textual criticism, developed in the nineteenth century by Karl Lachmann and other classical philologists, who wanted to be able to reconstruct the original texts of ancient writings preserved in relatively small numbers of manuscripts.[12] But even this method allowed a significant place for "the deliberate activity of the scribe" (Reynolds and Wilson 1974:210), who—far from being "passive"—could introduce emendations, bowdlerizations, or interpolations (Maas 1958:14–5, 34–5; Ap-Thomas 1966:42–8), and be responsible for conflation or "horizontal transmission," more commonly and pejoratively called "contamination" (Reynolds and Wilson 1974:192–4; Bévenot 1961), to say nothing of new revisions or recensions of the text. The very earliest papyrus fragments of the New Testament, for instance, reveal that some scribes transmitted the text quite freely, while others attempted to reproduce their exemplars with varying degrees of exactness.[13]

More importantly, however, the Lachmann approach is scarcely the only method of textual criticism practiced today, and thus its view of manuscript transmission can hardly be considered the only "Modern Paradigm." Since the beginning of the twentieth century the Lachmann method has been challenged repeatedly, even by classicists working with the kind of literature for which it was devised.[14] Among students of medieval literature, where the issues are already somewhat different than in classical studies, there has been considerable debate over what has been called "the logic

12. Classic statements of this method such as Hall 1913 and Maas 1958 have now been superseded by West 1973. The historical development of this approach is traced in Timpanaro 1971.

13. Aland and Aland (1989:58–64) see four types of texts: "free," "normal," "strict," and "paraphrastic," each representing a different attitude on the part of the scribes as to how to transmit the text. See also Epp 1989a, an extended review of Aland and Aland 1989, and Epp 1989b, an article on the papyri.

14. Some of the more important challenges are summarized in Metzger 1968:156–85; see also Pasquali 1962. A bibliography of writings for and against the Lachmann method, with brief annotations, is given in Boyle 1984:301–8. Recent collections of essays showing how the criticism of classical and early Christian texts is pursued today include Dummer et al., eds. 1987 and Grant 1989; see also Aland and Aland 1989:222–67, 280–316. A very interesting attempt to develop a mathematical model, showing that some traditional assumptions of the Lachmann method are consistent with probability theory, is Weitzman 1987.

of textual criticism" (Patterson 1987:77–113),[15] as well as continuing attempts to refine the traditional methodology for dealing with specific problems.[16] Scholars working with other literatures that have different kinds of transmission histories, and those who work with "texts" of unwritten or non-verbal media, have not hesitated to develop methodologies that are more pertinent to their material.[17] Musicologists, too, have held varying points of view on the applicability of Lachmannian procedures to the editing of early music and music theory.[18] More than one musicologist has pointed out that variants in music manuscripts need not be errors or even deliberate revisions—they may instead be important clues to the processes of transmission, reception, and performance that were active in the milieux from which the manuscripts came.[19]

However, few discussions of the problem by medieval musicologists have taken account of anything like the full range of text-critical approaches now available, or have even been informed by the far-reaching debates among medievalists over the goals and methods of textual criticism. The editing of chant in particular has received too little discussion from any quarter. Treitler is quite right seek to open a dialogue on these issues, and to insist that the basic presuppositions underlying our transcriptions and editions need to be thought through more deliberately. For progress to be made, though, musicologists and especially chant scholars will have to give more attention to some of the alternative approaches to textual criticism that may have something to offer.

One range of approaches with possible relevance to chant is being developed in the criticism of the New Testament.[20] This corpus of writings

15. See also Tanselle 1983, 1986; McGann, ed. 1985; Nichols 1990.

16. See, for instance, Paradisi, ed. 1971; Grier 1988b; Love 1984; Weitzman 1985; Wilson 1987; S. Wright 1986.

17. Many are chronicled in *Text: Transactions of the Society for Textual Scholarship* (1981 [1984]–) published in New York by AMS Press. A new bibliography on the subject of "editing documents and texts," compiled for the Association for Documentary Editing, is Luey 1990.

18. See for instance the articles in Fenlon, ed. 1981; also Brett 1988; Grier 1988a; Rapson 1989; Mathiesen 1990.

19. Atlas 1975/1:39–48; Fenlon, ed. 1981:249–399; Kirsch 1981; Pirrotta 1970, 1972, 1985.

20. The history of approaches to New Testament textual criticism is outlined in Metzger 1968:149–246, and, more recently, Aland and Aland 1989:222–67, 280–316. A call to give new attention to the oral environment in which the New Testament emerged is Achtemeier 1990.

resembles the Gregorian Graduale and other written chant collections in some important ways. Both contain material of varied origin and date, which moreover may have been edited numerous times before achieving its classic form. And both are preserved in thousands of manuscripts from many localities and periods—far too many to permit attempts to construct Lachmann-like stemmata. Thus biblical scholars for over a century have been trying out ways of working with "text types" or "group profiles," which permit large groups of manuscripts to be dealt with at the same time.[21] This approach inevitably shifts the emphasis away from individual manuscripts and from the personal decisions of individual scribes, toward comparisons among groups of manuscripts that are similar enough to be grouped together.

Something like this approach was finally adopted for the critical edition of the Gregorian Graduale (i.e., the repertory of chants for the Proper of the Mass) being prepared at Solesmes. The projected manuscript base would consist of nine "unities" or notational families, represented (usually) by one major early manuscript and one later diastematic source (Froger 1978).[22] As originally planned, the edition (Moines de Solesmes 1957–62), would have used "all the early manuscripts we know of."[23] The long list of manuscripts with detailed descriptions that was actually published, with the title *Les sources*, proved a great boon to chant scholarship, and is by far the most consulted of the three published volumes.[24] But as the basis for a critical edition it proved too unwieldy. Not only was there too much information to be effectively managed (Weakland 1961–2), but one critic even objected that some the most crucial manuscripts had not even been included.[25]

21. Numerous such studies could be cited, but see especially Ehrman 1987; Aland and Aland 1989: 48–71, 317–37.

22. I explored this issue with only partial success in an unpublished paper, "The Earliest Text-Types of the *Graduale*," read at the Seventeenth International Congress on Medieval Studies, Kalamazoo, Michigan, 1982. Portions of the paper were incorporated into Jeffery 1982, 1983, forthcoming.

23. "Nous continuons à l'accroître de tous les manuscrits anciens qui viennent à notre connaissance" (Froger 1954: 154). See also Cardine 1950.

24. Moines de Solesmes 1957. The bulk of the volume was actually authored by Michel Huglo, according to Spieth-Weissenbacher 1980.

25. "One can only be astonished that none of the direct ancestors of the [modern] Roman gradual has found a place among the 500 items [listed in the volume,] nor the ordinal [of the Papal curia] upon which this gradual and, for that matter, the whole Roman liturgy

Another editorial approach from which chant scholarship could benefit is often used for the texts of Latin liturgical manuscripts. Liturgical texts, like liturgical melodies, are relatively brief units that perhaps have very disparate origins, but that normally occur in the context of extensive collections or anthologies covering the entire liturgical year. The editor's purpose often is not to establish an "original" text by eliminating all the differences among the witnesses. Here every chronological and geographic stage of the transmission is equally of interest, and the goal is often to retrace the complete transmission history of the entire collection of texts. This approach is, then, very concerned with the peculiarities and historical contexts of individual manuscripts, and very open to appreciating the selection, revision, and editorial practices of individual scribes.[26] Compared with this, Hesbert's attempt (1963–79) to reconstruct the archetype of the Gregorian Antiphonale seems surprisingly naive (Huglo 1985, Moeller 1984, Ottosen 1986). But some better-informed essays on the criticism of chant texts—more prudently limited in scope—are also available (for example Chavasse 1984, Pinell 1984).

Thus the line between "the New Historical View" and "the Modern Paradigm" seems to me to have been too harshly drawn, and this has been done largely by attacking a characterization of the "Modern Paradigm" that is so narrowly conceived it is almost a parody. In reality there is no single "Modern Paradigm," but rather a whole range of approaches available for the would-be editor of medieval chant to examine and choose among—each reflecting a different way of looking at the written transmission and its interactions with unwritten processes. Even the most conservative approach to textual criticism allows for greater initiative on the part of the scribe than Treitler alleges. I hope that in the future, Treitler will outline more carefully how a critical approach based on the New Historical View would fit in among all the other schools of text criticism and editing that are practiced today. This would contribute to the advancement of a dialogue that has been neglected throughout the historical study of medieval music. For inseparable from the issues of criticism and editing is the underlying deeper issue—the nature of the transmission itself.

---

has depended since the second quarter of the thirteenth century" (Van Dijk 1960:98). See also Meeûs 1960.

26. Andrieu, ed. 1931–61/2:28–37, 1938–41/1:115–9; Vogel and Elze, eds. 1963–72/1:xi–xxii; Deshusses, ed. 1971–82/1:47–50, 75–8; see also Ottosen 1973.

D. Summary

To say that a hypothesis like the New Historical View needs further refinement or more explicit restatement is no condemnation—it only means that it is still a hypothesis. I hope that bringing some of the problems out into the open will help all of us who are interested in finding solutions for them. An important part of the process by which hypotheses become widely accepted, and entire fields renewed and strengthened, is scholarly debate, as those who agree on the importance of an issue respectfully listen to and reflect on each other's proposals for resolving it.[27] It is in that collegial spirit that I have offered these reflections.

My reflections on the New Historical View of Gregorian chant, briefly put, center on three problems: the problem of "grammar," the problem of confirmation, and the problem of criticism. Of these three, the most crucial is probably the second, which is a major cause of the other two. Our inability to verify the accuracy or plausibility of modern statements about the nature of early medieval chant transmission—or even to develop a precise theoretical vocabulary with which to make such statements—is one of the main reasons that we have not yet developed incisive approaches either to the analysis of the melodies or to their criticism and editing. The New Historical View, as presently formulated, does little to resolve this problem, because it is ultimately grounded in analogies between music and texts. Such analogies are inherently problematic, but in this case they may be even more so than usual, because they are framed according to a particular school of thought (the strand of literary scholarship that seeks to reinterpret the Parry-Lord theory in light of generative grammar). This school of thought is by no means universally respected even among students of literature. Other approaches to the study of oral literature, such as those employed by anthropologists (Goody 1977, Murphy 1978) have not even been taken into account.

What chant scholarship really needs to turn to is a field that studies the oral transmission of music itself rather than texts. From such a field we could learn directly about the ways musical oral traditions actually function across the spectrum of human societies and cultures. Such a field would be based on direct observation of oral music without the mediation

27. The ideal, in my view, was succinctly expressed by a biographer of G. K. Chesterton: "Even those whose opinions he attacked felt confident that it was only their opinions that were under attack" (Ffinch 1986: 3).

of other disciplines. If used at all, terms and concepts borrowed from literary studies, like "grammar" and "formula," would be no mere metaphors, but would clearly and immediately denote observable musical phenomena. Only when we can recognize and name in our own tongue the kinds of musical phenomena that occur frequently, occasionally, or rarely in the various contexts formed by interactions between oral and written transmission—only then will we be able to make educated guesses about what may have happened in early medieval Europe.

If chant scholarship were informed by the direct observation and evaluation of actual oral musics, those who theorized that the oral transmission of the chant may have operated in one way or another could then support their claims with evidence that other oral traditions actually have been observed to operate in much the same way. As it is now, historical speculation is not controlled by verifiable facts about the observable processes of musical oral transmission. As a result, it is always in danger of raging unchecked, ending up with no demonstrable relationship at all to the human realities of musical experience in any historical period, and with no accepted grounds by which the validity of any historical hypothesis can be confirmed. Attempts to explain the transmission processes behind the melodies are made virtually in an informational vacuum, so that no one can justify saying yea or nay.

Given the way the musicological discipline is currently divided, to say that chant historians need to learn about musical oral traditions is the same as saying that they should study ethnomusicology, the field of musical scholarship that has, in effect, been entrusted with all investigations of oral music. It is a sad testimony to the deep chasms that divide our specialties that historical musicologists, when they begin to wonder about oral tradition in music, should find it easier to turn to the study of oral literature than to the branch of their own discipline that actually studies oral music, even though the potential value of ethnomusicology to chant studies has been pointed out before.[28]

One reason some historical musicologists may be reluctant to become involved in ethnomusicology is that they sense it will not be easy.

28. No one has called more consistently for ethnomusicological investigations of early chant transmission than Leo Treitler, most dramatically by including Bruno Nettl and Poul Olsen in his panel on "Transmission and Form in Oral Traditions" at the 1977 meeting of the International Musicological Society (Nettl 1981; Olsen 1981). See also Treitler 1981a, 1984b:159, 1988:575.

They are right. One cannot merely read an authoritative book on oral transmission and apply some of its ideas to one's own work with medieval chant. What will be needed is a new type of chant scholarship that is profoundly ethnomusicological, the results of which would be as much a contribution to the overall field of ethnomusicology as they would be to historical musicology. This is inherent in the very nature of the subject, but in particular it reflects the fact that, in the current state of ethnomusicological research, oral transmission is a very open and controversial subject.

It would be a great mistake to imagine that ethnomusicologists have built up a vast store of information about the workings of oral tradition, which is valid for almost all cultures, and which therefore has only to be injected (with the appropriate modifications) into chant studies. In fact, so much of the human musical terrain remains completely unmapped that ethnomusicological research must still proceed culture by culture, often doing spadework that is still much too basic to permit the kinds of cross-cultural comparisons that would make a general theory of oral transmission possible. Hence responsible theories about musical universals of any kind may be expressed only in the most tentative language. As a result, "the general literature on oral transmission is actually based on a small number of repertories. For example, Lord's (1965 [1960]) highly influential book deals with Yugoslav epic poetry; Cutter (1976) and Treitler (1974, 1975), with Christian liturgical chant; Hood, with Java. Barry, Bayard, and Bronson have developed the concept as it works in Anglo-American folk music, Wiora in German song and Europe generally. The conventional wisdom is based mainly on knowledge of European and American folk music" (Nettl 1983: 189). This situation naturally encourages the perception that oral tradition represents a special situation, a peculiar and indeed rather limited approach to music-making that applies only to a few musical cultures, so that some of their most distinctive features, such as "formulas" (as in the Yugoslav epic) and "tune families" (as in European and American folk songs), have come to be seen as typical of oral transmission in general.

But this perception is in fact the opposite of the truth, for the subject of oral transmission is as broad as music itself. "The approaches developed in ethnomusicology can underscore something already understood but rarely expounded, that oral (or more correctly, aural) transmission is the norm, that music everywhere uses this form of self-propagation, that . . . it almost always accompanies the written [transmission], and that it dominates the musical life of a society and the life of a piece of music" (Nettl 1983:200). Oral transmission has been an essential part of almost every known musical culture, so that it is no easier to generalize about than any other aspect of music. Historical musicologists tracing the origins of chant traditions, then, cannot expect to succeed merely by borrowing a few concepts or a ready-made paradigm from ethnomusicological literature. They will only be able to deal adequately with oral transmission by adopting (temporarily, at least) a new perspective on their subject that is fully ethnomusicological. Building on the views of one eminent practitioner, we might characterize such a perspective as one that seeks to understand the chant as a "total musical system," in light of what can still be learned about its original cultural context, informed by modern fieldwork and comparative studies of all, or at least many, of the other musical cultures of the world (Nettl 1983:ix–x, 9). This does not mean that the traditional historical and paleographical approaches to medieval chant study are wrong, faulty, or exhausted, or that they will be any less important in the future. It only means that they can and should be pursued in a new way, a way that is open to all the evidence bearing on the unlimited variety of human musical activity past and present.

The notated chant manuscripts we study today should be seen as relics of a culture that is in many ways quite foreign to us—not merely an early stage of our own culture. Parts of the medieval cultural heritage are of course still with us, in many of the practices and customs that are still followed in modern universities and monasteries—in architecture, ceremonies, courses of study (cf. Culham and Edmunds 1989)—and even in popular science fiction (cf. Goethals 1990:150; Gaster 1987). In music, too, such concepts as the diatonic scale and the principles of staff notation have clearly developed from medieval antecedents.

In spite of all this, we are still natives of McLuhan's "Global Village," heirs as much (if not more) of the Renaissance and the Industrial Revolution as of the Middle Ages, supported by high technology and communicating by electronic media—and now even the Latin liturgy is gone (see Bugnini 1990). As we look back on medieval chant from more than a thousand years' remove, we find our own mental categories so different from those of early medieval clerics that we cannot necessarily trust our usual instincts—what seems a sensible inference to us may be completely inappropriate to the period we are studying. We must be willing to recognize that, though we have inherited much from the Middle Ages, we are no more at home there than in the modern "Third World" cultures whose exports we buy and use. To both we are cultural outsiders, trying to imagine how the insiders experience their own very different cultures, by listening carefully and impartially to a relatively small number of insider informants (cf. Nettl 1983:259–69). To understand the oral side of early medieval musical culture, then, we need to learn to see it as an ethnomusicologist might, drawing whatever assistance we can from the great stock of experience that ethnomusicologists have built up trying to understand modern musical cultures not their own.

In the rest of this essay I will make two kinds of suggestions about the new directions in which I think chant research should proceed. Of course I exaggerate somewhat in calling these directions "new," for in many cases both their existence and the value of exploring them has been evident to all for some time. But they need to receive new attention because of their special usefulness for studying the problem of early chant transmission—in fact their particular accessibility to ethnomusicological investigation helps to explain some of their past neglect by music historians.

The first group of suggestions (chapter 4) grows out of some of the concerns that ethnomusicologists typically bring to almost any subject matter. These concerns do not necessarily focus on oral transmission as such, but no study of musical orality can be conducted without them. It is remarkable how unerringly every one of these concerns points to an unjustifiably neglected area of chant research. The second group of suggestions (chapter 5) identifies musical processes that are known to have been active in the world of medieval chant, and that have interesting parallels in some other cultures of the past or present. Though some of these processes have not been looked at this way before, each of them should be investigated as a possible variety or type or means of oral transmission—one of the ways that human beings in some circumstances, with or without the aid of writing or of other oral/aural processes, have passed on the contents of their musical heritages to their listeners, students, and cultural descendants.

4

Some Ethnomusicological Concerns

A. Some Terms

It is helpful to begin with some terminological distinctions. While the words "tradition" and "transmission" originally had similar meanings (Latin for "handing over" and "sending over" respectively) the recent tendency in musical scholarship has been to use the word "transmission" more narrowly, as referring to the processes by which music is passed on. The word "tradition," then, is left to denote a somewhat larger range of meanings. "Tradition" can be the content or product of a "transmission" process, as when we say that there is a tradition linking Gregorian chant to Pope Gregory the Great: we have heard of this linkage because it was transmitted or handed down to us from long ago. Or "tradition" can denote the entire musical "dialect" or culture in which the transmission processes take place, as we might say that the Gallican chant tradition never developed a written notation while the Gregorian did. However, "the concept of tradition which implies the existence of a generally accepted and relatively solidified corpus of musical material and practice is probably the one most often used currently" (Harrison 1979 : 116). I would use the term "tradition" in this sense when speaking of a corpus of chants in terms of its historical development (i.e., diachronically), as distinct from the more "timeless" or synchronic implications of the term "repertory." One might remark, for instance, that a certain chant text had a long and important history in the Ambrosian chant tradition, but was not to be found at all in the extant Gregorian repertory. Thus there is a tendency for the word "tradition" to connote the relatively stable aspects of historical continuity, and "transmission" its more changeable aspects (Nettl 1982 : 3–4; Coplan 1991). A somewhat related distinction is that made between "content"—those features of the music that a particular culture regards as essential to the complete and correct transmission of the tradition—and "style"—the more transitory features that are not regarded as part of the musical matter, but are peculiar to particular versions, performers, performances, or other transient phenomena (Nettl 1983: 47–9, 115–7, 189–91). This sort of distinction has already been observed in cases where the "same" melody is found in more than one medieval chant tradition, expressed each time in the local stylistic vocabulary.[1] "When a piece is transmitted, style changes, content remains" (Nettl 1983: 190). Of course, the question of which features should be identified as "content" and which as "style" may change not only from culture to culture or tradition to tradition, but even from generation to generation within a single tradition. This is one of the many reasons why both historical and ethnomusicological approaches must be employed synergetically in the study of medieval chant.

B. Cross-Cultural Comparisons

Because the culture of medieval chant can no longer be observed directly, any attempt to study it ethnomusicologically will inevitably involve hypothetical analogies to other, more recent cultures. But cross-cultural comparisons are hardly new to chant scholarship—comparisons of Gregorian chant to folk music, Jewish music, and other traditions of religious chanting have been made for decades by many writers. Parry's and Lord's attempt to investigate ancient Greek poetry by means of analogies to modern Serbo-Croatian songs was itself founded on the principle that cultures can be meaningfully compared, and Treitler's attempt to extend Parry's and Lord's comparison to medieval chant amounts to a further endorsement of this principle. It is important, therefore, to look closely at what is really involved in comparisons of musical cultures, in order to determine how they may properly be undertaken and what they can reasonably be expected to accomplish.

1. Principles of Comparison

Ethnomusicologists are often wary of cross-cultural comparisons because of the simplistic ways in which they have frequently been abused. Never-

1. In one of his many studies of such melodies, Kenneth Levy observed "that chant dialects impose their own stylizations on whatever materials they contain" (1970: 210).

theless, Alan P. Merriam (1982) argued that such comparisons have at least three legitimate uses: (1) for what was called "inferential history" by Śarana (1975), that is, the attempt to recover the unwritten history of a culture by comparing its present state with that of another culture to which it was once related; (2) for the study of distribution and typology, as when one attempts to map the musical styles found in different parts of a given region; (3) as a basis for suggesting generalizations or universals. Comparisons have been used in chant studies for all three of these purposes, though usually without much consideration of the problems inherent in any comparative approach. And all three must play a role in current attempts to reconstruct hypothetically the conditions in which early medieval chant emerged.

Attempts to characterize the workings of oral and written transmission processes in the early medieval period could certainly be considered "inferential history." Because the oral component of early medieval culture is no longer directly observable, it can only be recreated inferentially, by comparing the written melodies with information derived from other sources (cultures) about the ways oral traditions operate. To make this comparison is necessarily to make use of generalizations or posited universals, otherwise one could not justify any comparisons between modern living cultures and lost ancient ones. The acceptance of some universal (or at least common or "supracultural") principles must also underlie studies of chant "distribution and typology," otherwise comparisons of the great Latin chant dialects (Gregorian, Roman, Ambrosian, etc.), for instance, would be pointless.

Of course, as Nettl points out (1983:36–43) we know far too little about the music history and anthropology of the human race as a whole even to begin to speak authoritatively about what is truly universal. A more manageable concept has been proposed by a student of music cognition (Serafine 1988:39–42), who distinguishes "generic processes," which are common to many cultures, from "style-specific processes," which are limited to only one (I would prefer, for the latter, the phrase "culture-specific" to avoid confusion with other usages of the word "style"). Using such language one could perhaps isolate processes that seem to operate similarly in more than one of the cultures that make use of liturgical or ceremonial chant, and distinguish them successfully from processes that seem to be limited to only one or a few related cultures, or "musical communities" (Serafine 1988:33–5). One could then avoid using the inevitably problematic word "universal," for it may be that nothing is truly universal except the human brain and the body it controls.

Hence familiarity with the study of musical cognition, or the psychology of music, should be indispensable to anyone attempting to deduce facts about one culture on the basis of comparisons with another. Indeed it is possible to argue that "a musical culture is essentially a cognitive entity, in other words to define a musical culture means defining 'the things a people must know in order to understand, perform and create acceptable music in their culture' " (Cook 1990:222, quoting Feld 1974:211). One who subscribed to such a cognitive definition of culture would presumably also agree that "the categories in terms of which musicians evaluate pitch and time exist only by virtue of acts of perception that embody culture-specific knowledge" (Cook 1990:219). Or, to switch from a cross-cultural to a historical frame of reference, "the conventions of eighteenth-century music ultimately reside in the minds of listeners" (Gjerdingen 1988:269).

It goes without saying that not everyone would agree with this attempt to define "musical culture" in terms of only one of its many factors. But it is hard to disagree with the notion that shared categories of perception and understanding are surely prominent among the elements that define a musical culture, that distinguish each musical culture from all the others, and that determine who is a member or "insider" to a culture, and by the same token who is an "outsider."

Anthropology and ethnomusicology, of course, have long been conscious of the differences between cultural insiders and outsiders, not least because scholars in these fields spend so much of their time studying cultures different from the ones in which they themselves were raised (Grenier and Guilbault 1990). Hence the special terms "emic" and "etic" for "inside" and "outside" (see Nettl 1983:140–1; Harris 1976), which have also been applied to the study of the past in the field of "ethnoarchaeology" (Gould 1990:64–92). An "emic" description of a cultural artifact attempts to reproduce the viewpoint of a member of the culture, even if the scholar doing the describing is actually an outsider, and whether or not the process being described is judged "generic" or "culture-specific." An "etic" description, on the other hand, is written from outside the culture (most often from a Western perspective, of course), and thus will often involve translating phenomena of one culture into the conceptual language of another. Underlying such cross-cultural analogies will often be an unavoidable implication that what is being described is some sort of "generic," if not "universal," phenomenon (cf. Ember 1977).

2. Some Comparable Cultures

A chant scholar who really wanted to follow Parry's and Lord's example, by comparing early medieval chant with some similar but more accessible modern culture, would not go about it by trying to force medieval chant into Parry's construction of the Slavic epic poem. One would operate instead by locating and investigating a modern culture that, in at least some important respects, appeared to resemble the early medieval clerical culture in which the chant arose. Such cultures are not difficult to find, and they reflect many different kinds and degrees of similarity to the early medieval church.

First of all, small pockets of orally transmitted Western chant have been reported to survive in several parts of modern Europe (papers on a number of them were read at a recent conference, see Arcangeli, ed. 1988). Even if one chooses to deny that these traditions have any direct historical continuity with the Middle Ages, the fact remains that in them we can see the same texts, sung to what are sometimes the same melodies, and in a context that is directly descended from the medieval Western liturgy. Thus we can observe the use of oral psalm tones (some of them known medieval tones, one apparently adapted from Verdi!) and simple oral polyphony in the Ossola valley, province of Novara, in the Italian Alps (Oltolina 1984). A similar but apparently more extensive tradition survives in the diocese of Udine in the Friuli (Ernetti 1978–9). In the more complex tradition found on the island of Corsica (Chailley 1982, Quilici 1971, Römer 1983), we find familiar medieval (and post-medieval) melodies performed with both vocal ornamentation and polyphony—and with a significant written tradition alongside the oral one. In Dalmatia (Yugoslavia), where the Roman rite has been celebrated since the ninth century in the Glagolitic or (as it is more properly called) the Old Church Slavonic language, medieval Gregorian melodies are still performed in highly ornamented and harmonized versions.[2] Lesser amounts of ornamentation are tradi-

2. On the history of the Romano-Slavonic use see Jelić 1906; Korolevsky 1957: 73–90; Smiržík 1959; Schütz 1963. On the modern ornamented and harmonized chant

tional in Hungary, where the Roman rite was celebrated mainly in Latin before the worldwide adoption of the vernacular beginning in the 1960s (Rajeczky 1985), a reform that now threatens the survival of most of these traditions.

In the Byzantine liturgical orbit, extant oral traditions appear to be even more substantial, though they have so far attracted only a few article-length studies.[3] Greater attention to these traditions is particularly advisable, however, because Byzantine chant has a written tradition reaching almost as far back as that of the West, and posing most of the same problems. But because some of the variables were inevitably different, we can sometimes see aspects of the oral and written transmissions more clearly than in the West. Particularly interesting are those unusual instances when an individual chant or group of chants is preserved both in Eastern and Western versions.[4]

The smaller oral and written traditions of the Armenian and Georgian churches have received serious study by native scholars, but deserve much more attention from the international scholarly community.[5] These traditions are especially important because they are in part directly descended from early medieval translations of the Greek chant repertory sung at Jerusalem, the Holy City whose liturgical rite exercised considerable influence on the worship and chant of the entire ancient Christian

---

melodies see Martinić 1981; Stepanov 1983. The musical tradition of this Romano-Slavonic use is also of interest because (due to the difference in language) it seems to have escaped the chant reforms of the early twentieth century, in which the Vatican Edition was universally adopted wherever the Roman rite was celebrated in Latin (Jeffery 1991b). Apparently, the only part of the Vatican Edition to be adapted to the Slavonic texts and officially adopted in the Romano-Slavonic use was the *Cantorinus*, the book of melodies for the prayers sung by the priest at Mass. They were first published in *Pěnije* 1914, and incorporated into all subsequent editions of the Romano-Slavonic Missal.

3. Baud-Bovy 1979; Dragoumis 1966, 1971; Raasted 1979b; Salvo 1952; Sciambra 1965–6; Stathis 1979; see also Jeffery 1988a:132. A symposium on the question of how recent oral and written traditions of Byzantine chant can help illuminate the medieval traditions (Raasted, ed. 1982) included the following papers: Engberg 1982; Stathis 1982; Touliatos 1982; Petrescu 1982; Borsai 1982; Kapronyi 1982.

4. Some older studies are listed in A. Hughes 1980:71, 72–3, 84–5. See also Levy 1970; Moran 1980; Strunk 1977:151–6, 165–90, 208–19, 297–330.

5. Among the more accessible publications on Armenian chant are Atayan 1968; Dayan 1952, 1957, 1960–; Ertlbauer 1985; Henrotte 1980; Nersessian 1978; Outtier 1973, 1985; Serkoyan 1973; Tʿahmizyan 1970, 1977, 1983. Concerning Georgian liturgical music, some articles in Western languages include Gwacharija 1967, 1977–8; Grimaud 1977, 1979a, 1979b; Outtier 1985; Tsereteli 1974.

world.[6] Relatively "pure" oral traditions of Christian liturgical chant are to be found in the Syriac and Coptic rites, where few notated documents were ever in use.[7] These come the closest of any modern cultures to resembling the ecclesiastical culture in Europe before notation was in use, and possibly even before the centralizing Romanization and Byzantinization of the Latin and Greek repertories was fully under way. The Ethiopian rite, which makes use of a notation that records melodic formulas rather than individual pitches, is particularly important for investigating the formulaic character of liturgical chant.[8]

It may also be possible to learn from some of the non-Christian religions whose worship includes the use of monophonic chant.[9] Judaism (Spector 1981–2), Islam, and Hinduism make use of scriptural cantillation and of prayer texts sung to traditional oral melodies, and many other religions make use of monophonic vocal music that in some respects resembles medieval Christian chant (see, e.g., Tatar 1982). Buddhist monastic communities, such as those found in Tibet, may perhaps have something to show us both about the society within the monastery and about its relationship to the culture outside (Tethong 1979).[10] Truly eye-opening opportunities "to see ourselves as others see us" can be found in attempts by musicians of other cultures to draw parallels between their own music and the traditions of liturgical chant that are more familiar to us.[11]

6. See Jeffery 1991a, forthcoming. The first full-length study of Jerusalem chant and its influence will be my book currently in progress, working title *Liturgy and Chant in Early Christian Jerusalem: The Sources and Influence of a Seminal Tradition,* which assembles all the primary sources of the Jerusalem chant repertory, and traces the historical development of that tradition from the fourth to the twelfth century.

7. The bibliography on the Syriac chant traditions is very extensive, but see Breydy 1971, 1979; Cody 1982; Hage 1972; Husmann 1966, 1967, 1969, 1971, 1972, 1974a, 1974b, 1975–8, 1979, 1980; Raasted 1979a; Ross 1979. On Coptic chant, see Blin 1888; Gillespie 1978; Menard 1952, 1959, 1972; M. Robertson 1984, 1985, 1987; the many publications of Ilona Borsai listed in the bibliography of this book and in Borsai 1980a; and the articles on Coptic music by Marian Robertson in *The Coptic Encyclopedia.* On the rare instances of notation in these traditions, see Raasted 1979a; Husmann 1974b, 1975–8.

8. See Shelemay and Jeffery forthcoming; Shelemay, Jeffery, and Monson forthcoming.

9. For an attempt to develop a universal theory of "chanting" as a distinct musical activity common to many religions and cultures, see Spector 1986–7, 1987.

10. An interesting study of Tibetan Buddhist nuns is Havnevik [1989]; for brief discussion of their music see 75–8, 106–7.

11. An attempt to describe medieval Gregorian chant in Indian terms is J. Higgins 1965. The encounter of an Indian student of Sāmavedic chant with Samaritan and Hebrew chant is recorded in Raghaven 1954. A remarkably unselfconscious attempt by an Israeli scholar to describe Syrian Christian chant in India in terms of Jewish liturgical categories is

In making comparisons of this sort, it is important to avoid the pitfall into which some older writers have fallen, by supposing that these very different liturgical chant traditions are somehow historically derived from one another. The temptation to trace a simple historical line from the Synagogue to the early Church has been especially difficult for many to resist (Jeffery 1987). But resistance is essential, for to know these chant traditions intimately is to see clearly that they are related only on a very fundamental level—the kind of level on which all dance music or all marching music or all musical theater might be said to be related. The liturgical chant traditions of the world's major religions are similar in some respects because they are used in similar contexts to achieve similar purposes, not because one is historically derived from another.[12] Many other cultures that lack liturgical chant as such nevertheless make use of ritualized, cultic speech that has properties in common with chant as we know it—in oral cultures, ritual chanting may fulfill some of the functions that writing performs in literate cultures (Akinnaso 1982). On a more basic level still, it is possible to see most types of chanting as developing from a kind of stylization of the pitch variations that are characteristic of all human speech, the phenomenon linguists call "intonation" (Bolinger 1989; Watt 1990). But then perhaps this could be said of almost all vocal music.

By making critical use of information learned from non-Western and non-Christian chant traditions, chant scholars will establish a much broader and firmer basis on which to speculate about the ways oral processes may have functioned in Europe a millennium ago. Chant scholarship will begin to expand out of its present niche within music history, and move toward becoming a field that is as much ethnomusicological as music-historical, one that studies liturgical chant holistically as a human activity, common—with many differences but also with important similarities—to much of the world. When this begins to happen it will be a boon to both the fields of ethnomusicology and historical musicology. For "until we know how oral transmission works, we won't know what music history is all about" (Nettl 1981 : 144; Treitler 1981a : 202, 1984c : 143). Wide acceptance of a comparative approach would also bring liturgical chant studies

---

Ross 1979. There are, of course, innumerable published descriptions of Jewish liturgy that attempt to describe it in terms of Christian liturgical categories!

12. Jewish and Christian chant share the additional similarity that they use many of the same texts—though in different ways, in different languages, and with different melodies.

up to the norm of modern liturgical studies generally, where it is taken for granted that every scholar is informed about all the Eastern and Western liturgical traditions of the religion(s) he or she works in. As one prominent liturgical historian has put it: "Liturgiology, like linguistics, is a comparative discipline: one can no more be a liturgiologist by studying one tradition than one can develop a theory of linguistics knowing only one language."[13] The problem of oral transmission in early medieval chant has brought us to the point where we must now be prepared to say the same. Given the very lopsided concentration of musicological literature on the Latin chant traditions of the West, this will not mean that every chant scholar will have to be equally conversant with every chant tradition. But the field as a whole needs to move toward the kind of inclusiveness that expert liturgiology has already almost achieved, in which studies of every liturgical tradition contribute on an equal footing to the ongoing progress of the whole liturgiological discipline.[14]

C. The Performers and Their World

A written text may have a "life" of its own, but an oral tradition lives only through the musicians who perform it. Oral music, therefore, cannot be studied in isolation, without reference to the lives of its performers. One could perhaps almost say that a singer is to an oral tradition what a manuscript is to a written one—each is the indispensable source, without which we would have no access to the music at all. A. B. Lord emphasized this by naming his classic study of oral poetry *The Singer of Tales*. The student of medieval chant, then, would do well to begin by studying the medieval singer of chants, asking some of the same questions an ethnomusicologist would. Questions about how ecclesiastical singers were selected and trained, how their liturgical duties were assigned, and what individual career paths they followed—all these and more have everything to do with

13. Taft 1984: ix. On the field of modern Christian liturgical studies, see also Jones et al., eds. 1978; Taft 1985; Wegman 1985; Neunheuser 1987, 1989; Kavanagh 1988; Thompson 1989; Caspers and Schneiders 1990; De Clerck and Palazzo 1990. On comparative approaches in Jewish liturgiology, see Sarason 1981, 1983; Hoffman 1987; Lardner 1989.

14. A step in this direction was taken at the fourth meeting of Cantus Planus, a study group of the International Musicological Society, in Pécs, Hungary, 3–9 September 1990. The proceedings will be published by the Institute for Musicology of the Hungarian Academy of Sciences in Budapest.

the problem of how the chant melodies were created and transmitted, both before and after the introduction of neumatic musical notation (cf. Nettl 1981: 144). But of course it is one thing to describe living singers on the basis of personal interviews—quite another to attempt to unearth comparable information about singers who died centuries ago. The tendency to overlook this problem is one weakness of the Parry-Lord approach, for historical study of the ancient Greek Homeric poets might have turned up some important differences between them and the modern Serbo-Croatian singers of tales—differences that would have called for greater caution in comparing the two (see now Nagy 1989).

The situations in which medieval chant was performed had little to do with what most modern people think of as "going to church." For the most part, the bulk of the repertory was not performed by or for a congregation on Sundays, but by and within religious communities that lived apart from the rest of society. In Western (i.e., Latin) Christianity these communities were made up of canons, monks, friars, or nuns, while in Eastern Christianity things were somewhat different.[15] The celebration of the liturgical services with their chant was a major reason such communities existed, but by no means the only one, either from the individual's

15. To give an oversimplified explanation of these terms as they were understood in the medieval West: Canons were priests committed to the common life and to the celebration of the liturgy "in choir" (i.e., communally and with music). They might be cathedral, or secular, canons, attached to the church that served as the "headquarters" of a diocese, where the bishop (the highest-ranking clergyman) had his throne or *cathedra.* Or they might be canons regular, members of one of the religious orders that followed the Rule [*regula*] of St. Augustine. Canons regular could also be cathedral canons, but if they were not attached to a cathedral their church was known as a collegiate church. Monks, who were not necessarily priests, were also committed to the common life and to the celebration of the liturgy, but they lived in monasteries and followed the Rule of St. Benedict. The most important medieval monastic orders were the Benedictines, the Cluniacs, the Cistercians, and the Carthusians. Friars were members of the new mendicant orders that began to be founded in the early thirteenth century, the Franciscans and the Dominicans being the most important. Canons regular, monastic orders, and mendicant orders all could have corresponding female orders of nuns; nuns whose mode of life was based on that of the canons regular could be called canonesses. Of course there was also liturgical and musical activity in other ecclesiastical settings, such as within the orders of chivalry (including the Knights of Malta and the Knights Templar), and in parish churches, palace chapels, and various kinds of memorial chapels established by bequest so that prayers could be offered for the souls of the deceased donors. For a good brief summary of this subject see Engels 1970. The Eastern church never developed orders of mendicants or knights, and the cathedrals and monasteries were organized somewhat differently. See Onasch 1981: 211, 267–70; Meyendorff 1983; Metz 1987.

point of view or from that of society. Thus it is likely that even the expert singers did not regard themselves primarily as musicians at all.[16] An ethnomusicologist who turned his attention to medieval chant would immediately want to learn as much as possible about both the structure of the communities and the lives and educations of the individuals who belonged to them. Yet chant scholars have devoted hardly any attention at all to this subject. In the musicological literature, one typically encounters only one acknowledgment that the chant was created and performed within a human community. This occurs in treatments of the ritual foolery that took place between Christmas and New Year's day, when the liturgical celebration was turned on its head: mocking songs were sung amongst the sacred chants, a donkey was given the place of honor in the liturgical procession, a choirboy was appointed bishop (Chambers 1903, 1:274–371, 2:279–89; Arlt 1970; Fassler forthcoming a). This sort of thing has always been regarded as an embarrassment by church historians and an anomaly by musicologists, but it is familiar ground to anthropologists, who know that "ritual clowning," temporary inversions of the social authority structure, or "periods of license" are a common phenomenon in many societies, "when the customary restraints of law and morality are thrown aside, . . . and when the darker passions find a vent which would never be allowed them in the more staid and sober course of ordinary life."[17]

The dearth of musicological research into the life of monastery society is not due to lack of material, but to our scholarly perspectives that have failed to value such information. Modern historical studies of medieval monastic life are readily available,[18] and anthropological studies of medieval monasticism and liturgy are becoming more common.[19] The

16. This was still the case in the fifteenth and sixteenth centuries, as the medieval system was finally beginning to wane. See Pirrotta 1966; C. Reynolds 1984; P. Higgins 1990. Much more research remains to be done, however, and even more so on earlier periods, where detailed records that permit us to trace particular individuals over the course of their careers are much scarcer. The earliest musical establishment for which substantial documentation bearing on the biographies of the singers has been found and published is the papal chapel of fourteenth-century Avignon (Tomasello 1983; Jeffery 1986b).

17. Frazer 1961:319–29; Handelman 1987; *The Encyclopedia of Religion* 16:191 at index entry "clowns"; E. Thompson 1987; Grimes 1990a:115–7.

18. Good introductions to the study of monasticism are Knowles 1969 and Leclercq 1982. A basic bibliography is Constable 1976.

19. See for example Turner and Turner 1978; McCormick 1985; J. Nelson 1986; Bynum 1987; J. Smith 1987b; Barnes 1990; Paxton 1990; all of which cover only specific

medieval "bylaws" of many religious communities still survive in numerous customaries, ordinals, and typika from almost all historical periods. Many have been edited, and await only the detailed investigation and interpretation of their musical evidence.[20] It is thus not surprising that one of the very few musicologists ever to study this material (Harrison 1980) was also one of the few scholars to distinguish himself in both medieval musicology and ethnomusicology. Yet in the more than thirty years since the first edition of his book appeared (1958), hardly anyone has attempted to follow his example (but see Summers 1986 : 139–40). One recent exception is an article outlining the historical development of the office of armarius/cantor, the official who controlled not only the teaching and performance of the chant, but also the copying and correction of musical and non-musical manuscripts (Fassler 1984). It shows how many anachronistic assumptions underlie much modern writing about the circumstances surrounding the copying of manuscripts and the performance of the chant, and how little musicologists know about these activities, despite the ready availability of substantial amounts of evidence.

D. Books and the Oral/Written Continuum

It is by now a commonplace that oral and written transmission are not to be seen as bipolar opposites, but as overlapping areas on a continuum. Nevertheless the specific shape and extent of the continuum needs to be worked out. It quickly becomes evident that a single one-dimensional continuum cannot possibly serve to adequately describe the several ranges of variables. Instead one needs to envision a number of interrelated continua, each one stretching out in two or three or more dimensions.

---

aspects of the subject. For the history of the use of anthropology in Christian liturgiology, see Stringer 1989. Examples of anthropological studies of non-medieval or non-Christian rituals include Baal 1971; d'Aquili et al. 1979; Sahlins 1981; R. Wagner 1984; Gorman 1990; Pandian 1991 : 131–82; Shaw 1991. On the emerging discipline of "ritual studies" see Grimes 1982, 1985, 1990a, 1990b, and the *Journal of Ritual Studies* (1987–), published by the Department of Religious Studies at the University of Pittsburgh. But the application of "ritual studies" approaches to medieval Christian liturgy is still unusual, to say the least.

20. For lists of published and unpublished medieval ordinals see Moines de Solesmes 2 (1957) : 189–96; Vogel 1986 : 366. Monastic customaries are edited in Hallinger, ed. 1963–, see also Angerer 1977. The main published typika are listed in Wegman 1985 : 259–60; an introduction to the study of the typikon is Schmemann 1986.

1. The Historical Continuum, from Oral to Written

In the historical continuum, which is relatively easy to describe as a one-dimensional line of chronological development, it is best not to think of a clean break between the period of oral transmission and the period of writing, but rather of a gradual shift from the predominance of one kind of transmission to the predominance of the other,[21] a shift that can be seen to have happened in stages.[22] In the first stage there was the Bible, from which most of the chant texts were excerpted or paraphrased; it was always a written source during the medieval period, yet chant texts often give indications that they were not merely excerpted from a book, but rather developed from the way texts were quoted from memory during sermons and other oral renditions. From the sermon literature of the late fourth and early fifth centuries we can see that certain psalms were already customarily sung on specific feasts, and we often are told that a particular verse served as the responsorial refrain, sung by the congregation after each psalm verse was performed by a soloist, who was known as the *cantor* ("singer") in Latin, the *psaltēs* or psalmist in Greek. In several dozen cases these fourth-century psalms and refrains are already the same texts that will turn up later in the Gregorian and other medieval chant repertories, particularly in the graduals, tracts, and (to a lesser degree) alleluias of the Mass. During the fifth, sixth, and seventh centuries, chant texts were beginning to be collected in books, a development that is first attested at Jerusalem and indeed may have begun there.[23] At first, chant texts were written down as supplements to the Bible in one way or another. Thus at Jerusalem the chant texts seem first to have accumulated around the lectionary, the anthology of biblical excerpts to be read at Mass each day of the year. Only later, as the number of chant texts and genres grew, were

21. The historical continuum has already been traced in Huglo 1973, and further developed in Treitler 1981b: 474–5, 488–91. A. B. Lord, too, observed that "when writing was introduced, epic singers . . . did not realize its 'possibilities' and did not rush to avail themselves of it. . . . Oral transmission did not become transferred or transmuted into a literary tradition of epic, but was only moved further and further into the background, literally into the back country, until it disappeared" (Lord 1960: 124, 138).

22. The outline that follows is a summary of the chronology laid out in my book in progress, *Prophecy Mixed with Melody* (see above, chapter 1, n. 2). See also Jeffery 1990, a transcript of a lecture on this topic.

23. See Jeffery 1986a; 1988a: 133–4; 1991a; forthcoming; and especially my work in progress, *Liturgy and Chant in Early Christian Jerusalem* (see n. 6, above).

they separated out from the lectionary and collected into a book of their own. The earliest true chant book—that is to say, the first book exclusively devoted to chant texts and containing at least the complete Proper repertory—is the one representing the rite of Jerusalem, and it probably dates from the seventh century. Though it was originally composed in Greek, it now survives only in a tenth-century translation into the Georgian language (Jeffery 1991a). It is interesting that the Georgian name for this book, *Iadgari*, may have been derived from a (Persian) word for "memory," perhaps recalling the momentousness of the first instance of writing down the complete repertory that had formerly been stored only in the memories of the singers (Tarchnišvili 1955 : 454).

In the West, lectionaries that include chant texts already existed by the sixth century (CLLA 250).[24] Some other early chant collections depend on the psalter rather than the lectionary. Thus a manuscript of the psalms from the sixth century also includes a collection of responsorial refrains (Huglo 1982). The late seventh-century Irish "antiphonary" of Bangor (CLLA 150) is a more extensive psalter supplement, containing a disordered collection of canticles, hymns, antiphons, and collects.[25] The Mozarabic Orationale of Verona (CLLA 330; early eighth century) is a better-organized collection of prayers to be said after (mostly) the psalms of the Office; before many prayers the incipits of the corresponding antiphons have been given, making this the earliest witness to the Mozarabic chant tradition.

The earliest extant Western source that could be considered an antiphoner strictly speaking is the Ambrosian double palimpsest fragment now at St. Gall (CLLA 550, dated ca. 700). From late in the eighth century come the earliest manuscripts of the Gregorian Proper chants,[26] and from about the year 900 date the earliest extant manuscripts in which these texts have neumes (cf. Jeffery 1982). Diastematic neumes began in the eleventh century, though staffless neumes were common in German and Eastern European manuscripts as late as the fourteenth century. Neumated Byzantine manuscripts begin in the tenth century, and the notation became fully diastematic late in the twelfth. In the other Eastern rites notation developed (if at all) at various dates, ranging from the earliest Byzantine

24. The abbreviation CLLA refers to the numbering of liturgical sources in the catalogue of Gamber 1968, 1988.

25. This is explained further in my unpublished paper "Eastern and Western Elements in the Irish Monastic Prayer of the Hours."

26. The checklist I published in Jeffery 1983 is already in dire need of extensive revision, expansion, and improvement; see also Jeffery forthcoming.

Slavonic source (perhaps late eleventh century) to the earliest Ethiopian one (sixteenth century; Shelemay and Jeffery forthcoming).

By delineating the stages of the historical continuum, one is actually laying out important chronological milestones that can help date other features of the medieval repertories.[27] For certain texts it is possible to determine approximately when they entered particular repertories, depending on whether they first appear in sermons of the fourth and fifth centuries, in provisional chant collections of the sixth and seventh centuries, in the first fully developed chant books of the eighth and ninth centuries, or only in chant books that are later still. When a significant number of texts from different periods ended up in the same melodic group, they can become the basis for reconstructing part of the musical history of the group. For instance, it is sometimes possible to detect melodic features that are consistent among texts of similar date, as well as features that are consistently different among texts of different dates. These features may reflect aspects of the developmental state the melodic group was in at the time the texts were introduced, and thus they are very important clues to the "History of Gregorian Style" (Apel 1958:507)—or, indeed, the history of the transmission of every medieval chant repertory for which this kind of evidence survives.

2. Uses of Books in Liturgical Celebrations

Alongside the historical continuum one can detect other continua, reflecting changes in the ways oral and written transmission interacted in different periods of the Middle Ages. More difficult to map than the chronological continuum would be one describing the uses of books during the actual celebration of the liturgy. For example, one type of liturgical book seems to have served more as a badge of office than as a score to perform from. Already in the fourth century, an ecclesiastical council decreed that "No others are to sing in church, except the official cantors, who ascend the ambo and sing from a parchment" (McKinnon 1987:118). The early eighth-century liturgical rulebook known as Ordo Romanus I shows that this "parchment" had developed into a complete book, known as the *cantatorium;* the cantor who sang the solo verses of

27. This paragraph summarizes material in *Prophecy Mixed with Melody* (see above, chapter 1, n. 2).

the gradual, tract, and alleluia carried it as he ascended the ambo (Andrieu, ed. 1931/2:86). By the tenth century, if not before, the ceremony for ordaining a cantor consisted of his receiving the book (now called *antiphonarium*) from the hands of a priest or bishop (Vogel and Elze 1963:14–5).

The early medieval cantatoria that actually survive are every bit as impressive as such a ritual object should be, with their fine ivory covers, their parchment pages died purple and inscribed in letters of silver and gold.[28] Sources from later in the middle ages treat the cantatorium as more or less interchangeable with another authority symbol of different origin, the cantor's staff (Jeannin 1933:15).

The fact that the cantatorium served a symbolic purpose, that the singer did not actually need to read it while singing, led the ninth-century liturgical commentator Amalarius of Metz to extend the symbolism, transforming the book from a mere sign of ecclesiastical office into a figurative statement of multiple religious truths. An inveterate allegorizer, Amalarius characteristically compared the Christian cantor holding the book of David's psalms to the Old Testament Levites (the musicians who performed in the Temple in Jerusalem) holding the instruments they had been assigned to play by the same king David (1 Chronicles 25). He was able to expand the symbolism even further by spinning out a whole series of allegories based on the facts that the covers were ivory tablets, that there were two of them, and that the cantor held them in his hands.

> Bede writes in his commentary on Esdras, "The Levites will praise the Lord through the hands of David, either with the instruments that he made, or by singing the psalms that he instituted." In their place the cantor holds tablets in his hands, without any need of reading [from them], so that they might signify the words of [David] the Psalmist, "Let them praise his name in the chorus, and with tympanum and psaltery let them sing psalms to him" [Psalm 149:3]. . . . The tablets that the cantor holds in his hand are customarily made of bone, for they signify the perseverance of good thoughts and good works. . . . Or they signify love of God and neighbor, which love is vain

28. For more on the ivory covers of the cantatoria see Jeannin 1932–3; Smits van Waesberghe 1932; Hourlier 1963; Rasmussen 1983:78–80; Duft and Schnyder 1984: 117–8.

> unless it [also] has works. For that reason they are held in the hand, that the love [expressed by] the voice may be carried out by [good] work. . . .[29]

Cantatoria, however, were not the only kinds of liturgical chant books. Far more numerous are the thousands of manuscripts of the graduale, the book that contained all the Gregorian chants of the Proper of the medieval Latin Mass—both the solo chants that were also in the cantatorium and the choir chants that were found only in the graduale. But even these books may not have been what they at first seem. There is reason to think that many of the earliest ones were not intended to be used by singers during the musical liturgies, but rather by higher clergy during liturgies that lacked music. This is because almost all the early copies that survive as intact books, rather than mere fragments, have come down to us bound with copies of the two other liturgical books for the Mass, namely the sacramentary (containing the prayers said by the priest) and the lectionary (containing the readings from the Bible). In other words, these gradualia are sections within primitive missals, the historical antecedent of the plenary missals in which prayers, chants, and readings were interspersed in the correct liturgical order (Vogel 1986 : 105–6). If this was their original state (which often seems likely but in some cases remains to be demonstrated), then it is clear these gradualia were not meant for the singers at all, but for priests, who would read the chant texts quietly, along with the prayers and the readings, during private Masses at which there was no congregation and no singers.[30] If so, such books would tell us little about how the chant was being transmitted among the singers during the same period, and the fact that the earliest manuscripts lack music notation would be of little significance to the debate over the origins of notation. A book that was made for a priest reciting a private Mass obviously cannot tell us whether contemporary singers used books at all, whether singers'

29. "Scribit Beda in tractatu Esdrae: 'Laudabunt autem Dominum levitae per manus David, sive in organis quae ipse fecit, sive psalmos quos ipse instituit concinentes.' Eorum vice cantor sine aliqua necessitate legendi tenet tabulas in manibus, ut figurent illud psalmistae: 'Laudent nomen eius in coro, et tympano et psalterio psallant ei.' . . . Tabulae quas cantor in manu tenet, solent fieri de osse, qui fortem perseverantiam signant bonarum cogitationum et bonorum operum, . . . vel signant dilectionem Dei et proximi, quae dilectio, nisi opera habeat, vana est. Quapropter tenentur in manu, ut dilectio vocis exerceatur per opus" (Hanssens 1948–50/2 : 303–4).

30. Jeffery 1983 : 317. On the origins of the private Mass see Vogel 1986 : 156–9.

books (if they existed) were used for learning or performance, or whether they were notated or not. Until this question is settled, then, the mere existence of early graduale manuscripts without notation cannot be cited in support of any theory about the date at which singers began to use notation (cf. Treitler 1988:567, 1984c:145).

Nor does the situation become much clearer after notation has emerged. Notation is frequently found in plenary missals as late as the twelfth century, even though these books too were presumably meant for the priest and not for the singers. The notated gradualia of the same period, though they lack the priest's texts and thus may have been meant for singers, are often so small that it is difficult to imagine them being used during performances. Many of them can only be read by one individual holding the book fairly close to his face; thus they are more likely to have been used for learning or studying the chant rather than for actually performing it during the liturgy (Hucke 1980d:447–8). This is still the pattern in the modern Ethiopian rite, where manuscripts are copied by students as part of their training to be full-fledged singers. After they become singers (*dabtaras*), they continue to use manuscripts for study and teaching, but always perform from memory during the actual liturgy (Shelemay and Jeffery forthcoming). Again, the musical signs of the Hebrew Bible appear in the printed books used for study purposes, but (like the vowel signs) they may not be included in the Torah scrolls that are actually used in the liturgy. The reader knows he will find only the consonants in the liturgical scroll, and must supply the rest from memory, though in my own visits to Orthodox synagogues I have observed that worshippers in the congregation, following along in printed books, do not hesitate to correct the reader whenever he makes a mistake.[31]

31. The central rite of the bar mitzvah ceremony is when a thirteen-year-old boy reads from the Torah scroll for the first time, commemorating the fact that he is now old enough to participate as an adult in liturgical services. Because every Jewish male with a traditional upbringing goes through this rite of confirmation, there is a large market for aids that assist one in learning to read the musical signs. Published transcriptions into staff notation are quite common, though Binder 1959 and Ne'eman 1966–7 are especially detailed. More typical are the brief lists of transcriptions found in books like Chiel 1971:6–8, and in some printed editions of the Hebrew Bible. Cassette tapes are also widely used. However, after learning the portion they need for their own bar mitzvah, many adults never go on to master the entire system for the complete text of the Bible. When it is their turn to read during the services, therefore, they stand next to a specialist, the *Baʿal Kore* ("master reader") who reads in their

In the medieval Latin church, the shift from the miniature early books to the huge choirbooks of the fifteenth and sixteenth centuries, which could easily be read by an entire choir,[32] certainly points to a comparable shift in the way books were used during performances, but it is not so clear when or how this shift took place. At least some medieval liturgical regulations imply that the practice of singing from books during liturgical celebrations spread only very gradually, coming at different times and at different rates in different localities. As late as the sixteenth century, in at least some places, there were still regulations obliging singers to perform without books under certain circumstances (Harrison 1980:102–3; 1972:317–8; C. Wright 1989:325–35), so that memory, and perhaps other oral processes also, still played a role in musical performance.

3. Performance Practice

All this reveals yet another continuum, for at some point the problem of oral transmission turns into the problem of performance practice. Indeed from some perspectives the difference may be primarily terminological, for "performance practice," can be seen as merely a customary term for the oral component of all Western art music, the unwritten conventions performers use to interpret the written sources. Performance practice is one of the most neglected areas of contemporary chant study—surprisingly, given its importance to the study of every other kind of early music.[33] The long-lasting hegemony of the Solesmes method, and the deadlocked debate over Gregorian rhythm, may be two of the reasons. But now that

stead. An interesting example of a book intended to train people for the Baʿal Kore role (*Tiqqun* 1946) contains facsimiles of a scroll and of a typical printed edition on facing pages.

32. Many pictures of the period also show entire choirs gathered around a single book. Examples include C. Wright 1989:331; McKinnon, ed. 1990:235. Yudkin 1989:455 is unusual in that it also depicts a rebec player performing with the choir. The painting of Johannes Ockeghem's choir in *The New Grove Dictionary* 13:492, though it seems to show the choir singing from a single sheet of parchment, nevertheless offers a good depiction of a typical late medieval bookstand, which could hold a book on each side and be swiveled around as the choir needed to switch books; also note the storage space for books underneath. On the earliest large manuscripts of choral polyphony, see Bukofzer 1950.

33. Vinquist and Zaslaw 1970 appears to have no chant entries in the index. Jackson 1988:36–40 lists only sixteen items related to chant. Some other interesting items that could have been included are Associazione 1984; Bas 1909; Berry 1965–6, 1967; McKinnon 1983; Potier 1939; Raes 1952; Thomas 1947.

even Solesmes is changing its approach to performance practice (Jeffery 1991b) renewed attention to the question is long overdue. New interest in the study of performance practice in non-Western cultures offers yet another opportunity for dialogue between ethnomusicological and historical approaches.[34]

E. Cultural Contexts

1. Musical Contacts between Clergy and Laity

Though medieval liturgical chant was the business of the monks or canons of the religious community, the laity may have performed some of it at Mass, during processions, and at some other ceremonies. While there seems to have been a decline in the amount of congregational singing from the fourth and fifth centuries to the end of the Middle Ages (we do not know very much about this), it is clear that some congregational singing did persist in some places (see Anglès 1969?, Mahling 1972, Janota 1980, Rajeczky 1984). But for the bulk of the medieval services, particularly the hours of the Office, the laity may not have been present even as the "audience," for these services were seen as the responsibility of the clergy. Indeed, large portions of the most musical services took place in an enclosed part of the church building that the laity could not enter; by the twelfth century the low wall that enclosed this area had begun to develop into a high wall (the Western rood screen or Eastern iconostasis) through which, when the doors were closed or the curtains drawn, the laity could not even see.[35]

Yet the knowledge of the chant was not entirely limited to the clergy, and there is evidence, at least from the later Middle Ages, of two-way interaction between the chant and the music of the surrounding culture. For one thing, some musicologists have claimed to find in medieval secular songs influences of the melodic style, the modes,[36] and even the poetic/musical forms (Fernandez 1976) of liturgical chant. Of course these melodies survive at all only because they were written down in chant notation

34. See, for instance: Béhague 1984; McLeod and Herndon 1980; Sawa 1989; Shelemay and Jeffery forthcoming; Yung 1987.

35. Mallion 1964; Onasch 1981 : 49–50, 56–9; Mathews 1982; Farkas 1985; Schulz 1986 : 33–4, 44–6, 72; Whittington 1988.

36. For instance, it has been claimed, "It is clear that trouvère song was strongly influenced by the Church modes" (Tischler 1986 : 333).

(Stäblein 1975:168–73, 176–81, 190–1, 196–7, 200–1, 208–13; Conomos 1979). Many researchers have believed they could detect the formative influence of liturgical chant in the modern folk songs of various European countries.[37] If these perceived interrelationships are genuine, they would seem to show that liturgical chant played an important role in shaping the overall musical culture. And it may be that the lines of influence went both ways, for there is at least one medieval report of an adaptation in the opposite direction, in a story about a musician who turned a peasant love song into a liturgical sequence, though the piece in question seems not to have survived in either form.[38]

One entire genre of medieval chant purports to represent a category of non-liturgical "women's music." This is the *planctus* or lament, representing the kind of mourning song that women in many cultures sing for the dead. The liturgical planctus often represent the Virgin Mary standing by the cross of Jesus (Smoldon 1980:376–81), a theme also encountered in the Byzantine *staurotheotokia* (Wellesz 1961:239, 243; Onasch 1981: 339), and in the well-known sequence *Stabat mater dolorosa* (Mies 1932, 1933; Szövérffy 1964–5/2:287–90).[39] Laments also survive for other Biblical women characters, particularly in the context of liturgical dramas: Mary Magdalene and the three Marys at the tomb of Jesus, Mary and Martha weeping for Lazarus, Rachel at the slaughter of the Holy Innocents.[40] These Latin liturgical planctus are not themselves folk songs, of course; they are highly artistic creations, intersecting on the one hand with the liturgical sequence repertory (cf. Crocker 1977:132–4; Stäblein 1962), on the other hand with a great many secular lais and other musical and literary works, some of which mark the deaths of kings, nobles, or other historical or fictional personages (Yudkin 1989:237–42; Stevens 1990:428–33). Yet they stand for a kind of song that women have sung

37. For example: Abrahamsen 1923; Anglès 1964; Hervé 1924; Járdányi 1959; Kodály 1971:100–1; Laub 1904; Rajeczky 1969b; Smits van Waesberghe n.d.

38. The sequence *Christe Deus Christe meus Christe rex et Domine* ("Christ God, my Christ, Christ King and Lord") by Frater Henricus Pisanus, who died in 1239. According to the chronicler Salimbene, Henricus based it on a song he heard sung by a servant girl, *E s' tu no cure de me / e' no curarò de te* ("And if you do not care for me, I will not care for you"). Scalia 1966/1:263; Baird et al., eds. 1986:172–3. Anglès (1967, 1968) also claimed to detect the influence of folk music in medieval sequences.

39. An Ethiopian hymn on the same theme is published in van den Oudenrijn 1960.

40. For basic information see Young 1933/2:580 (see "Lament") and 594 ("Planctus"); Smoldon 1980:168–9, 217–20. Recent studies include Rankin 1981, 1989/1:72–160; Traub 1990.

in many parts of the world for much of recorded history (Jarrett 1977), and that was probably familiar to most people in medieval Europe.[41]

Nor is medieval Christianity the only religion that elevated this genre to a religious ceremony, redirected to honor a mythical or religious figure instead of mourning an ordinary human being. In ancient times women engaged in rites of lament for Tammuz, Adonis, and Osiris (Frazer 1961:164–71, 249–50, 183–99, 250–1), and customs descended from ritual laments over various fertility gods, who die and rise each year, are reported still to survive in certain places (Frazer 1961:243–7, 251–3, 285–6).[42] An old Finnish tradition of lament has survived in Soviet Karelia "with the indirect support of the Russian Orthodox church" (Honko 1987:335).

One way to investigate the interactions of sacred and secular traditions is to look more carefully at those areas of medieval life where music played a role in contacts between the two subcultures of the clergy and the laity. One obvious arena for such contact was the educational system of the period.[43] Members of the upper-class laity would have had access to some ecclesiastical education (see Bäuml 1980), and could thus have learned some music theory and chant without ultimately joining the clerical subculture. But we do not yet know much about the educational process as it relates to medieval music, particularly musical performance.[44] Of course we know even less about influences moving in the other direction: When a young monastic or clerical singer, having just left the world of the

41. Edsman 1962, Lloyd 1980, and Birlea 1987 do not begin to do justice to the wide cross-cultural distribution and variety of this type of song. Kim 1989 describes a striking Korean example in which lament performances help to preserve the memory of a violent 1948 uprising, despite government attempts to eliminate all recollection of it.

42. For a more up-to-date discussion than Frazer 1961, see Smith 1987a.

43. On educational contacts between the learned clerical culture and the lay culture, see Bischoff 1989; Gurevich 1988; Le Goff 1980:159–88, 330–41; McKitterick 1989:211–70; McKitterick, ed. 1990:36–62, 109–33; Riché 1976; Stock 1983; *Dictionary of the Middle Ages* 7:557–70, 594–602, and 11:59–78. The subject is a complex one, with wide differences from region to region and century to century.

44. We know more about the study of music theory treatises in the medieval university (Chartier 1987; Bernhard et al. 1990; Huglo 1990) than about the actual processes by which singers were trained. A little information given by Chaucer about the training of singers in fourteenth-century England is discussed in Courtenay 1987:9–10, 17–20. That there was a wide gulf between the academic study of theory and the practical training of liturgical singers is evident from the music theory literature itself, which makes much of the distinction between the *musicus*, or student of theory, and the *cantor*, who is said to sing without understanding; see Reimer 1978.

laity to enter that of the clergy, began to learn the medieval chant repertory, how much "preparation" had he already received from the culture he was first raised in, outside of the ecclesiastical institutions? To investigate such questions is to investigate the processes anthropologists call "cultural transmission" (Tindall 1976), "enculturation," or "culture acquisition" (Pitman et al. 1989), the problem of how a person learns the ways of a culture and thus becomes a full-fledged member of it. Beginning in the seventh century we have some important information about the Schola Cantorum (School of Singers) in Rome, which trained poor and orphan boys for a wide range of clerical positions, and whose alumni included a number of popes (Jeffery forthcoming). This kind of training still exists in modern Ethiopia (though it is increasingly threatened by Western-style education and government hostility to the Church), where young boys are taught reading and music in a quasi-monastic setting, from about the age of five. After about thirty years, those who complete the training join the ranks of the dabtaras, whose duties include both the performance of liturgical chant and dance and the copying of all kinds of manuscripts. Some of those who do not complete the full training become priests, whose occupation does not require as high a level of literacy. Thus the dabtaras, though lower in ecclesiastical rank than the priests and other clergy, are in fact the most literate and highly educated group in traditional Ethiopian society (Shelemay and Jeffery forthcoming, Shelemay, Jeffery, and Monson forthcoming).[45]

2. Liturgical and Quasi-Liturgical "Folk Songs"

Some very preliminary research (Jeffery 1981) has identified other avenues of musical interaction between the clerical and lay strata of medieval society, at least in later medieval Western Europe. First, there survive a number of medieval hymns in vernacular languages that are clearly derived (often in both text and melody) from chants in the Gregorian repertory;[46] at least one of them subsequently developed in the other direction, by being adapted again into a liturgical melody (Hermelink 1970). But we do not

45. The significant role of boy singers in the transmission of medieval chant will be examined further in my *Prophecy Mixed with Melody* (see ch. 1, n. 2, above); the importance of this topic was made clear to me by Margot Fassler.

46. See, for instance, Ameln 1966, 1970; Aubry 1898; Dobszay 1971; Gottwald 1964; Janota 1980; Lipphardt 1960, 1961, 1963, 1966, 1983; Smits van Waesberghe 1962.

know how these adaptations came about. Did they arise "spontaneously" in attempts by the lay congregations to join in the liturgical singing of the clergy? Or were they composed by priests who deliberately intended to teach them to the laity? Or were they composed by educated laity?

There are even entire genres of vernacular song that appear to be derived from liturgical chant, such as the German Leisen (Ursprung 1952; Hucke 1963; Gamber 1977; Lipphardt 1979; Riedel 1980), which incorporate "Kyrie eleison" in their refrains; the word "Leise" may even derive from the word "eleison" (for an English example see Trend 1928). In the early twentieth century, in certain French villages, one could still hear examples of the Kyriolé or Criolé, in which young women sang verses in French at the Kyrie of the Mass, in alternation with the (male) choir singing the liturgical chant (Tiersot 1905; Bleyon 1910–11); in some respects this practice may resemble the performance of the medieval Latin prosulae or tropes, depending on one's view of how they were performed (Marcusson 1979; Kelly 1985).

Second, there are references to music in medieval sermons, at least from the time of the mendicant orders (the thirteenth century and later), whose wandering friars incorporated popular singing and dancing into their preaching. In England some of these songs seem to have been related to the repertory of Christmas carols, which often mixed passages in Latin and the vernacular (Stevens, ed. 1970, 1975). The German Christmas custom known as the *Quempas* derives its name from the Christmas carol *Quem pastores laudavere* ("Whom the shepherds praised"), which was sung by students as they went door to door seeking alms (Klammer 1963; W. Thomas 1965).

Third, and particularly interesting, are the liturgical books written and used in religious communities of women. Because they did not belong to the ordained clergy and had had less education, medieval nuns seem to have stood somewhere between the illiterate majority and the monks. One result of this was that they made greater use of vernacular songs within their liturgical services.

3. Regional Chant Dialects

Directly related to the problem of the relationship between chant and folk music is the claim that there were regional dialects of Gregorian chant. Certainly by the fifteenth century, European musicians were aware of regional differences (Harrán 1989: 43–64). But we do not really know how early these differences arose, whether they really amounted to "dialects," and to what degree they may have reflected local differences in the nonliturgical musical culture(s). Certainly the neumatic notation, from the very earliest period (the ninth century), already existed in different regional scripts.[47] These earliest manuscripts also exhibit differences in repertory, reflecting a variety of recensions within a broader geographic division between East (the countries where Germanic and Slavic languages now predominate) and West (the countries where Romance languages are spoken), with "zones of transition" standing between them, on a line from England through Alsace to northern Italy (Huglo 1988: 113–4). But if such regional variations also included consistent differences in melodic content, these differences have yet to be systematically plotted on a grand scale. In the Greek world, too, there are differences in the notation, repertory, and melodic content of Byzantine chant among the various medieval centers (Greece and Asia Minor, Palestine, southern Italy or "Magna Graecia"), but we still await the large-scale study that will show whether we may speak of regional dialects and what the distinctive characteristics of each dialect may be.

Unfortunately, much of the existing literature on the question of dialects in Gregorian chant has been tainted by the nationalistic rivalries of the nineteenth and early twentieth centuries,[48] and by the related controversy over the relative merits of the Ratisbon editions of the chantbooks, published in Regensburg (called "Ratisbona" in Latin, hence "Ratisbon" in English) on the basis of the seventeenth-century Medicean edition, as compared with the Vatican/Solesmes editions, edited by French monks working from early medieval manuscripts.[49] In the years leading up to the First World War, when the Church withdrew its approval of the Ratisbon editions in favor of the Vatican edition, many German-speaking musicians understandably felt that they were being forced to replace their own hoary

47. The notations of medieval monophonic music are introduced in Stäblein 1975, with many helpful reproductions. Recent discussions of the origins of these different early notational styles include Levy 1987a, 1987b; Treitler 1982b.

48. For example, Haberl 1902; Molitor 1904; Weidinger 1903. See also works cited in chapter 5, footnote 5, below, on the so-called "German" chant dialect.

49. On the Ratisbon editions, see Haberl 1902; P. Wagner 1903; Weidinger 1903; Meier 1969; Donakowski 1977: 259, 379. On the history of the seventeenth-century Medicean edition, see Molitor 1901–2; Hayburn 1979. On the Vatican/Solesmes editions, see P. Wagner 1907; Moneta Caglio 1960–3; Combe 1969.

German tradition with a foreign French one, as if unaware of the fact that, while the sources of the Ratisbon editions were Italian, the St. Gall manuscripts so valued by the editors of the Vatican edition were German Swiss.[50]

Recently, though, some less tendentious but still limited attempts have been made to reopen the matter.[51] In pursuing this issue one is almost inevitably led to ask questions about the survival of medieval traits in the folk music of modern Europe, a question that ethnomusicologists have already begun to examine in other connections (Etzion and Weich-Shahak 1988).

4. Art Music vs. Folk Song in the Liturgy

Since the 1950s, the relationship of liturgical chant to folk music has become embroiled in another controversy, spawned by the movement to reform the modern Roman Catholic liturgy, which saw its agenda officially adopted at the Second Vatican Council (1962–5).[52] Gregorian chant, which up to that time had been valued for its sacred character, its high artistic quality, and its role in an internationally uniform Latin liturgy,[53]

50. Molitor 1904 is an interesting attempt by a German writer to persuade other Germans to accept the Vatican edition. The fact that it was published in New York, in English, shows that nationalistic opposition to the Vatican edition ran high among Americans of German background as well. I myself have encountered American Benedictines of German extraction who still believe that the alleged "German tradition" of Gregorian chant is superior to the "French tradition" enshrined in the Solesmes editions; this is what they were taught as young monks, as recently as the 1930s and 1940s. Substantial portions of a D.M.A. dissertation on the history of the Medicean and Ratisbon editions were incorporated into Hayburn 1979, an unsuccessful attempt to expand the dissertation into a survey of twenty centuries of papal teaching on music. It includes much useful and interesting information and a fairly large bibliography; the author also used many unpublished sources but did not always identify them adequately. For further bibliography on the Vatican edition see Jeffery 1991b, especially n. 6.

51. For example, Avenary 1977; Deusen 1982; D. G. Hughes 1986; Mezei 1990; Rajeczky 1973, 1974. Several more articles on the problem of regional variation in Western chant will be found in *Studia Musicologica* 27 (1985). See also chapter 5, footnote 5, below.

52. See Jeffery 1991b, as well as an article I am working on, to be titled "Art Music vs. Folk Song, Myth vs. History: Catholics Debate Gregorian Chant."

53. Sanctity, "goodness of form," and universality were identified as "the qualities proper to the liturgy" which "are possessed in the highest degree by the Gregorian chant," in the highly influential motu proprio of 1903, issued by Pope Pius X (reigned 1903–14). See Seasoltz 1966:4–6 or Nemmers 1949:199–201 for complete English translations, Romita 1936:290–301 for the original Italian and Latin texts. On the authorship and historical

suddenly seemed out of place amid reforms that were characterized by a new openness to modernity and worldwide cultural diversity, a greater emphasis on congregational participation, and the substitution of modern vernacular languages for Latin.[54] The resulting debate over the continued suitability of Gregorian chant for modern worship can be seen as a striking example of what Grimes has called "ritual criticism . . . the interpretation of a rite or ritual system with a view to implicating its practice" that, in one way or another, is carried on in most cultures and religions in parallel with the ritual practice itself (Grimes 1990a:17).

Disagreement over Gregorian chant was a central factor in provoking a split among Catholic church musicians, dividing those who dedicated their efforts to "permitting the people to sing and . . . having the liturgical texts sung in the vernacular" from those who were determined "to safeguard the heritage of church music that has come down to us from the past, as well as to keep watch over the artistic character of church music, choral singing, and the Latin language" (Hucke 1966:72). The former group quickly came to name its ideal by the term "pastoral music," that is, music shaped by the kinds of concerns a good pastor should have for his flock.[55] The most notable innovation of the pastoral musicians has been the "Folk Mass," in which the congregation is urged to join in on guitar-accompanied songs reminiscent of Anglo-American popular music. The latter group rallied around the traditional concept "sacred music," often preferring the Latin form *musica sacra*, with all the centuries of philo-

---

background of this document see the 1961 installments of Moneta Caglio 1960–3; Donakowski 1977:259, 379; Hayburn 1979:195–249. For its far-reaching effects on twentieth-century church music, see Henry 1915; Harnoncourt 1974:90–4.

54. For the history of the Liturgical Movement see Chandlee 1986; Collins 1987; Donakowski 1977; Franklin 1987; Franklin and Spaeth 1988; Harnoncourt 1974; K. Hughes, ed. 1990; Jeffery 1989a; Musch, ed. 1975; B. Thompson 1989:46–53; Unverricht, ed. 1988. For a variety of perspectives on the liturgical reforms, see Bugnini 1990; Dinges 1987–8; Flannery, ed. 1975; E. Foley 1989; International Commission 1982; Jeffery 1991b; Murray 1977; Overath, ed. 1969; Quinn 1989; Schmitt 1977; Seasoltz 1966, 1980; Weakland 1967.

55. An extensive and detailed statement of the "pastoral" position is Universa Laus 1980, 1981, on which see also Stefani 1980 and Rainoldi 1981. Other notable expressions of the "pastoral" viewpoint include Deiss 1976; Pol-Topis et al., eds. 1979; E. Foley et al. 1989, with replies in Jeffery 1989b, Mannion 1990, E. Foley 1990b, Halmo and Ridder 1990; and the writings of Stefani. For further bibliography see Overath, ed. 1969; Costa 1971; Godard 1971; Stefani 1971; Hameline 1977; Deyrieux 1977; Huijbers 1980; Winter 1984; Jeffery 1991b: n. 1.

sophical baggage that this expression carries with it.[56] The musicians of this group soon found themselves to be the sole defenders of Gregorian chant, and indeed of all classical music in the liturgy.

The most influential early exposition of the "pastoral" viewpoint (Gelineau 1962, English translation 1964) sought to give this position a historical basis. It claimed that the ideals of the pastoral musicians represented a return to the spirit of the early church, and that Gregorian chant had originally been a kind of congregational folk song, much like the music the pastoral musicians were promoting. This original tradition was asserted to have been betrayed during the Middle Ages, as cultural changes and the emergence of musical professionalism transformed it into the Gregorian repertory we know.

> When we look at the patristic era (especially the fourth, fifth and sixth centuries), we find that the people's singing in the liturgy was taken for granted. . . . The first blow suffered by active participation of the faithful in worship came at the end of the ancient culture when the barbarians invaded the West. From that time those who entered the Church were strangers to the Mediterranean culture which had been the setting wherein the liturgical rites had evolved . . . . The psalms, the very basis of liturgical chant, were hardly explained to them; Latin was only more or less well understood by the barbaric tribes converted to the Church. The liturgical chant was chiefly sustained in the sacred offices only by the local clergy or the monks. In the eighth and ninth centuries, Charlemagne, following Pepin, labored to replace the Gallican liturgy with that of Rome; and the latter did not escape the disadvantages of an imported liturgy, admired by the educated but too remote from the ordinary people. The sacred action became more and more the affair of clerics. At the same time there came a wave of poetry and music from the East (the Mélodes of Jerusalem, in the seventh century). This profoundly modified the structure of the traditional chants. By the beginning of the eighth century there arose in many places the *scholae* of professional singers and virtuosos who developed the ancient melodies or created

56. On the history of the concept of sacred music, see Romita 1936, 1947, 1952; Weissenbäck 1937; Stenzl 1976; for a Protestant perspective see Söhngen 1967. An attempt to reformulate the concept in contemporary terms (at least as it relates to Gregorian chant) is Jeffery 1989a.

> new repertoires. The execution of these highly artistic pieces was reserved to them. The people listened to them, at least in those places where they were performed—in cathedrals and monasteries. . . . Developments in polyphony finally excluded the people altogether from strictly liturgical singing . . . . (Gelineau 1964:82–3)

According to Gelineau, all of this profoundly affected the development of the Gregorian chant repertory, rendering it unsuitable for congregational use.

> When responsorial and antiphonal psalmody developed into the forms now found in our responsories, Graduals and anthems [the English translator should have used the word "antiphons"], we come to a new stratum of more elaborate melodies. This found its typical and definitive form in the *Antiphonarium Missae*, which seems to have been fixed about the ninth century in some school of singers within the Frankish empire (Metz?). From there, if one can believe in the travels of the old manuscripts, it became diffused gradually throughout all the West. For the first time in the history of the Church, a musical repertoire as such, recognized as superb, obtained an authoritative status equal to that of the texts themselves. The practical art of the cantor, who re-created the word by singing it in a way handed down by tradition, suffered eclipse behind an achievement of fine art, musically defined and fixed. For this repertoire of melodies, one of the most astonishing in the whole known field of music, is a work of the highest quality. It was created by specialists in vocal technique and was intended for elite singers so highly trained expressly to perform it that one might call it *bel canto*, even though, at that time, the term had not yet been invented. . . . The active and intelligent participation of the faithful in the basic rites then became more and more reduced. In the singing they were replaced by cantors or clerics whose powerful trained voices could now be heard from the ambo, the rood-screen or the choir. We have already pointed out that melodic ornamentation reduced or even suppressed the psalmody. . . .
>
> Judged solely as Christian art, this category of chants possesses an immortal beauty; but judged according to the functional laws of liturgy implying the active and intelligent participation of the people, it is far from satisfactory. Even

> when the psalmodic verses have survived, it is very difficult to hear their text because of all the melismata. The refrains from the psalms are far too difficult for the people to sing. . . . For all these reasons we have to conclude that this repertoire of Gregorian chant does not provide music fitted for the needs of the average community celebrating the liturgy. (Gelineau 1964:196–8)

This account, intended as it is to support a very specific agenda, includes many historical errors and oversimplifications. First of all, it is not at all clear how universally "taken for granted" congregational singing was in the pre-medieval period or in the early church. Responsorial psalmody, in which the congregation sang a refrain in response to a soloist who sang psalm verses, certainly existed by the late fourth century, but it was regarded as an innovation at that time, and had many opponents, who seemed to prefer an earlier state of affairs in which there had been no congregational singing (Dyer 1981; Ferguson 1983; Jeffery 1984a). In any case the soloists, young men in the lower ranks of the clergy, were already in some respects specialists, since no one could carry out this role unless he had been officially ordained or appointed to it (see "Uses of Books in Liturgical Celebrations," above). It is by no means clear that every genre of Mass chant was originally sung by the congregation; the introit in particular may have been reserved to the choir from the beginning, if indeed its origin may be traced to a fourth-century adoption of imperial Roman ceremonial by Christian bishops.[57] Medieval congregations do seem to have done less singing than in the late antique period,[58] but the question has received very little study. In any case there are many possible reasons why congregational singing could have declined, and we cannot assume a priori that it was caused by a change in the character of the music. It could, for instance, have had more to do with an increased isolation of the clergy from the laity rather than with changes in musical style, just as changes in

57. This possibility, suggested in Klauser 1979:33–5, is a good example of a very significant question that has never been investigated historically. The fact is that, for most of the chants of the Ordinary and Proper of the Mass, we do not know when or how they originated, what their original purpose or meaning was, and who originally sang them. Many other questions, such as the prevalence, personnel, and liturgical roles of choirs in the early church, are equally unexplored. Some of these questions will be discussed further in my *Prophecy Mixed with Melody* (see ch. 1, n. 2, above); see also Jeffery 1984a.

58. Anglès 1969?; Mahling 1972; Atkinson 1977:7 n. 14; Janota 1980; Rajeczky 1984; see also "Melodic Embellishment," below.

musical style (if they actually took place) could have been caused by many factors besides a desire for "virtuosity" (cf. Jeffery 1989a:25–6, 29). The migration of Germanic tribes into the Western Roman empire may indeed have had some effect on the musical culture and the history of liturgical chant; but we can only guess what it was, for they took place well before the melodies were first written down. It is hardly certain that the invaders encountered a vigorous tradition of congregational singing or did anything to weaken it, and it is certainly wrong to claim they did not learn Latin. On the contrary, Latin was the common tongue that enabled Franks, Anglo-Saxons, Visigoths, Lombards, Celts, Western Slavs, and other peoples to create a unified medieval culture extending all over Europe.

Nor can the barbarians in the West be blamed for the more or less contemporary decline of congregational singing in the Byzantine realm (Conomos 1980). Whatever happened in the East must have been caused by some other factors, and identifying them might lead us to the real "culprit" responsible for whatever it was that happened in the West. The alleged "wave of poetry and music from the East" that "profoundly modified the structure of the traditional [Western] chants" cannot have been the source of the problem, for it simply never occurred. The *kanōn* poetry of John of Damascus (died ca. 749) and the other hymnodists of Jerusalem (who belong more to the eighth century than to the seventh) were very important for the development of the Byzantine chant repertory, but were virtually unknown in the West, where hardly anyone understood Greek.[59] The repeated references to the "artistic magnificence" of Gregorian chant sound more like Gelineau's opponents (the "sacred" musicians) than like the medieval literature on *ars musica* (cf., e.g., Fladt 1987:149–67); as descriptions of how chant was perceived in the Middle Ages, they are more suggestive of the nineteenth century than the ninth. The description of Gregorian chant as full of "melodic ornamentation" and "melismata" is a half-truth, not only because many Gregorian melodies would not fit this description, but because even the most melismatic Gregorian chants (the graduals and alleluias) are less elaborate than their counterparts in the local chant traditions that the Gregorian tradition replaced (Baroffio

59. For a rare exception, a series of Western antiphons derived from a kanōn by the Mēlode Andrew of Crete, see Strunk 1977:208–19. But these pieces stand out precisely because they are so exceptional. The work of the hymnodists of Jerusalem is described in Jeffery forthcoming, and will be discussed much more fully in my *Liturgy and Chant in Early Christian Jerusalem* (see ch. 4, n. 6, above).

1980:316). That the Gregorian repertory was "fixed about the ninth century in some school of singers within the Frankish empire" is only one possible scenario, among the many that have been or could be proposed to solve the problem of the origins of Gregorian chant. Finally, the characterization of Gregorian chant as an art that was always completely removed from ordinary people ignores the many parallels that scholars have repeatedly claimed to detect between it and European folk music (see Rajeczky 1984, and "Liturgical and Quasi-Liturgical Folk Songs" and "Regional Chant Dialects," above).

In short, Gelineau's construction of the history of Gregorian chant is in no sense a critical, dispassionate musicological investigation, but rather an attempt to provide "historical" support for a religious or political position (the "pastoral" critique of Gregorian chant) that has already been arrived at by other means. But there are at least three reasons why chant scholars and ethnomusicologists cannot afford to ignore such a tendentious abuse of music history, even if they feel personally uninvolved in modern ecclesiastical politics and unaffected by the virtual disappearance of Gregorian chant from liturgical use in the wake of the "pastoral" arguments. First, the "pastoral" representation of chant history proffers simplistic ideological answers to what are in reality very important and complex questions: In what ways was medieval chant genuinely related to the music of the early church, and how can historians establish such historical relationships? What roles did professionalism and "congregationalism" actually play in the historical development of Christian liturgical music, and how did their interrelationships change over time?[60] And of course, what was the relationship of liturgical chant to the larger musical culture of both the late antique and medieval periods? The relative lack of serious scholarly attention to these questions has only made it easier for those with a partisan agenda to fill the void with "answers" of their own.

Second, Gelineau's views have had considerable impact in the field of liturgical scholarship, where (for want of any challenge) they are widely

60. In view of all that has been written about this question during the last few decades of liturgical reform, it is quite surprising how little critical research has actually been done on it. Some essays on professionalism in Byzantine chant are included in Kouyumdjieva and Todorov, eds. 1989. Congregational participation in the history of Western Catholic and Protestant liturgies is examined in Caspers and Schneiders 1990, but without much specific consideration of music.

accepted as an established part of the scholarly consensus (see, e.g., Vagaggini 1976:291–3, 321, 988, 990; Costa 1971; E. Foley 1982, 1990a: 858–60). Thus they affect much scholarly writing on the history of the liturgy that musicologists may unwittingly consult and rely upon. Even the "sacred" musicians have only rarely criticized the "pastoral" revision of chant history, preferring instead to reaffirm their belief that the higher artistic quality of Gregorian chant and European classical church music renders them inherently more suitable for use in sacred rites than music inspired by modern popular songs or non-European cultures (e.g., Ratzinger 1986:118–9, 121). This position too, and the "pastoral" rebuttals of it, raise many further issues of scholarly importance. How have our views of Gregorian chant been shaped by the historic Western dichotomy between "sacred" and "secular" music?[61] To what degree did distinctions between classical or art music (on the one hand) and folk or popular musics (on the other) play a role in the transmission of medieval chant? Questions like these are important enough to "pure" chant research that they deserve to be discussed by disinterested specialists, rather than being merely abandoned to ecclesiastical controversialists.

Third, it is not widely recognized that echoes of Gelineau's opinions can even be detected in the New Historical View of Gregorian chant, for Helmut Hucke, a leading member of the "pastoral" camp, frankly admires Gelineau's writings.[62] Thus Hucke's opinion that "communal song in the musical language of our own days" has "created a link with the old forms of singing in Christian worship that were lost in the Roman rite" (Hucke 1965:131) has much to do with his historical hypothesis that "none of the forms of Western chant can be traced back to . . . early Christian times." For instance, it is stated as fact that "until the fifth century the position of the gradual in the service was occupied by a different chant-form, the *psalmus responsorius* [responsorial psalm]" (Hucke 1980d:439, see also

61. "Pastoral" replies to the "sacred" viewpoint include Hucke 1967, 1971, 1979a, 1979b, 1979c, [1982]; Schalz 1971, 1985; Stefani 1974, 1975, 1976, 1980; Weakland 1967. Less partisan discussions of "sacredness" in music will be found among the following publications: Irwin, ed. 1983 (see the reviews Jeffery 1984b, Shelemay 1986b); Jeffery 1989a, and the other works in Collins et al., eds., 1989; and the music articles in *The Encyclopedia of Religion* 10:163–216, especially Ellingson 1987. "Musica sacra" is the subject of two issues of *The World of Music*: 24/3 (1982), and 26/3 (1984).

62. "Gelineau's book has put the approach to the renewal in Church music on a new footing" (Hucke 1965:126). Other publications espousing "pastoral" viewpoints include Hucke 1966, 1969, 1971, 1979c, Hucke ed. 1974.

464–5), even though there is no consensus among chant historians concerning how related the two really were.[63]

What other "pastoral" presuppositions can be detected underlying the New Historical View? What about Hucke's conception of the medieval cantor, who "in performing a gradual verse . . . had a general pattern to follow, and certain rules to observe," but also had "opportunities . . . to demonstrate his artistry" (Hucke 1980d:460)? Is the word "artistry" a hint that we are to identify this cantor as one of Gelineau's "virtuosos?" If so, what kinds of "patterns" and "rules" should we envision? Did the cantor begin with the simple old congregational folk songs and elaborate them with (as Gelineau would say) "complex and subtle" ornaments that in another age would have been dubbed "bel canto"? Or had the old recitative-like melodies simply disappeared, replaced outright by a new cantorial art? And if this new specialist art did not develop out of the older tradition, but represented a clean break with the past, where did it come from? Why did the old, simpler tradition disappear with so little resistance? Why did it not have some champions whose opposition to its demise would have left some traces, however obscure, in medieval writings about music, even if only in the writings of their opponents?

Because the relationship of Gregorian chant to medieval and late antique culture has been discussed largely in the context of the highly charged debate between "pastoral" and "sacred" musicians, even scholars who are personally insulated from internal ecclesiastical politics will find it difficult to avoid this bitter controversy, for they will have trouble finding anything to read that has not somehow been shaped by it, even unconsciously. Yet the effort to explore the relationships between liturgical chant and its culture must be made, for so many important scholarly questions depend upon it. One thing that is clearly needed, then, is a wider and more open dialogue among all those who are interested in the problem: liturgical historians, church musicians of all stripes, and musical scholars representing a full range of musicological opinion. Such a dialogue would most profitably begin with discussions of the primary sources that actually tell us something about musical "stratification" (Nettl 1983:303–14), examined

63. For instance, Huglo 1982 describes some very important evidence of a direct continuity between the ancient responsorial psalms and the medieval graduals. I have presented much other evidence for the same view in a series of unpublished papers, and this material will appear in my forthcoming book, *Prophecy Mixed with Melody* (see ch. 1, n. 2, above). Hucke's view is set forth at greater length in Hucke 1973:150–5.

in the context of modern research on the sociology of the ancient and medieval worlds (e.g., Duby 1980).

The medieval Latin author who devoted the most attention to such issues was Johannes de Grocheo, who wrote about the year 1300. Rather than a simple dichotomy, such as between "art" and "folk" music, he described the music of his time according to a trichotomy. Simple, civil, or vulgar music, which included secular monophonic songs and dances, was to be distinguished from measured music, that is, polyphony employing precisely measured consonances, which "ought not to be propagated among the vulgar, since they do not understand its subtlety . . . , but it should be performed for the learned and those who seek after the subtleties of the arts" (Seay, transl. and ed. 1974:26; Rohloff [1967]:144). Yet to identify these two categories with "folk" and "art" music would overlook the fact that some of the monophonic genres classified as "vulgar" were performed in court settings for the upper classes of society, notably the *cantus coronatus* composed by and performed for kings, nobles, and princes (Seay, transl. and ed. 1974:16; Rohloff [1967]:130). Gregorian chant, on the other hand, was classifed by Grocheo in a third category, ecclesiastical or church music. It was among the arts that every churchman (*vir ecclesiasticus*) had to know, yet it was made (*efficitur*) from the first two categories, and like the "vulgar" music it was also "civil," for it was "needed for use by citizens and . . . of value for the benefit and protection of the whole state" (Seay, transl. and ed. 1974:30, cf. 12; Rohloff [1967]:150, cf. 124; Fladt 1987:168–84).

In medieval culture, then, one is dealing not only with the differences between the clergy and the laity, but with several social strata along a continuum from king to noble to peasant, which strata persisted in both the clerical and lay segments of society. In both clerical and lay music there was some sort of continuity perceived between what we would call the "folk songs" and the "art" music—but in Grocheo's view it was at Gregorian chant that all these categories intersected.

Only impartial historical investigation of the medieval cultural contexts for liturgical chant, then, can free us from the dubious presuppositions and anachronistic categories imposed by the ecclesiastical politics of modern liturgical reform. New attention to the historical evidence bearing on the relations between clergy and laity, studies of extant music that appear to bridge the categories of liturgical chant and vernacular song, and attempts to identify more exactly the alleged regional dialects of medieval chant will open up three avenues leading us deep into the neglected and abused subject of chant in medieval culture. As we follow each of these avenues, the careers of performers and the uses of books provide two stable foci on which to fix our attention, and the careful use of suitable cross-cultural comparisons can assist us in evaluating the surviving evidence and inferring what is not actually attested.

›5‹

Some Possible Means of Oral Transmission in Liturgical Chant

While neither formulaism nor any other musical phenomenon is exclusively characteristic of oral transmission, several kinds of musical features seem to be frequently associated with orality, at least in the opinion of modern scholars. For medieval chant, such features include the use of formulas, melody types, added syllables, melodic ornamentation, and "improvised polyphony." Perhaps all these phenomena can occur in contexts where oral transmission is not the dominant factor, but at least sometimes they appear to have been among the means or vehicles or agencies in which the content of the tradition was formulated and by which it was handed on.

In attempting to find a common designation for these very different realities, I was uncertain whether to characterize them rather statically as "types" or "varieties" of transmission, or more dynamically as "processes" (which could make them sound like uncontrollable natural forces) or "strategies" (which could attribute a greater role to human choice and decision making). In view of how little we actually know about them I decided to use the less colorful word "means," modified by the adjective "possible." Thus, if in a particular chant tradition oral transmission can be said to operate largely through melodic formulas, then formulas are a means of transmission at least for that tradition.

A. Formulas

The formulaic character of medieval chant is the feature that has most often been linked, in recent writing, to the oral processes of transmission. Yet in this area we have not moved very far beyond the situation that prevailed thirty years ago, when a Byzantinist could write, "The study of melodic formulae is still in its initial stages" (Velimirović 1960, 1:61). Because we lack an empirical methodology for analyzing chant melodies into their component formulas, we are often forced to fall back on more impressionistic and descriptive means, which are inherently vulnerable to attack from those who have a different impression. As Treitler put it:

> The identification of a formula is an assertion of the existence of a piece of more-or-less fixed or stereotyped stuff—material that the composer put into this or that place or that the singer held in readiness for performance upon reaching a certain point in the melody. Either way, we want to be able to say with some confidence, here is that formula, there it is not, and there again is a variant of it. If we cannot do these things with confidence and with criteria that are demonstrable, . . . we . . . have no reason to think that the formula was any more distinct in the mind of the composer or the singer than in that of the analyst. (Treitler 1975 : 16–7)

But it may be unfair to insist that the formulas detectable by modern scholars must have been equally "distinct in the mind of the composer or singer," for it often happens that performers/composers are unaware of features that are clearly evident to a musicologist. "The degree to which improvising musicians adhere to patterns may exceed their own knowledge" (Nettl 1983 : 289).[1] It may well be that the creation or recall of a formulaic melody is at least partially an unconscious process, governed by the physiology and psychology of human memory as much as, or even more than, by deliberate choices made in keeping with consciously applied rules. One psychologist has compared the performance of formulaic poetry to ordinary human speech, stating that Lord's "singer of tales" would know "thousands of formulas, not from having memorized them but from having heard and used them, as we know the words and phrases of our own language" (U. Neisser, quoted in Sloboda 1985 : 141). Unfortunately modern research in musical cognition has not given much attention to traditional formulaic music, understandably focusing on the kinds that are more important in our own culture: common practice classical music, children's songs, and jazz (but see Pressing 1988 : 146–7). There have, on the other hand, been some fascinating studies of formulaism in the "songs" of another mammalian species.[2]

1. One attempt to analyze jazz piano improvisation by means of "the theory of formulaic composition" is G. Smith 1983.

2. Guinee and Payne 1988 describe the songs of humpback whales, in which contiguous "phrases" often either begin or end with the same series of sounds, a phenomenon they

If the choice of formulas was not entirely conscious, it may have been constrained not only by the physiology and psychology of individual musicians (whether composers or singers), but also by the stylistic idiom the musician had learned from his teachers. Many of the variables that would have gone to make up this idiom would have changed with the passage of centuries, affected by such factors as the rise and fall of renowned teachers or regional schools, or the establishment or modification of corpora of classic models used for teaching and defining stylistic limits. Thus the applicable conventions (whatever they were) may have either tightened or loosened from one century to another. Would (for instance) a tenth-century musician who created a melody for a new text have had a wider or a narrower range of options than his counterpart in the sixth century? We are so little able to envision the operating procedures of, and constraints upon, early medieval singers that we cannot even answer broad, simple questions like these.

Furthermore, the use of formulas may actually be more deliberate in some written transmissions than in some oral transmissions. From the ninth century on, as medieval Greek missionaries brought the Byzantine church and liturgy to the Slavs, the Byzantine chant repertory was translated into the Old Church Slavonic tongue with the help of the new Cyrillic and Glagolitic alphabets created for this very purpose. As much as possible the Slavonic translations were kept to the same number of syllables as the Greek originals, so that the melodies would fit, and in fact these melodies were notated using a neumatic notation similar, but not identical, to the one used by the Greeks. The melodies, too, appear to follow the Greek note for note in many places, but there are also a significant number of departures, only some of which are easily explained by differences in the number of syllables and so on. When the Slavonic melodies do depart from the Greek, however, this often happened in ways that respected the formulaic structures of the melody (Ulff-Møller 1986, 1989:30–9), as if the adaptor was fully cognizant of their existence and function(s). Though we do not know how oral and written means of transmission may have inter-

call "rhyme-like" by analogy to human poetry. "It is interesting to find that humpback whales use rhyme-like structures in their songs during the periods when their songs contain the most material and are the most rhythmically regular," for which reason they speculate that "in this context their mnemonic function is enhanced" in a way reminiscent of Parry's and Lord's concept of the oral formula (1988:305).

acted to produce the Slavonic melodies, it is difficult to dispel one's impression that written processes were very important, that Slavic scribes, copying or adapting from notated Greek manuscripts, made many of the decisions regarding the adaptation of melodic formulas to texts.

There are many other unresolved issues that continue to hold us back. One of these is our inability to spell out even a provisional definition of what the term "formula" ought to mean, or indeed whether "formula" is even the best word to describe this musical phenomenon. To recognize the seriousness of this problem, we have only to consider Parry's definition: A formula is "a group of words which is regularly employed under the same metrical conditions to express a given essential idea" (Lord 1960: 30; Treitler 1974:355–6). This definition is scarcely applicable to music at all. Melodies do not include groups of words, they do not necessarily operate within "metrical conditions," and they rarely "express ideas" of the sort that words do. But if all this is excised from the definition, there is nothing left.[3] It is of course possible to "translate" Parry's definition into "equivalent" musical terminology, such as "a group of notes which is regularly employed under the same architectonic conditions to fulfill a given musico-syntactical function." Such attempts would inevitably entangle us in the inherent problems that accompany the application of linguistic

3. There is at least one medieval repertory where something like Parry's definition could be applicable. Many of the sequence melodies composed at the Parisian Abbey of St. Victor, in the twelfth century, are built up of stanzas and phrases derived from the melodies of more famous sequences. The borrowings are often intended to call attention to related ideas in the two sequence texts, according to "the Victorine belief that a melody adapted to a new text brought with it the meaning of the older text, permitting the mind to ponder both at once in a vivid exegesis" (Fassler 1983:116). In this case it would be possible to describe a derived phrase as "a group of notes which is employed under the same metrical conditions to express a given idea," although the "metrical conditions" would not apply when the derived music is an entire stanza. We still could not say, as Parry did, that the derived phrase was "regularly employed," because many options would be available to fit "the same metrical conditions": the concept of "thrift" (Lord 1960:50–4; Treitler 1974:368–70; Cutter 1976; Edwards 1983:159) is scarcely applicable to this repertory. Ironically, the fact that Parry's definition of "formula" almost fits the Victorine sequence demonstrates how poorly it captures the diagnostic characteristics exclusive to orally transmitted music (whatever they may be). These sequences were not created through oral composition or re-composition by means of a "generative system." Some of the texts may well have been composed by an individual poet, presumably Adam of St. Victor (Fassler 1984). The melodies were created by a highly sophisticated technique of recension, through the artifice of a specific though anonymous redactor (or perhaps several redactors), resulting in a definitive, written version of the melody. There will be a full discussion in Fassler's forthcoming edition of the Parisian sequence texts and music, and in Fassler forthcoming b.

analogies to music (Powers 1980b), and in any case we would have no confirmation that this "definition" describes any musical reality that actually exists. If there is such a thing as a musical formula, it cannot be defined by analogy to texts, but only on the basis of critical study of actual formulaic music, preferably on many such musical traditions rather than merely a few.

A similar criticism has been leveled at the word "centonization" as applied to melodic formulaism in medieval chant. It originally referred to the creation of a textual "patchwork" or mosaic of quotations from and allusions to the Bible, Vergil, or some other pre-existing literary source. Thus when John the Deacon claimed in his ninth-century biography that Pope Gregory had compiled an "antiphonary cento" (Migne, ed. 1844–55/75 : 90), he meant that Gregory had combined extracts taken from many parts of the Bible into a complete annual cycle of chant texts (Jeffery 1984a:163–5). The use of such a concept to describe formulaic music has therefore been attacked as too strongly implying a written/textual metaphor, forcing us to envision a composer writing a melody on parchment rather than a singer generating it during a performance (Treitler 1975 : 14–5). But the possibility of a link between textual centonization and musical formulaism should not be so readily dismissed. First of all, even the centonate character of liturgical texts may not be a purely literary phenomenon, but at least partly the result of oral practices.[4] Second, more than one specialist in Byzantine chant has noted instances wherein textual formulas seem linked to musical formulas, as if the occurrence of a stereotyped textual phrase prompted the creator of the melody to use a musical phrase traditionally associated with it (H. Schmidt 1979 : 198–201; Petrescu 1982; Ulff-Møller 1986). Comparable instances can be found in Gregorian chant, for example in many of the antiphons that begin with the words *O quam, Benedictus qui venit,* or *Hodie*, though no study of them from this perspective has yet been published.

Clearly, comparative study of the "formula" concept in different musical traditions or cultures leads almost immediately to a bewildering complexity, because the specific characteristics that define a formula, and that determine the ways formulas can be combined into melodies, will vary (perhaps greatly) from one culture to another. Yet isolating a few characteristics that appear to be common to many formulaic musical traditions

4. Examples of this will be given in my *Prophecy Mixed with Melody* (see ch. 1, n. 2, above).

may make it possible to knock together at least some sort of working definition by which to proceed with the analysis of medieval chant.

1. Repetition

The most obvious attribute of formulas—their stereotyped character which is the reason for calling them "formulas"—was captured in one way by a scholar who opted for a strictly notational definition, defining a formula as "a recurrent sequence of neumes, i.e. a string of signs which occurs several times in the material" (Amargianakis 1977 : 10; see also Ulff-Møller 1986). Such thinking often underlies the work of scholars who have published lists of formulas without specifying any criteria for their identification beyond simple recurrence (some recent examples: Kaufman 1975 : 407–32; Crochu Lozac'hmeur 1985).

2. Ranges of Variability

Yet many formulas can be quite flexible or variable, so that it is necessary for the scholar to determine the limits of this flexibility: " . . . a melodic formula, as far as one can define it, is . . . a framework, within which there are elements of fixation, yet [it is] still subject to transformation. . . . The melodic formula is by no means an ossified melody which always appears in exactly the same form. It is a mere melodic outline, within which slight variants and changes may occur, which may diversify its appearance, yet still not destroy [its] basic quality" (Velimirović 1960, 1 : 62). Another view (Treitler 1982a : 28–9) prefers to speak of "pitch groups" or "modules" rather than "formulas." These are defined by their "underlying structure" rather than by surface details. "Pitch groups" that are superficially very different may nevertheless have the same "underlying structure" (such as an upward motion to a specific pitch followed by a descent to the final), "because there is no fixed way in which the melody moves through [these structural] pitches" (1982a : 39).

One type of flexibility, of course, is seen when the "same" formula is applied to different texts, with different numbers of syllables or patterns of accentuation; this type has been examined in parts of the Gregorian chant repertory (recently by Milanese 1987, C. Schmidt 1980). Another type of flexibility may be seen in the variants that emerge between different sources of the same repertory, particularly if families of variants tend to correspond to regional and/or chronological groupings among the sources. Such variants, as they occur in written manuscripts of Byzantine chant, were a focus of some of Strunk's articles (1977: 157–64, 191–201, 255–67, 277–84). More recent studies of the same sort have been undertaken using other groups of Byzantine chant manuscripts (Busch 1971; Isobe 1982), the printed and handwritten sources of Byzantine Ukrainian chant (Antonowycz 1974), and Eastern European sources of Gregorian chant, where the problem impinges on the question of the alleged German regional chant dialect.[5] The most ambitious attempt to deal with regional variants in Latin chant, however, was published before questions about oral-formulaic procedures had been widely raised, and envisioned the problem as one of comparing written variants after the manner of the textual critic, without considering the potential oral-formulaic character of the melodies.[6]

Just as formulas may vary from place to place, so they may also vary over time, a possibility that is particularly troublesome for anyone concerned with historical questions. One way this problem has begun to be investigated is in the comparison of modern sources of Byzantine chant with medieval manuscripts (Touliatos 1982, Petrescu 1982)—in other words, written sources of the same tradition created at different periods.

3. Concepts of "Formula" and "Centonization" in Selected Cultures

Because of the ways formulas can vary, a major problem in working with them is the problem of identity. When are two melodic passages so similar that they should be considered variants of the same formula? And when are they so different that they must be classified as different formulas? One reason these questions are so hard to answer is because we are separated by so many centuries from the mental world of those who actually created and transmitted the melodies. To attempt to gain an insider's perspective, one must turn to traditions where emic conceptions of "formula" are expressed in the indigenous music theory, or at least where individual formulas are identified by means of names or notational symbols.

All of these conditions are met in late Byzantine-Slavonic chant,

5. See for instance Brenn 1956; Falvy 1964; Horn 1901–2; Lipphardt 1952; Mezei 1990; Miazga 1980; Molitor 1904; Wagner 1926, 1930, 1932; Weidinger 1903.

6. Moines de Solesmes 1960, 1962. For more recent attempts to apply this approach, see Hiley 1980–1; Underwood 1982.

where in recent centuries the melodies inherited from the Middle Ages have come to be understood as constructed from a finite series of short melodic phrases. The largest group of formulas, known as *popevki*, are excerpts from actual chants, each one identified by the word(s) to which it is sung in the chant from which it is excerpted. Two other types, the *litsa* and the *fity*, are identified in writing by stenographic notational signs, the melodic realization of which was originally known to the singer through oral tradition.[7] Since about the seventeenth century, the pitch content of all three types of formulas (there are about a thousand altogether) has been fully spelled out in diastematic neumatic notation in the Slavonic theoretical treatises.[8]

A very different approach to notating formulas is found in medieval Byzantine Greek manuscripts and in the Slavonic *kontakaria* (eleventh to thirteenth centuries). Above or below the neumes, which prescribe the melody interval by interval, there are larger symbols called "Great Signs" or "Great Hypostases," which may derive from cheironomy (hand signals used for "conducting"; see Gerson-Kiwi 1980), and which seem to occur at places where there were standardized formulas in the melody. Exactly what information they conveyed, however, is not fully clear (Conomos 1974: 325–67; Levy 1978: 207–9).

The chant of the Ethiopian Orthodox Church also makes use of formulas that are regarded as excerpts from specific chants. The notational sign is an abbreviation of the word accompanying the melodic formula in the chant from which the formula was excerpted. However, the pitch content of each formula is known to the singer only by oral tradition, for the realization of each notational sign is not itself defined in writing as in Byzantine-Slavonic chant. The especially interesting relationship of oral and written elements in Ethiopian chant make this little-known tradition an excellent candidate for combined historical/ethnomusicological investigation. The results of the first such study should appear in print shortly, but there will be room for many more.[9]

In the chanting of the Hindu Vedas (Sāmavedic chant), a formula is called a *parvan*, which means "division" (Howard 1977: 528–9, 543–4).

7. The occurrences of all three kinds of formulas in the most important chants of the repertoire are tabulated in Sava 1984.

8. Gardner and Koschmieder, eds. 1963: 31–330; commentary in Gardner and Koschmieder 1972; see also Ulff-Møller 1989: 28; Gusejnova forthcoming.

9. A dictionary of the signs and other material appear in Shelemay and Jeffery forthcoming; Shelemay, Jeffery, and Monson forthcoming.

This name may refer to the fact that, in written manuscripts, the beginning and end of each parvan are indicated by breath marks in the text of the chant, since a parvan is to be sung with one breath (Howard 1977: 12–13).[10] Parvans are understood to be excerpts from various chants in the repertory, but their specific melodic content is not spelled out in writing anywhere. Unlike Slavonic and Ethiopian chant they do not have a text-derived notation. In one school of chanting, the approximately three hundred parvans are represented in writing by a syllable notation, but this was developed in an attempt to classify them using the structure of the Sanskrit alphabet and is not related to the texts of the source chants from which the parvans were derived (Howard 1977: 115–24).

Sāmavedic chant is of special interest for the problem of oral transmission, for it is sung to texts that were handed down orally for up to a thousand years before being committed to writing—an event which itself may have happened more than two thousand years ago. A similar history, more than a millennium of oral transmission followed by many centuries of written, can be demonstrated for the Avesta, the scriptures of the Zoroastrian religion composed in the ancient Iranian language.[11] Like the Vedas, the hymns of the Avesta (some of which are attributed to Zoroaster himself) are still performed in religious services today (Boyce 1979: 30–8), though the chant seems not to have been investigated yet.

In Latin chant, too, pre-existent melismas may be excerpted from one chant to serve in another context (for instance as the melody for the dismissal formula *Ite missa est* or *Benedicamus Domino)*, or as the tenor of a polyphonic composition—or both simultaneously. When this happens, their source is often formally acknowledged by the fact that an excerpt of the original text is transmitted along with the written music. One recent study has tried to depict this process as "mirror[ing] in many respects the kind of oral composition that Leo Treitler has outlined for the

10. A similar concept may underlie the use of the Greek loanword *pneuma* ("breath") in medieval Latin chant to mean "melisma," a passage sung on one syllable or breath. This should not be confused with the other Greek loanword *neuma* ("sign"), which may be the source of the word "neume," meaning a notational sign. The two were often confused in the medieval West, and the confusion survives even in the second edition of the *Oxford English Dictionary*, wherein the definitions of liturgical terms are generally notoriously poor (*OED*, "neuma," "neume," "pneum," and "pneuma"). Thus the etymologies proposed in Treitler 1982b: 244, 1984c: 152, and 1986: 47 remain hypothetical until the history of these two Greek words in Western usage has been fully sorted out.

11. On the problems of dating the origins of the Vedas and the Avesta, see Widengren 1968; Renfrew 1987: 9–12, 42–7, 178–210; Mallory 1989: 35–56.

transmission of chant before the development of musical notation" (A. Robertson 1988:52), but it is hardly a case of oral generation from a stock of traditional material and according to traditional rules. The melismas are simply excised from one context and inserted into another, usually with minimal change, and with the new words applied by a process of contrafacture (see A. Robertson 1988:18–26). It is all much more like centonization than like the processes envisioned in the New Historical View.

These examples from the Byzantine-Slavonic, Ethiopic, Sāmavedic, and even Latin repertories suggest that attempts to discredit the concept of centonization[12] may be somewhat premature. In these traditions, at least, the formulas are (or in time came to be) understood as belonging originally to one specific chant, from which they could be borrowed and arranged into a mosaic to create other chant melodies. "There are such things in music" (Treitler 1975:14), and there are such things in at least some traditions of liturgical chant.

At least in the Slavonic and Ethiopic repertories, the development of a formalized centonization system seems to have taken place during a period of standardization and consolidation, coinciding with the creation (in Ethiopia) or further refinement (in the Slavonic world) of the notational system. Yet we cannot say that the "mosaic" approach to melody construction was a complete innovation then, utterly unknown to earlier generations of singers. Indeed, two Byzantine Greek manuscripts show that a musician can think this way about his music even when it is not officially sanctioned by the notational system. They contain "bits of interlinear text" in some of the lesser-known chants that served to remind the singer of passages in more familiar ones, "whose melodies he could supply from memory" (Strunk 1977:212).

4. "Formulas" with Syntactic Functions

The most venerable approach to the study of melodic formulas in Christian chant, based on the example of the psalm tones, involves cataloguing them according to their apparent function in marking syntactical divisions in the text. The formulas are classified using psalm tone terminology ("in-

12. Treitler 1975. See also Hucke 1980d:450: "The cento principle . . . requires a fixed and written tradition. It cannot by any means explain an oral tradition."

tonation," "reciting pitch," "medial cadence," "termination"), and their ways of adapting to the varying accentuation patterns of different texts are noted (Ferretti 1934:64–88, 118–31; Apel 1958:258–304; Wellesz 1961:417–27; Szigeti 1967). This approach has the advantage of implicitly acknowledging the widespread, perhaps universal, importance of punctuation, or points of repose, in vocal melody—as well as the fact that cadences are not mere stopping places, but involve an element of cultural encoding (Francès 1988:160). Recent attempts to improve on this approach to formula classification have operated by giving even more attention to textual accent (Ribay 1988), or by classifying formulas according to hypothesized underlying reciting pitches (Claire 1981; Madrignac 1986), or by emphasizing pitches deemed to be structurally important for whatever reason (Viret 1986:151–65). One recent attempt at a comparative analysis of Gregorian and Old Roman first-mode introits especially emphasizes the cadences (Klöckner 1988:37–53).

In the Jewish synagogue, the cantillation of the Bible also makes use of melodic formulas related to textual syntax. These formulas are traditionally linked to written signs that originally indicated pauses (or the absence of pauses) between words and phrases. The signs convey not only the locations of the pauses, but their relative strength or importance.[13] Because the signs were not originally intended to convey musical information, the musical formulas used to interpret them vary greatly from one Jewish community to another.[14] In most communities there is generally one musical formula for each graphic sign, but among the Yemenites the relationships among sign, musical formula, and textual syntax are more flexible (Sharvit 1980, 1982). Particularly fascinating is the way many of these formulas seem to spawn other kinds of music that are never notated at all: the liturgical prayer modes (Levine 1982–3; Spector 1984–5;

13. On the two most important systems of signs, the Palestinian and the Tiberian, see Revell 1977, 1979; Yeivin 1980. Yet another system is used among the Samaritans (Spector 1965).

14. The bibliography is extensive, but see, for instance, Binder 1959; Herzog 1963, 1971; Idelsohn 1929:35–71; Lachmann 1978; Levine 1982–3; Ne'eman 1966–7; Rosowsky 1957; Spector 1984–5. On the other hand, the widely publicized book of Haïk Vantoura (1976a) though it won a national book award in her native France, nevertheless completely misrepresents both the history of the Hebrew cantillation signs and their musical interpretation. Thus the accompanying recording (1976b) and transcriptions (1978–81, 1985) are without merit as representations of ancient Hebrew music. For extended reviews see Claire and Morin 1977; Ringer 1981; Werner 1981–2; Jourdan-Hemmerdinger 1986.

Nulman 1984–5), and even some non-liturgical folk songs (Gerson-Kiwi 1965).

An interesting example of a tradition that deliberately avoids both formulaicism and notation is to be seen in the Islamic chanting of the Qurʾān, where, "ideally, the recitation is new every time with no imitation or memorization" (K. Nelson 1982: 42; 1985: 178–84).[15] In practice, though, individual singers seem to be known for their distinctive cadences, which can be quoted by other singers and recognized by the audience, and which are important for establishing the *maqām* or for modulating to another maqām (K. Nelson 1985: 128, 169).

The fact that we do not yet have even a definition for "musical formula" shows that ethnomusicology can do more for chant studies than simply providing a different point of view. Engaging ethnomusicology would mean that chant scholars could contribute to, and be enriched by, wide-ranging interdisciplinary attempts to develop a precise theoretical vocabulary for many musical phenomena. The present lack of such a vocabulary is one of the reasons the discussion of chant transmission has as yet achieved so little consensus.

Yet, in exploring the idea of "formula," the wide cross-cultural range of possibilities shows how complicated a general, generic scholarly definition may need to be, and how the values of each parameter may differ from one musical culture to another. To have a viable definition even for one tradition, it will be necessary to control both the degree of "sameness" or "repetitiveness" among different occurrences of the same formula, and also several ranges of variability according to a number of criteria. The possible relationship of formulas to syntactical divisions in the text must be taken into account, and so must the possibility that formulas may be conceived emically as excerpts or borrowings from certain well-known model chants. This leads us, of course, to the problem of "melodic models" or "melody types."

B. Melody Types, Melodic Models, and Tune Families

1. Melodic Groups and Types

Formulas cannot usually be assembled at random; they operate within the context of complete melodies, or at least long-range melodic plans of

15. On the other hand, see the nine Moroccan performances compared in Schneider 1954.

one sort or another. Thus it is not enough to deal with the individual formulas—one needs to consider whole melodies also. Focusing on melodies, rather than formulas, is probably the oldest ethnomusicological approach to the oral transmission of monophonic repertories, classically formulated in the concept of the "tune family" developed by students of Anglo-American and Western European folk songs.[16] In liturgical chant repertories, too, it is easy to find large numbers of more or less closely related melodies, which a scholar is naturally tempted to organize into groupings. Once grouped, the individual melodies are readily seen as concrete representatives or realizations of a more abstract design, but such an abstraction may be called by a variety of names, depending on the individual scholar's view of its exact nature. Names that tend to imply relative rigidity include "melody-types" (Kapronyi 1982), "type-melodies" (Connolly 1972:159), "melodic stereotypes" (Nowacki 1981:191), or "melodic models" (A. Robertson 1988:52–5); deliberate attempts to weaken the implication of rigidity include "melodic families" (Treitler 1975:9), "melody type[s], or set[s] of idioms" (Crocker 1986:443–4), "formulaic systems" (Treitler 1974:352).

2. Melodic Outlines and Contours

One common way of abstracting a melody type from a group of related melodies is by paring away all variants to arrive at a bare outline, a melodic "skeleton" (Seeger 1966) or "Kernlinie" (H. Schmidt 1979:186). But it is difficult to determine how much historical reality this abstraction should be accorded. There is often a temptation to dub this the "original" tune, "archetype" (Connolly 1972), or "proto-melody" (Boilès 1973), and sometimes this is intended or assumed to affirm that all extant melodies in the group are historically descended or derived from it by processes of variation or corruption. But was this "original" (if indeed it ever existed) an actually performed tune? Or was it an idealized scheme in the mind of

16. For a succinct exposition of the history of this concept, see Nettl 1983:104–27, 193–6. A classic study is Seeger 1966; more recently see Shapiro 1975. For further bibliography see Shapiro 1972. The proceedings of an entire symposium on the classification of folk tunes is published in *Studia Musicologica* 7 (1965): 213–355; another such symposium is Elschek, ed. 1969; see also Dobszay 1988. An attempt to formulate the concept according to generative grammar principles is Burman-Hall 1978.

the singer that was somehow "fleshed out" during the performance?[17] Or does it have no historical reality at all except in the mind of the scholar who abstracted it? Some writers have sought to move even beyond the "original" to an even more abstract and (in their opinion) primitive level: an underlying pentatonic structure for instance,[18] or a monotone psalmodic reciting pitch.[19]

The legitimacy of such hypotheses probably varies from one repertory to another, and confirmation is (to say the least) difficult when there are no written sources to document early developmental stages of the alleged archetypal melody. More "objective" approaches, such as "melodic contour typology" (Adams 1976) or the "Wrocław Dendrite" (Czekanowska 1976), may offer detailed classification schemes or other advantages, but they tend to keep one completely outside the mental world of the musical culture one is studying.[20] Preliminary evidence from psychological experiments on melodic recall suggests that, in any case, contour may be less important for long-term memory than specific series of intervals heard in their scalar context. "Interval information is encoded more precisely when a key can be established. . . . Contour information is immediately available regardless of novelty, familiarity, transposition, or non-transposition . . . [but] it is easily lost. . . . Increased familiarity with melodies makes interval information much more resistant to decay than contour information. . . . [Contour] appears to be less important in familiar melodies and melodies retained over a period of time. . . . Repeated exposure to a melody seems to consolidate interval information but has

17. Thus Nowacki (1985–6) argued against comparing isolated Gregorian and Old Roman antiphons, and in favor of considering all extant examples of a given melody type. While most of the texts are shared by both repertories, only about 60 percent are assigned to the same melody type in both. Even within one Old Roman manuscript, "all . . . examples . . . are viewed as equally plausible embodiments of the melody-type in question, and comparisons with the Frankish [i.e., Gregorian] dialect are made on the level of the melody-type per se," not on the level of selected individual antiphon texts (1985–6:273).

18. Chailley 1980. For an even more ambitious attempt to discern pentatonicism in Gregorian chant, see Hansen 1979; Huglo 1984.

19. Claire 1962, 1963, 1975, 1981. Claire's views have influenced many French and other continental writers, but see especially Turco 1987.

20. Nettl 1983:89–92. As List (1985), for instance, shows, the ways melodies are conceived within a culture may be quite different from the ways they are likely to be perceived by scholars whose background is in Western classical music. Any attempt to describe early medieval melodies as they were conceived by early medieval singers should therefore be undertaken with great circumspection.

little effect on the availability of contour information" (Edworthy 1985: 182–4). Perhaps the tendency of some to see the contour of a melody as more important than its specific intervals ought to be reconsidered more carefully. And perhaps further studies of music perception will tell us something about why, in both East and West, neumatic notations that originally conveyed contour information gradually changed until they communicated mainly interval information.

Many attempts to reconstruct the history of individual melody types seem quite simplistic when compared with the great variety and flexibility that can actually be observed in the field.[21] One proposed typology (Nettl 1983: 193–200) suggests that there are "four types" or "hypothetical kinds of history" by which both individual tunes and entire repertories can develop. But these "types" only represent "generalized tendencies," and more than one kind may be present to varying degrees in any given situation. In addition, all kinds of histories can be affected by numerous variables, reflecting such parameters as (1) "density" or "sparsity," that is "the degree to which separate units of a repertory are similar," (2) "broadness" or "narrowness" depending on the range of possible variation, and (3) "historical density" or rate of change. One might say, for example, that in general the repertory of Gregorian tracts for the Mass was dense, narrow, and resistant to change, while the chants for the Ordinary of the Mass were both less dense and less narrow, and the trope repertory the sparsest and broadest of all.

Recently a specialist on Irish folk songs (Cowdery 1984, 1990) has sought to reformulate the "tune family" concept in a way that may be useful to chant scholars, because it recognizes the functioning of formulas and standard phrases within each melody of the family. His reformulation breaks the overall concept down into three "principles." The "outlining principle" focuses on the overall melodic contours of complete melodies, and "allows us to compare wholes to wholes." The "conjoining principle" covers tunes that have "sections in common," and "provides for comparing sections to sections" (a "section" is, of course, not necessarily the same thing as a "formula"). "A third principle arises from this: the 'recombining' principle, whereby we may compare sections to sections *and* wholes to wholes without requiring a fixed overall contour" (1984: 497–8, em-

21. Among the many studies that seek to trace the history and/or distribution of a single melody or a single song (i.e., melody plus words), see: Kolinsky 1978; Ling and Ramsten 1985; List 1979; Seeger 1966.

phasis original). Cowdery's view permits a highly flexible conception, in which "certain melodic moves are seen to belong together not as a fixed chain of events, but more as a system of potentialities. These motives can recombine in various ways, expanding or contracting, to make new melodies which still conform to the traditional sound," a phenomenon he himself likens to Gregorian centonization (1984:499).

Cowdery's three-pronged approach is much more easily adapted to liturgical chant than ideas borrowed from literary scholars like Parry and Lord, because it seeks to describe the behavior of music rather than the behavior of texts. And Cowdery's three principles are easily supplemented by others dealing with other features of music, such as the characteristics of different scale types, or of modal ranges and finals, or the use of formulas to mark textual divisions.

3. Kinds of Melodic Models: A Continuum

To investigate the range of ways that melody types or tune families can be understood by musicians who actually use them, it is informative to study traditions where the melodic models or groups are formally recognized, either by being given names or by having some sort of theoretical system to govern or explain their behavior. Even in these traditions, the relationships of the models to their "derivatives" can be quite varied, and this can be illustrated by placing them on a kind of continuum. At one extreme (let us call it the "left"), one would place instances where the model is imitated so exactly that its application to a new text is no more than a process of contrafacture. At the other extreme (the "right" in this case) would be examples of much more open-ended models that offer considerable room for creativity in their adaption to different texts. It must be remembered that even such a continuum is an oversimplification, both because it is one-dimensional and because some of the musical cultures placed on it have been more fully researched than some of the others.

Beginning at the "left," then, one would find the example of the Byzantine *heirmoi* (Velimirović 1973) and *automela,* often called "model stanzas." Each is defined by a specific poetic structure (including a fixed number of lines, a fixed syllable count, and a distinctive accent pattern) and a specific melody, and named for the textual incipit of the original stanza that serves as the model. Great numbers of other texts, designed by Byzantine poets to have virtually the same poetic structure as the model, were thus also sung to the same melody with few if any significant changes (Wellesz 1961: 198–203, 243–4), though today many of these texts are more likely to be recited without tune (Velimirović 1973: 205). Moving slightly away from this extreme might be the Syrian type of model stanza, called *resh qala* in the East Syrian (Assyro-Chaldean and Syro-Malabar) rites, *rish qolo* in the Syro-Maronite rite (in either case meaning "head chant"), or simply *qala* ("chant") in the West Syrian or Jacobite rite. These too are model poetic stanzas as well as model melodies,[22] most of which are named for their textual incipits. But there is greater room for melodic variation as the melody is applied to new texts. This is partly because, in the absence of written music notation, the melodies cannot be fixed as rigidly as in notated Byzantine manuscripts.[23] But it is also because greater variability is permitted in the poetic structure of the texts, even though they are transmitted in writing (Husmann 1972: 76–80; Hage 1972: 41, 64, 67). Indeed, remarkable conflicts between "melody type" and "text type" are possible (Hage 1972: 132–6). In addition, the East Syrian tradition recognizes variant forms of some resh qala melodies (Husmann 1972: 77–8), while each West Syrian qala has been expanded into eight forms, each corresponding to one of the eight modes in the West Syrian *oktoechos* (Husmann 1971; Kuckertz 1969). One scholar has observed that the Maronite rish qole can themselves be grouped into still larger "type-melodies," permitting us to observe a greater amount of variation in the "same" melody over an even broader range of texts (Hage 1972: 54–131).[24] Coptic chant, too, makes use of models called in Arabic *alḥan* (singular *laḥn*, meaning "melody"), though some of them are also called "echos," a loanword that in the original Greek would mean "mode." The alḥan too have both poetic and melodic characteristics (Borsai 1980a: 732–3; 1980b), but are fewer and less systematized than among the Syrians. Clashing textual and melodic shapes have been observed here also (Borsai 1971).

Further to the "right" is where one might put melody types that were

22. The texts of the Maronite model stanzas are edited in Breydy 1979. His commentary also explains the relationships to the East Syrian and West Syrian model stanzas, and refers to published musical transcriptions when possible.

23. One can compare the models and their derivatives by using the indices of melody names in Husmann's transcriptions of the East Syrian (1967: 200–1) and West Syrian (1969) ferial offices.

24. Complicating matters further, it is also possible to discern text types that change as they are applied to different melody types; see Hage 1972: 132–6.

deliberately designed to expand and contract in order to fit any text, for instance by including reciting pitches that can be repeated any number of times. The eight *samohlasen* tones of the Byzantine-Ruthenian stichiry offer a good example;[25] the eight responsorial psalm tones of Latin chant offer another.[26] In each case, the eight tones correspond to the eight church modes.

As we move toward the "right" end of the spectrum, the "models" become increasingly difficult to distinguish fully from "modes."[27] The two concepts already began to intersect in the West Syrian qala, and to be confused in the Coptic use of the Greek word "echos." They are identified even more closely in the samohlasen and responsorial psalm tones, because in these traditions there is (theoretically) only one melodic model per mode. An even closer identification of "model" and "mode" would seem to be exemplified by the melodic models that have been used in Armenian chant since at least the sixteenth century. There is one of these for each mode of the Armenian oktoechos (which in fact contains more than eight modes), and apparently the Armenian word for "mode" (*jayn*) is also the word for the modal model (Tʿahmizyan 1970 : 36). Modern Armenian musicians regard these models as very ancient in spite of their relatively recent appearance in the manuscripts (Outtier 1973 : 183), and they appear to assume that all the melodies of each mode somehow arose as adaptations of the one model.[28] This may indeed be the way the models function in Armenian chant today, because the medieval neumes can no longer be deciphered (Atayan 1968). Armenian singers either know the melodies through oral tradition, or else they perform them from nineteenth- or twentieth-century transcriptions from oral tradition. But in view of their late origin, the Armenian model melodies may at first have been more like the "antiennes-types" of Latin chant, the most famous being the series that began "Primum quaerite regnum Dei" (Huglo 1971 : 386–8). These were

25. Roccasalvo 1986 : 98–128, 144–5; for the liturgical context in the Ruthenian oktoechos see Papp and Petraševič 1970 : 53–92.

26. Apel 1958 : 234–41; Crochu Lozac'hmeur 1985; Frere 1901–24 : 3–61; Hucke 1973 : 180; Randel 1969.

27. On the range of concepts that can be denoted by the word "mode," see Powers 1980a.

28. Differing transcriptions of the models will be found in Serkoyan 1973 and Tʿahmizyan 1977 : 171–3. Serkoyan also gives examples of some of the "adaptations." The attempt to analyze these models in Outtier 1973 can only be understood in the context of the presuppositions and methodology of Claire 1962, 1963, 1975, which Outtier takes for granted.

examples of typical modal patterns used for training singers to distinguish the modes, but they were not considered the ultimate sources of all the other melodies in the repertory.

Approaching the "right" extreme of the continuum, one may perhaps locate the "prayer modes" of the Synagogue, called *nusach* in Hebrew, *shtayger* in Yiddish (see Levine 1980–1:13–5 on terminology). These "modes" are used by the *chazzan* or cantor to sing the prayer texts of the service; the cantor is not necessarily the same person as the master reader in charge of Bible cantillation. There is no traditional notation for the prayer melodies, though in recent centuries many cantors have published their own collections in modern staff notation.[29] Some of the prayer modes are named for the type of prayer text they are used with, others bear the name of one particularly prominent liturgical text that is sung in that mode.[30] The fact that modern writers tend to call them "modes" shows that it is hard to pin down a specific melodic prototype comparable to the examples given to the "left" on our continuum—to us the shtayger look more like "scales." Scholarly discussion of the shtayger has therefore been greatly clouded by writers who have insisted on identifying "mode" with "scale," and fitting the evidence into their own views of what the underlying scale may be. More plausible is a recent attempt to redefine the prayer modes as "aggregates of characteristic phrases" (Levine 1980–1:34). Even more than the cantillation melodies, the shtayger have also influenced Yiddish folk and popular songs.[31]

The prayer modes have also been compared (Frigyesi 1982–3) to the maqāmāt of Arab music, which perhaps belong toward the extreme "right" of our continuum.[32] The liturgical repertories of both Christian and Jewish communities in the Middle East have experienced direct influence from the maqām system. In the two Syrian Christian chant traditions that make use of an oktoechos, West Syrian or Jacobite chant (Husmann 1974a; 1980:475–6) and Byzantine-Melkite chant (Cohen 1971, 1973),

29. One series of books for instructing cantors is Ne'eman 1968–9, 1972. See also Nulman 1984–5. Some of the classic collections of prayer melodies by historically important cantors are listed in Idelsohn 1929:287–95; some of these collections have been reprinted in Hecker et al., eds. 1953–4. See also Ephros 1957; Edelman 1978–9.

30. See the brief introduction in Idelsohn 1929:72–89, 129–44.

31. Wohlberg 1977–8; Slobin 1982:32–6, 168–73, 182–97.

32. The concept is briefly explained in Powers 1980a:423–8, see also al Faruqi 1981:169–70 and the various cross-references there. Entries on the individual maqāmāt are indexed under "melodic modes (names of)" in Appendix I, p. 428. For some more extended discussions see Elsner 1981; Shiloah 1981; Powers 1988; Scott 1989.

the eight modes have actually become identified with eight particular maqāmāt (see also Husmann 1979). Musicologists studying the two Syrian traditions that lack the oktoechos, the East Syrian or Assyro-Chaldean (Husmann 1972:81–4; Ross 1979) and the Syro-Maronite (Husmann 1972:86; Hage 1972:19), have detected the influence of the maqāmāt there also. Attempts have even been made by Greek Orthodox singers to assimilate the modes of modern Byzantine Greek chant to the Turkish Makam system (Husmann 1979; Powers 1988:214–5). The influence of Islamic music theory has also been detected in the gamut of pitches used in Armenian chant (Chabrier 1989), though the modes of the Armenian oktoechos never became linked to specific maqāmāt. The Egyptian Copts seem to have resisted the influence of the Arab maqāmāt more successfully, though they appear to have lost large portions of their medieval repertory in the process.[33]

As with the word "formula," any attempt to develop a musicological definition of "melody type" (or whatever it should be called) requires controlling many intersecting ranges of possibilities. A melody can be examined in terms of its component formulas and phrases (which are not necessarily the same thing) in all their potential variety. Similar melodies can be grouped on the basis of resemblance alone, or on the basis of their alleged theoretical or historical derivation from a common model of some sort. And at some point the concept of "model" itself fades into the concept of "mode." Different interrelationships of variables are inevitable as one moves from one tradition to another, but they may also be possible within a single tradition, where some pieces of music may function rather differently from others. For example, the single tradition of Tibetan Buddhist chant includes a continuum almost as long as the multi-cultural one outlined above. It includes strophic melodies repeated with little change for multiple textual stanzas (*rta*), elastic "recitation chants" that can fit

33. In ethnomusicological terms, the loss of much of the Coptic repertory can be seen as an example of "impoverishment"—one of the ways minority music cultures attempt to resist the encroachments of a surrounding musical culture (Nettl 1983:350–1). On the other hand, the Syrian approach of absorbing features of the maqāmāt system would be an example of "syncretism" (Nettl 1983:353–4). The difference reflects the differing attitudes of the two different groups toward the dominant Arabic culture that they inhabit. For while the Syrians generally take pride in being Christian Arabs, the Copts take pride in the fact that they are descended from the non-Arab people of pre-Islamic Egypt. Hence their music is assumed to be historically connected with the musical culture of the pharoahs and the pyramids (Menard 1952; Borsai 1968a, 1968b), thereby posing a problem of "inferential history" no less daunting than the issue of oral transmission in early Christian chant!

a variety of texts (*ʾdon*), and composed, notated chants that use "tone-contours" rather than discrete pitches (*dbyangs*) (Ellingson 1979; Kaufman 1975). Clearly, any etic attempt to identify analytically the "melody types" of a specific repertory will have to take all the ranges of possibility into account, using them as the backgrounds against which to map the observable features of the individual repertory being investigated.

4. The Impact of Modal Theory

Reconstructing medieval concepts of "melody type" can become especially tricky when dealing with musical repertories that have a highly developed music theory, if the theory seems to ignore the formulaic or "melody-typic" aspect of the tunes. In Gregorian and Byzantine chant, for instance, one would have to decide how much importance to assign to the traits medieval theorists used to classify melodies: traits such as modal final and ambitus, and the relationship between the opening pitch and the end of the preceding psalm verse (Strunk 1977:35–6). It may be that these features became important only after the introduction of the eight-mode system, when theorists felt the need to bring theory and practice into agreement. If that were so, then perhaps they could be ignored by a modern scholar bent on recovering the "original" or "pre-oktoechal" system of "melody types" (e.g., Claire 1975). But we do not know. The problem is one that, in my opinion, tends to be underemphasized in some recent writing on Western chant transmission: To what degree might the earliest written melodies already reflect the work of editors trying to bring them into conformity with the incipient modal theory? Is it possible that the oldest written melodies we have are actually revisions that had never in that form been part of the "pure" oral tradition before the introduction of the modes and the neumes? How are we to know?

The development and spread of the modal system, and the gradual adaptation of individual chant repertories to conform to it, were crucial events in the early history of Christian chant, events that no theory of chant origins can afford to slight. The earliest musicians who certainly used the eight-mode system were Syrian hymnographers who wrote in Greek, monks at Palestinian monasteries during the late seventh and early eighth centuries. The most prominent of these was John of Damascus (ca. 670–ca. 750), whom tradition credits with the compilation of the Great Oktōēchos or Paraklētikē, a liturgical book of hymns arranged according to the eight modes, which hymns are still sung through a repetitive cycle of eight weeks, one mode per week, throughout the Byzantine rite liturgical year. It is now clear, however, that the eight modes may date from a century or more before John, for they already occur in the Jerusalem Iadgari of the sixth or seventh century, sections of which are arranged by mode in numerical order (Jeffery 1991a). How or from where the urban rite of Jerusalem obtained the modes, however, is still unknown.[34]

From its apparent origins in or near Jerusalem, the modal system spread rather quickly. It was already fully in place in Constantinople by about the year 900, when the earliest extant typikon of the local rite of this city was made (Mateos 1962: x–xviii). The eight modes are said to have reached nearby Armenia before the year 735 (Outtier 1973: 182), and they may have reached the West by the end of the eighth century (Huglo 1971: 25–9, but see Hucke 1980d: 442–3 n. 25), though Gregorian chant was the only Western tradition to adopt them (Hucke 1975, 1980b). Their first appearance in the Syriac-speaking churches was in the ninth century, at first only in spheres that were open to Greek influence (Cody 1982: 92, 98, 103); the full assimilation of the Syrian Jacobite repertory to the modal system took centuries to complete. But the assimilation process took just as long in the Gregorian repertory. In short, whatever the relationship between the earliest notated melodies and the oral tradition that preceded them, the adoption of the modal system was a significant factor in the transition from one to the other. Like the invention of notation, the adoption of the modes was a historic watershed, its role in shaping the melodies so subtle yet pervasive that it can no longer be hypothetically "factored out" by those who would like to recover the "pre-oktoechal" melodies of an earlier time.

In my opinion, the most prudent approach to retracing the impact of the modal system when it was still new is the one attempted by Crocker, who begins by focusing on modally organized series of antiphons that "we know to be of Frankish origin, from the ninth century or following," because these provide us with "the first Western music we know to be modal,

34. One important source of evidence remains uncollected and uninterpreted, namely the incidences of modal terminology in papyrus fragments of Greek hymns. A preliminary list appears in Jourdan-Hemmerdinger 1987: 93 nn. 35 and 41, cf. p. 99. To this list I would add John Rylands papyrus 466 (Roberts 1938: 28–35, see also the Addenda at the end of the Roberts volume), a primitive kanōn in the first plagal mode, dated to seventh-century Egypt. For further information on the development of the modes and the kanōn see my *Liturgy and Chant in Early Christian Jerusalem* (see ch. 4, n. 6, above).

the first certain to have been composed with evident attention to the system of eight modes" (1986:443, 490). He then asks what "procedures" or "models" may have been available to the "Frankish cantors" who presumably created these series. While he finds this first study "largely negative in result" (1986:488), I believe this is simply because of the limited range of material that was able to be included. The direction itself is a correct one, freeing us from anachronistic concepts of mode and forcing us to imagine ourselves in a fixed time and place that is relatively documentable and close to the time the modal system was first introduced in the West.

C. Interpolated Syllables

In some liturgical traditions, melismatic chants are remembered and performed with the help of meaningless syllables interpolated among the syllables of the text (Raghaven 1954:110, Touliatos 1989). These appear to assist the singers by breaking up the sustained vowels of long melismas, helping to stabilize the number, duration, and relative pitch of the notes, and thus perhaps helping the members of the choir stay together while singing. Such syllables are a prominent feature of the Byzantine Greek book called the Asmatikon, a collection of the choral sections of responsorial chants (some of them liturgical counterparts of the Gregorian gradual and alleluia) developed by the highly trained choir of the Great Church Hagia Sophia in Constantinople.[35] For that reason they are sometimes called "asmatic letters" (Strunk 1977:321, 329–30). They are also important in the Kondakar, the Byzantine-Slavonic counterpart (more or less) of the Asmatikon (Levy 1978:200–1). In later Byzantine Greek sources such syllables also turn up in other kinds of chants, where they are called *teretismata* because the syllables *te* and *re* are especially common (Conomos 1974:261–86). Equivalent Slavonic terms include *anenayki* and *khabuvi,* because common interpolated syllables in Slavonic chant include *a, ne, na, kha,* and *vu* (Palikarova Verdeil 1953:145). Coptic chant makes use of such syllables also (they are printed in red in Blin 1888 to distinguish them from the text proper). There is probably much that we still do not know about how the use of such syllables assisted the singers,

35. The solo sections for these same chants are collected in a different book known as the Psaltikon, see Strunk 1977:45–54.

but a recent article suggests a new direction for research. David W. Hughes, in a very provocative paper, argued that some Asian and European musical traditions utilize nonsense syllables in very sophisticated ways as a kind of notation, to represent, either mnemonically or in writing, essential musical information regarding articulation, "tone color, resonance and/or pitch" (1989:3). Though the Byzantine use of nonsense syllables does not closely resemble the systems on which this article focuses, Hughes has pointed out some important ways that linguistic phonemes can be made to represent musical phenomena, opening up several avenues that may possibly lead to a better understanding of the Byzantine practice.

Though interpolated nonsense syllables were apparently not used in Western chant, it has been suggested that some of their functions may have been exercised by the proses and prosulae—"trope" texts composed to fit syllabically to the melismas of specific chants (Conomos 1974:286–7). The issue of whether this is true is, of course, inevitably bound up with the problem of how proses and prosulae were performed (Marcusson 1979, Kelly 1985). But no less a figure than Notker (d. 912) wrote that the prose texts he composed helped him to "bind fast" the "very long melodies" which, though "repeatedly entrusted to memory," just as repeatedly "escaped from my poor little head" (Crocker 1977:1, cf. Hucke 1983). If there is any truth at all to this claim, then the prose and prosula texts of medieval Western chant must have been among the practices associated with musical memory and transmission, at the same time that they may also have fulfilled other functions.

D. Melodic Embellishment

Throughout the written history of Byzantine chant, a process of increasing melodic ornamentation can be detected (Wellesz 1963:143–50; Strunk 1977:41, 157–61, 193–4, 254). Beginning already by the ninth century, it apparently led to the *kalophonic* or "beautiful-sounding" style of the fourteenth and fifteenth centuries (Williams 1968, Conomos 1974). The melodies of Neo- or Meta-Byzantine chant, the kind performed in Greek Orthodox churches today, sometimes seem to be heavily ornamented versions of the simpler melodies preserved in the medieval manuscripts (Dragoumis 1966). The relationship is such that Greek church musicians categorically reject the transcriptions made by Western scholars from the medieval notation, asserting that an unwritten performance practice of ornamenting in the modern way was always part of the tradition (Stathis 1979, 1982; Jeffery 1988a: 132–3). No doubt they see some confirmation of their view in certain modern Greek folk music, wherein the traditional melodic outline, called *skeletos* (meaning "skeleton"), is never performed as such, but always in an expanded, ornamented form that varies with each performance and social context (Brandl 1989: 114–6).

Something like this process was also active in the West. In certain places during the late medieval period, Gregorian chant was performed in a manner that seems very foreign to us today. The melody was sung very slowly, but it was heavily embellished. Such a practice is documented in Toledo Cathedral from at least 1448 to 1851 (Gümpel 1981), where it was called Eugenian chant, after a seventh-century bishop of Toledo. A similar practice in French cathedrals, called *machicotage,* is documented from 1391 through at least the eighteenth century.[36] The medieval melodies surviving in Dalmatia are also highly ornamented sometimes (Martinić 1981, 1: 127–32). Another interesting case of what appears to be the "same" process can be seen in the Spanish songs sung in the Mystery of Elche (Trend 1920; Rubio 1965, 1968), a traditional ceremony sometimes described as the last survival of medieval liturgical drama (on its origin see Gironés 1977). Some very conservative Protestant communities also have a practice of singing traditional hymn tunes in a highly ornamented manner, which they call the "Old Way of Singing" (Temperley 1981, Miller 1984). A process of gradual ornamentation may also have taken place in the chant of certain Japanese Buddhist sects, for the notation of one of the earliest manuscripts (dated 1238) indicates only what appear to be "Skelettmelodien" of the melismatic tunes notated in fifteenth-century sources and still sung today.[37]

It is easy to see this type of embellishment as a way of preserving or transmitting a traditional melody by surrounding it with ornaments, like a rare jewel preserved in an elaborate but more recent setting, or an ancient text enveloped by commentary. And it is noteworthy that in at least some of these traditions people recognize a difference between the embellished performance practice and the "straight" performance of the "real" melody: Eugenian chant is distinguished from Gregorian chant, the "Old

36. Lebeuf 1741: 69–115; d'Ortigue 1854; Apel 1969; Berry 1980. On a fifteenth-century discussion of chant ornamentation in France, see Harrán 1989: 43–64.

37. Giesen 1977: 26–36, 139–45, 347–9, 351–2. Further manuscripts of Japanese Buddhist music are described in Arai 1986 and S. Nelson 1986.

Way" from the "Regular Way." It is thus reasonable to see such practices as a common and important means of orally transmitting or preserving ancient melodies.

Although the embellishment of Gregorian melodies may only be documented from late in the Middle Ages, something like it may have gone on much earlier, even during the formative period. There are scholars who believe that the Gregorian melodies as we know them developed by a gradual process of ornamentation from simple recitations comparable to the psalm tones (Claire; Hourlier 1973; cf. Cutter 1967: 181) If this happened, it may have been through some practice of ornamentation analogous to late medieval machicotage. The fixation of the melodies in writing during the ninth or tenth centuries may have halted the original ornamentation process, permitting it to start over again later in the Middle Ages.

The opinion that the melismatic medieval melodies developed from simpler originals, by a process of gradual ornamentation, has been pressed into service to explain the apparent decline of congregational singing in the liturgy. The first person to make this connection may have been the Solesmes monk Jacques Froger:

> It seems, therefore, to judge by the evidence, that the people's share in the singing of Mass was relatively important in the very early days and that it was gradually and steadily reduced. The cause of this was undoubtedly the elaboration of the music. As long as the melodies were very simple and in the nature of psalmody or recitative, they could be sung, at least in part, by the congregation. But when the music became complicated, it was necessary to confine the performance to trained and skilled singers, for music of such complexity could not be sung by ordinary people lacking specific musical training. (Froger 1949: 61, as translated in Murray 1977: 21)

At the time, this opinion would have seemed to corroborate the experience of many church musicians involved in the chant revival led by Solesmes, because, even after decades of effort, many congregations and parish choirs still were capable of performing only the simplest melodies.[38] Since the difficulty of the melodies seemed the source of the modern prob-

38. Ellard 1948: 74–81, 274–91, 1956: 183–213; Deiss 1976: 232; Murray 1977: 35–45; Combe 1987; Carroll 1989; Jeffery 1991b: 1042–3.

lem (i.e., that modern congregations could only perform small parts of the Gregorian chant repertory), it was easy to blame it also for the historical problem (i.e., why congregational singing seems to have declined since ancient times). Thus many musicians naturally came to the conclusion that it was "the gradual elaboration of the music" that ensured that "the people were reduced to silence . . . . The liturgy thus became a performance of the rites and ceremonies by the clergy and their ministers at the altar to the accompaniment of music sung by quasi-professional singers in the choir" (Murray 1977: 21). What was missing was an explanation of why or how the melodies came to be "gradually elaborated."

It was this explanation that Gelineau sought to supply, and he did it by reversing the order of events Froger and others had supposed. Instead of supposing that the increasing ornamentation of the melodies made it "necessary to confine the performance to trained and skilled singers," Gelineau claimed the opposite, that it was the incursion of professionals into the liturgy that caused the complexification of the melodies. This claim became in fact the cornerstone of his version of chant history.

> The art of the *psaltes* or chanter consisted in adapting received musical models to the various texts. They remained close to recitative, and the tones for reciting were classified according to eight modes which corresponded to the eight weeks from Easter to Pentecost. Such a classification was originally ritual rather than musical. The Frankish chanters of the turn of the eighth century, perhaps in Metz, may be credited with the greatest revolution in the history of Christian singing. They introduced a melodic 'repertoire,' and with it, a concentration on music as such. They began with the *cantilena Romana* and the texts of the antiphonary as this had been fixed by Gregory the Great. On this basis they elaborated a sumptuous melodic version whose prestige was such that it gradually spread throughout the whole West. This phenomenon was made possible by the emergence, at about the same time, of a primitive form of music notation which enabled the tunes of this oral composition to be more or less fixed and handed on in writing. Spreading like ripples in a pool, the melodies of what we now call Gregorian chant cross Europe in manuscript form. By the thirteenth century they have even supplanted the indigenous Roman chant known as Old Roman—a somewhat debatable

appellation, since a certain amount of evolution had occurred in the intervening period. (Gelineau 1978:447)

But we do not know whether or not the cantors of the pre-medieval Church sang simple melodies "close to recitative." This is based simply on the assumption that, if it were not so, the congregations of that period would have been unable to sing the responses—something we also do not know and cannot assume merely on the basis of modern experience. We do not know that the modal system was "originally ritual rather than musical," and it probably was not yet in use during the fourth and fifth centuries, the period from which most of our information about early responsorial psalmody survives. We cannot say for certain that it was "Frankish chanters of the turn of the eighth century" who first elaborated the melodies that had until then been simple, and few scholars would now accept the statement that these simple melodies (if indeed they existed) could be traced back to Gregory the Great. The relationship of the preserved Old Roman chant melodies to earlier musical traditions is, of course, one of the most debated questions in current musicology.

To some it may seem axiomatic that the melismatic chant melodies would have developed from simpler originals. But this cannot be assumed without question, for throughout history many things develop in the opposite direction, from complex to simple. This is most evident in the history of languages: classical Latin, for instance, is clearly more complex than the modern romance languages descended from it, just as Anglo-Saxon uses many more inflections than modern English. In the history of liturgies, too, it has been noted that there is a simplifying process operating alongside the complexifying process (Baumstark 1958:19–23). In Byzantine chant, the elaborate melodies of the *kontakia,* the *prokeimena* or responsorial psalms, and the alleluias of the Mass (preserved in the medieval Asmatikon and Psaltikon manuscripts) have all been abandoned; when these texts are used today they are generally recited in a monotone. The *samohlasen* tones of Slavonic chant also represent the simplification of a formerly richer melodic tradition (Roccasalvo 1986:99–100). Therefore, we cannot state that in principle the melodies of Gregorian chant are more likely to have developed from simpler to more complex than in the opposite direction (cf. Apel 1958:507–8).

The historical question of whether the melismatic Gregorian melodies developed from simpler originals by a process of ornamentation is yet another issue that is difficult to investigate without becoming deeply entangled in the debate between "pastoral" and "sacred" musicians. Scholars who wish to explore this issue impartially must work with especially great care, not only because it is so difficult to maintain one's own objectivity when so many other writers on the subject have not done so, but because the answer to the historical question could have such a profound impact on present-day ecclesiastical policies relating to the liturgical use of Gregorian chant.

E. Organum

Unwritten, note-against-note harmonizations of Gregorian chant are at least as old as the *Musica Enchiriadis* (Schmid 1981, Phillips 1983), that is to say, as old as the earliest notated manuscripts of the chant itself. Up to the eleventh century, our information about polyphony comes less from written-out examples of finished polyphonic works than from theoretical instructions telling how to "improvise" or create it during performance. But even after it became common to write out polyphonic compositions in mensural notation, chant continued to be performed with relatively simple unwritten harmonizations throughout the Middle Ages and beyond, with the help of techniques that did not necessarily require the use of writing (K.-J. Sachs 1983; C. Schmidt 1983; Petrobelli 1980). We know this both from the remarks of theorists and from occasional written-out pieces of music, witnesses to the performance practices underlying such phenomena as organum, cantus binatim (Fischer 1971, 1973–4; Gallo 1966; Vecchi n.d.; Römer 1983:70), singing upon the book (Bent 1983; Peyrot 1913; Prim 1961), faburden (Trowell 1978) and fauxbourdon (Hoffman-Axthelm 1972; C. Wright 1989:349–54). From our modern point of view these practices seem relatively marginal, readily eclipsed by the many surviving written-out polyphonic compositions that we find more interesting. But in the Middle Ages they may have been quite common, even a normal way of performing the chant. Pope John XXII seems to have advocated the use of such unwritten harmonizations in his famous bull of 1322, in which he objected to some of the features of the more elaborate written polyphony of the Ars Nova—the type we think of as typical of the period.[39] Medieval

39. Fellerer 1970, Hucke 1984a. A convenient copy of the Latin text with an English translation is Wooldridge 1929:294–6. The standard edition is Richter and Friedberg 1922/1:1255–7.

"improvised" polyphony poses some of the same investigative problems as oral transmission in the chant repertory itself. In both cases we must try to surmise how extant written pieces of music were connected with an oral practice we can no longer observe directly, in order to learn how much can be inferred from the written pieces about what the oral practice was like.

Extempore polyphonic performance of Western chant can still be heard in the oral traditions of the Ossola, the Friuli, Corsica, and Dalmatia. It is also found in some modern Syriac Christian chant traditions (Husmann 1966, Ross 1979), and among the modern Samaritans (Ravina 1963). Temperley has noted that "popular harmonization" has a role in the Old Way of Singing (1981:529, see also Tallmadge 1984, Miller 1984). The study of musical cognition reveals that the tendency to harmonize spontaneously can easily be related to one of the ways that human beings recall melodies. Recent psychological experiments on immediate melodic recall (long-term memory is obviously more difficult to study under laboratory conditions)[40] suggest that "there is evidence that harmonic structure may be encoded even when exact melodic structure is lost. On some occasions, [when a subject is asked to reproduce a sample melody from memory,] this leads to a radically new melody, although, more commonly, subjects make small variations on the original melody that are harmonically and metrically consistent" (Sloboda and Parker 1985:160). The amount of musical training can also be a factor. "Musicians and nonmusicians differ significantly [in] the ability to retain the harmonic structure of the original" (*ibid.*; see also Oura and Hatano 1988).

Note-against-note polyphony may not be the only kind that can serve as a process for transmitting ancient melodies. Melismatic organum, the type that reached its highest stage of (written) development in the works of the Notre Dame School of twelfth- and thirteenth-century Paris (C. Wright 1989:235–300), can also be seen as indebted to two kinds of transmission: "vertical" harmonization combined with "horizontal" melodic embellishment. As in machicotage, the chant melody is performed slowly, but in this case it is in long drawn-out notes, with the ornamentation in quicker notes written on a different staff to be performed by a different person or persons.

At least two interesting parallels can be adduced from Asian traditions of instrumental music. In the type of music known as Tōgaku, proper

40. On the different types of musical memory, see Sloboda 1988.

to the Japanese imperial court, the *biwa* ("lute") and *shō* ("mouth organ") perform slow, harmonized (shō) or ornamented (biwa) versions of melodies inherited from the ancient Tang dynasty of China (tenth to twelfth centuries), which modern musicians regard as mere accompaniment or harmonization. Meanwhile the *ryūteki* ("flute") and *hichiriki* ("oboe")—both regarded by modern musicians as the melody instruments—play ornamented formulaic melodies of more recent origin, which modern performers now regard as the focus of musical interest.[41]

The repertory of the Indonesian gamelan also developed in a court setting where it was connected with religious ceremonies, particularly with dramatic performances of traditional Hindu myths by actors and puppets. The music centers on a "nuclear theme or melodic core" (Hood 1954:3) called the *balungan* (literally "skeleton")—a traditional, notated melody, played slowly in relatively long notes on the *saron* (a metallophone), while other instruments elaborate it according to traditional unwritten principles, and various types of gongs mark its subdivisions into phrases.[42]

Thus in melismatic organum, in Tōgaku, and in gamelan music, it could be said that traditional ritual melodies of great age have been preserved in a "wrapper" of newer music, in effect "encased" both "horizontally" and "vertically" in a "protective coating" of notes. The apparent fact that these three unrelated musical traditions rely on a similar process of transmission may be connected with their similar social and cultural functions. Because all are associated with religious and/or court ceremonial, they may all have been subject to comparable constraints, calling for an extremely conservative respect for the melodic heritage of the past—a heritage that is always re-presented in an atmosphere of reverent solemnity and awesome ceremonial.

Finally, the slow performance of the traditional melody in these three types of music may represent only one form of a more general process of "slowing down" that may often affect musical transmission. One readily thinks of two instances in the history of European art music: (1) the slowing of harmonic rhythm between the eighteenth and the nineteenth centuries, despite the continued use of some of the "same" musical forms, and (2) the repeated shifts to smaller and smaller note values in the history of mensural notation, so that (for instance) the semibreve, which was the

41. Markham 1985; Markham et al. 1988; Marrett 1985, 1986, 1988. Critical editions of this repertory are being published in Picken et al., eds. 1981; 1985–.

42. For an attempt to develop a grammar for gamelan music see D. W. Hughes 1988.

shortest note value in the thirteenth century, had by the seventeenth century become the whole note, the longest commonly used durational sign in the Western notational system. The latter process greatly influenced the performance of Gregorian chant right up until the reforms of Solesmes early in this century, because the square and lozenge-shaped notes of Gregorian notation were often regarded as longs, breves, and semibreves, and thus performed and transcribed as whole and half notes (Tack 1960: 52–67, Cardine 1988, Hiley 1990: 49–52). This is probably why, for example, the Credo intonation of J. S. Bach's B Minor Mass is notated in a breve and whole notes, and the *Dies Irae* in Berlioz's *Symphonie Fantastique* first appears at the speed of one pitch per measure (see also Kramer 1975: 80–1). Following modern Solesmes practice, these melodies would be transcribed in eighth notes today, and performed accordingly. The loss of the older practice during the chant revival led by Solesmes is itself an example of the way changing interpretations of the past can cause changes in performance practice—this process, too, has also been observed in other cultures. One scholar who has attempted to isolate and describe it in Chinese music has dubbed it "historical interdependency," the process by which one generation of musicians may preserve, reinterpret, or react against musical traditions inherited from the past (Yung 1987).

6

Summary and Conclusion

In recent chant scholarship, few issues have received as much discussion as the problem of how oral and written means of transmission may have shaped the melodies of the Gregorian and other medieval chant repertories. The purpose of this essay has been to show that this question cannot be isolated from other areas of chant study—by its very nature it touches on almost every other aspect of medieval chant. Attempts to investigate it, then, require us to reformulate the entire field of chant research, broadening our view beyond the fields of vision that traditional approaches to chant study have permitted. The way to do this is to learn to approach the whole field of medieval chant as an ethnomusicologist would—not abandoning the traditional historical approaches but carrying them out in a new way, open to new kinds of evidence, asking new kinds of questions, informed by new kinds of information. It is not that ethnomusicological methodologies should merely supplement or (on the other hand) completely replace the historical methodologies to which we are so accustomed. It is that chant scholarship must become a new kind of endeavor that is simultaneously historical and ethnomusicological.

This transformation of chant research would begin with the recognition that every medieval chant tradition, Eastern and Western, was a complete musical culture, on average as extensive and diverse as we might expect any musical culture to be today. In each of these cultures, many different kinds of musical activities played a role in both oral and written transmission, though the specific activities and the ways they interacted varied greatly from one place and period to another. Though each chant culture was more or less self-contained, it was free to, and at times did, interact with other musical cultures, both of ecclesiastical chant and of non-liturgical music. The interactions among all these factors in the processes that shaped the extant chant repertories were not random or unpredictable, but broadly resembled processes that can be observed in other cultures past and present.

Ethnomusicology, by definition, accepts every kind of music as a worthy object of study. There is no reason to exclude medieval chant from ethnomusicological investigation, and in fact ethnomusicologists sometimes have written about it. The obstacle to a fully ethnomusicological investigation of medieval chant is, of course, the fact that medieval cultures can no longer be directly observed by the methods of anthropological fieldwork. Thus many kinds of information that would normally be obtained through fieldwork can only be supplied imaginatively, on the basis of general knowledge of the ways music can be and has been transmitted in human society. Such an act of historical imagination cannot quite be termed "reconstruction," for it is both more complex and less tied to physical evidence than the kinds of activities we usually call "reconstruction," such as hypothetically completing a piece of music, a liturgical order, or a manuscript or historic site (Sorensen 1989) that survives only partially. No individual, and no group, could imaginatively recreate a culture of the past that either covered every possible detail or was accurate in every possible way. The effort to imagine what a culture of the past was like is more like viewing a landscape from afar: "Looking" back over centuries of intervening history, we can "see" some things clearly, others less clearly. There are still other things we cannot see but can only imagine, while there may be much we cannot know at all. Thus, by "re-envisioning" I mean trying to "see" (with the eye of the mind at least) what a culture of another time would "look" like if we could visit and observe it today.

Re-envisioning a culture of the past means not only seeing clearly the evidence that survives, but imaginatively filling in the gaps where evidence is missing. Traditional historical methods of studying medieval chant have not equipped us well to do this, for they (quite rightly) require us to keep our imaginings close to what can actually be documented. When it is necessary to infer what we cannot actually witness, we have had little to rely on except unsupported opinions of what medieval processes of transmission may be supposed to have been like, because we have little objective information about what the oral and written transmission of music actually is like in our world, in all the cultures and societies that make up the human race.

The only way to obtain the kind of objective information we really need is by direct, critical observation of musical cultures that, unlike medieval Europe, are still functioning and accessible to ethnomusicological investigation today. Only by casting as broad a research net as possible can we hope to assemble an accurate understanding of the ways music can be shaped by the means people use to transmit it, and only on the basis of such wide-ranging knowledge can we begin to speculate responsibly on what may have happened in the distant past. In other words, we need to practice historical musicology in a new way, a way that is so fully informed by and conversant with ethnomusicology that it will actually become a kind of ethnomusicology, without ceasing to be music history also. The purpose of this essay has been no more than to point out some of the paths we might take, and to offer suggestive glimpses at what we may find.

Though both serious and popular writers have often likened Gregorian chant to folk music, and though the fact that the chant was once an oral tradition has been accepted for a long time, only recently have Leo Treitler and Helmut Hucke forced chant scholarship in general to face squarely the issue of oral and written transmission, with their "New Historical View" of chant origins that proposes an original and far-reaching theory of how these transmission processes may have operated. Yet reflection on the New Historical View, with its indebtedness to the Parry-Lord theory reinterpreted by means of generative grammar, reveals at least three basic weaknesses.

The first is a certain vagueness in the conception of the "grammar" that underlies the melodies. Treitler and Hucke have not presented an exhaustive analysis of a sample melodic group, actually extrapolating a list of what they deem to be its "rules." The difficulties of doing so on their terms would be considerable, and some of these are illustrated by reconsidering two of Treitler's musical examples. Part of the problem is that neither formulaicism nor susceptibility to generative grammar analysis is in itself proof of orality, even when one is dealing with texts. The attempt to apply all these textual analogies to music multiplies the uncertainties. If we would study the oral transmission of music, our most important sources of information will have to be musical.

The second weakness has to do with the possibilities of proof and confirmation. Many of Treitler's and Hucke's statements about the ways oral transmission processes would have operated during the European Middle Ages cannot at present be confirmed, and are based on premises that should not be taken for granted. A more empirical basis for hypothesizing about the oral transmission of medieval chant needs to be found, and the main place to find it is ethnomusicology.

The third weakness relates to issues of textual criticism and editing. Treitler's disagreement with many accepted procedures of textual criticism and manuscript study threatens to paralyze efforts to produce critical editions of medieval chant melodies. But it derives in part from an overly narrow and rigid conception of written transmission. He thus accuses other chant scholars of believing that medieval scribes were engaged in a purely mechanical or passive activity in which their own decision-making faculties could not intervene, as if a scribe were merely a primitive and fallible antecedent of the photocopy machine. The obvious incorrectness of this view is seen by Treitler as proof that oral processes were active alongside written ones. But in fact, traditional textual criticism has always allowed much more room for scribal choices than Treitler claims. Thus scholarly attention to the processes of oral transmission need not require as dramatic a departure from conventional manuscript study as Treitler believes. Bringing the experience of ethnomusicology to bear on the problem would in fact promote a more realistic view of both oral and written transmission and their interaction, and would help historical musicologists take better advantage of the many approaches now available in all the modern schools of textual criticism.

Ethnomusicological investigations of medieval chant would begin with the kinds of questions ethnomusicologists almost invariably ask about any music. The application of such questions to medieval chant opens up long-neglected areas of obvious importance, extending even beyond the oral transmission question itself. Methods of making and using cross-cultural comparisons will have to be perfected and exploited to their fullest, as chant scholars will have to find responsible ways to develop meaningful comparisons between medieval chant and the pockets of oral tradition that still survive for Latin and especially for Greek chant, the "pure" oral traditions of the Syriac and Coptic churches, and the partly written, partly oral traditions of Armenian, Georgian, and Ethiopic chant. The liturgical chant traditions of Judaism, Islam, Hinduism, and Buddhism also offer certain parallels to medieval Christian chant that, when handled carefully, can teach us something about the interplay of oral and written transmission in liturgical contexts.

Chant researchers will need to delve into the lives, training, and responsibilities of individual singers within medieval clerical communities, and to retrace the lines of musical communication between these communities and the surrounding culture of the medieval world. They will need to trace the multidimensional continua that characterize the ever-changing interrelationships among the different processes of oral and written transmission, including not only the historic continuum leading from a purely oral chant repertory to an essentially written one recorded in books, but also other continua relating to such things as the rules governing when books were used and the relationship between oral transmission and performance practice.

Among the musical characteristics of the chant that may be investigated as means of oral transmission, the most obvious are the "formulas," stereotyped but not completely unvarying musical gestures or phrases. Attempts to clarify and define this concept more accurately would have to find ways of dealing with ranges of concepts of identity and variability, ranges of similarity and difference, the theoretical articulations of cultures that emically recognize such phenomena, and the tendency of formulas to mark syntactic units in the text. "Melody types," "melodic models," or "tune families" represent the long-range melodic plans in which formulas operate, plans that are shared by groups or families of melodies. A critical attempt to refine this concept would have to deal with the problem of describing or characterizing melodic contours, with the theoretical systems of cultures that emically articulate this phenomenon, and with the complicating problem of modal or scalar theory in cultures that possess it. Other practices related to oral transmission may include the use of added "trope" texts or of meaningless or nonsense syllables, and the addition of melodic or harmonic embellishment and "improvised" polyphony.

The ethnomusicological re-envisioning of the lost cultures of medieval chant will be difficult, because the enterprise must be carried out on the broadest scale. Every surviving chant repertory will have to be examined, "category by category, mode by mode, chant by chant" (Levy 1984:96), with the aid of every tool that can be put at our disposal, whether from traditional medieval disciplines like paleography and liturgiology or from newer ones like musical cognition. In short, chant scholarship will have to become more ethnomusicological, not by sacrificing any of the special historical approaches it has already developed or borrowed from other historical fields, but by reformulating them so that our future research will simultaneously contribute to both music history and ethnomusicology. As with the Western music of any other historical period, we will get much of our information from written sources, such as the statements of theorists, liturgical regulations, archival materials, and of course the notated melodies themselves. But a wide-ranging knowledge of ethnomusicology, or rather of world music, will be indispensable for interpreting these historical documents wisely. Without it, we will miss or misunderstand many of the clues. For when we ask what oral tradition is, we are in a sense approaching the matter from the wrong end. Oral transmission is not a peculiar feature of some music at certain times, but rather a universal characteristic of almost all music at almost all times. What we call "oral transmission" is what most human beings throughout history have known simply as "music"—something to play or hear rather than something to write or read. We modern Westerners are the ones who do things differently, and our preference for writing is our handicap. Only by learning from the ways ethnomusicologists have dealt and are dealing with this universal aspect of music can historical musicologists begin to re-imagine realistically the nature of oral traditions that fell silent centuries ago.

Works Cited

Abrahamsen, Erik
1923 *Eléments romans et allemands dans le chant grégorien et la chanson populaire en Danemark*. Publications de l'Académie grégorienne de Fribourg (Suisse) 11. Cophenhagen: P. Haase.

Achtemeier, Paul J.
1990 "*Omne verbum sonat:* The New Testament and the Oral Environment of Late Western Antiquity." *Journal of Biblical Literature* 109:3–27.

Adams, Charles R.
1976 "Melodic Contour Typology." *Ethnomusicology* 20:179–215.

Akinnaso, F. Niyi
1982 "The Literate Writes and the Nonliterate Chants: Written Language and Ritual Communication in Sociolinguistic Perspective." *Linguistics and Literacy,* 7–36. Ed. William Frawley. Topics in Language and Linguistics. New York: Plenum.

Aland, Kurt, and Barbara Aland
1989 *The Text of the New Testament: An Introduction to the Critical Editions and to the Theory and Practice of Modern Textual Criticism*. Translated by Erroll F. Rhodes. 2nd ed., rev. and enlarged. Grand Rapids: William B. Eerdmans; Leiden: E. J. Brill. Originally published as *Der Text des Neuen Testaments: Einführung in die wissenschaftlichen Ausgaben sowie in Theorie und Praxis der modernen Textkritik*. 2nd ed. Stuttgart: Deutsche Bibelgesellschaft, 1988.

Alexander, J. Neil, ed.
1990 *Time and Community: In Honor of Thomas Julian Talley.* Washington, D.C.: Pastoral Press.

Allen, J. P. B., and Paul Van Buren, eds.
1971 *Chomsky: Selected Readings*. Language and Language Learning. London: Oxford University Press.

Amargianakis, George
1977 *An Analysis of Stichera in the Deuteros Modes.* Université de Copenhague, Cahiers de l'Institut du Moyen-Age grec et latin 22–3. Copenhagen: Erik Paludan.

Ameln, Konrad
1966 "'Quem pastores laudavere.'" *Jahrbuch für Liturgik und Hymnologie* 11:45–88.
1970 "'Resonet in laudibus'—'Joseph, lieber Joseph mein.'" *Jahrbuch für Liturgik und Hymnologie* 15:51–112.

Andrieu, Michel, ed.
1931–61 *Les Ordines romani du haut moyen-âge.* 5 vols. Spicilegium Sacrum Lovaniense 11, 23, 24, 28, 29. Louvain: Spicilegium Sacrum Lovaniense Bureaux.
1938–41 *Le Pontifical romain au moyen-âge.* 4 vols. Studi e Testi 86–88, 99. Vatican City: Biblioteca Apostolica Vaticana.

Angerer, Joachim F.
1977 "Die Consuetudines Monasticae als Quelle für die Musikwissenschaft." In Stein, ed. 1977: 23–37.

Anglès, Higini
1963 "El canto religioso popular en los manuales litúrgicos de la Tarraconense." *Anuario Musical* 18:103–8.
1964 "Relations of Spanish Folk Song to the Gregorian Chant." *Journal of the International Folk Music Council* 16:54–6. Expanded version in Anglès 1975/1:103–6.
1967 "Die volkstümlichen Melodien in den mittelalterlichen Sequenzen." *Festschrift für Walter Wiora zum 30. Dezember 1966* 214–20. Ed. Ludwig Finscher and Christoph-Hellmut Mahling. Kassel: Bärenreiter. Reprinted in Anglès 1975/1:336–44.
1968 "Eine Sequenzsammlung mit Mensuralnotation und volkstümlichen Melodien (Paris, B. N. lat. 1343)." *Speculum Musicae Artis: Festgabe für Heinrich Husmann zum 60. Geburtstag* 375–86. Ed. Heinz Becker and Reinhard Gerlach. Munich: Fink.
1969? "The Various Forms of Chant Sung by the Faithful in the Ancient Roman Liturgy." In Anglès 1975/1:57–75. [According to the editor of Anglès 1975, this article was originally published in Overath, ed. 1969, but in fact it does not appear there.]
1975 *Scripta Musicologica.* 3 vols. Ed. José López-Calo. Storia e Letteratura 131–3. Rome: Edizioni Storia e Letteratura.

Anglès, Higini, ed.
1952 *Atti del congresso internazionale di Musica sacra organizzato dal Pontificio Istituto di Musica Sacra e dalla Commissione di Musica Sacra per l'Anno Santo (Roma, 25–30 Maggio 1950).* Tournai: Desclée.

Antonowycz, Myroslaw
1974 *The Chants from Ukrainian Heirmologia.* Utrechtse Bijdragen tot de Muziekwetenshap. Bilthoven: A. B. Creyghton.

Apel, Willi
1958 *Gregorian Chant.* Bloomington: Indiana University Press.
1969 "Machicotage." *Harvard Dictionary of Music,* 496. 2nd ed. Cambridge: Harvard University Press.

Ap-Thomas, D. R.
1966 *A Primer of Old Testament Text Criticism.* Facet Books Biblical Series 14. Philadelphia: Fortress Press.

Aquili, Eugene d', Charles D. Laughlin, Jr., John McManus, et al.
1979 *The Spectrum of Ritual: A Biogenetic Analysis.* New York: Columbia University Press.

Arai, Kôjun
1986 *Musik und Zeichen: Notationen buddhistischer Gesänge Japans: Schriftquellen des 11.–19. Jahrhunderts.* Ed. Roger Goepper and Robert Günther. Kleine Monographien 4. Cologne: Museum für Ostasiatische Kunst.

Arcangeli, Piero G., ed.
1988 *Musica e liturgia nella cultura mediterranea: Atti del Convegno Internazionale di Studi (Venezia, 2–5 ottobre 1985).* Quaderni della Rivista Italiana di Musicologia 20. Florence: Leo S. Olschki.

Arlt, Wulf
1970 *Ein Festoffizium des Mittelalters aus Beauvais in seiner liturgischen und musikalischen Bedeutung.* 2 vols. Cologne: Volk Verlag.

Arns, Evaristo
1953 *La technique du livre d'après Saint Jérôme.* Paris: E. de Boccard.

Arranz, Miguel
1976 "Les grands étapes de la liturgie byzantine: Palestine—Byzance—Russie: Essai d'aperçu historique." In Triacca, ed. 1976:43–72.

Associazione Amici della Musica di Arezzo
1984 *L'Interpretazione del canto gregoriano oggi: Atti del Convegno Internazionale di Canto Gregoriano, Arezzo, 26–27 agosto 1983.* Ed. Domenico Cieri. Rome: Pro Musica Studium.

Atayan, R.
1968 "Armenische Chasen." *Beiträge zur Musikwissenschaft* 10:65–82. Reprinted in Nersessian, ed. 1978:131–47.

Atkinson, Charles M.
1977 "The Earliest Agnus Dei Melody and Its Tropes." *Journal of the American Musicological Society* 30:1–19.

Atlas, Allan
1975 *The Cappella Giulia Chansonnier (Rome, Biblioteca Aposto-*

lica Vaticana, C. G. XIII. 27). 2 vols. Musicological Studies 27. Brooklyn: Institute of Medieval Music.

Aubry, Pierre
1898 "Le 'Letabundus' et les chansons de Noël au treizième siècle." *Tribune de Saint-Gervais* 4:276–86.

Avenary, Hanoch
1963 *Studies in the Hebrew, Syrian and Greek Liturgical Recitative*. Tel Aviv: Israel Music Institute.
1977 "Northern and Southern Idioms of Early European Music: A New Approach to an Old Problem." *Acta Musicologica* 49: 27–49. Reprinted in Avenary 1979:63–85.
1978 *The Ashkenazi Tradition of Biblical Chant between 1500 and 1900: Documentation and Musical Analysis*. Documentation and Studies 2. Tel Aviv: Tel Aviv University.
1979 *Encounters of East and West in Music: Selected Writings*. Tel Aviv: Faculty of Visual and Performing Arts, Tel Aviv University.

Baal, J. Van
1971 *Symbols for Communication: An Introduction to the Anthropological Study of Religion*. Assen, Netherlands: Koninklijke Van Gorcum.

Bailey, Terence
1976 "Accentual and Cursive Cadences in Gregorian Psalmody." *Journal of the American Musicological Society* 29:463–71.
1977 "Ambrosian Psalmody: An Introduction." *Studies in Music from the University of Western Ontario* 2:65–78.
1978 "Ambrosian Choral Psalmody: The Formulae." *Studies in Music from the University of Western Ontario* 3:72–96.

Baird, Joseph L., Giuseppe Baglivi, John Robert Kane, eds.
1986 *The Chronicle of Salimbene de Adam*. Medieval and Renaissance Texts and Studies 40. Binghamton, New York: MRTS.

Bakker, Egbert J.
1988 *Linguistics and Formulas in Homer: Scalarity and the Description of the Article "per."* Amsterdam/Philadelphia: John Benjamins

Barbour, Stephen, and Patrick Stevenson.
1990. *Variation in German: A Critical Approach to German Sociolinguistics*. Cambridge University Press.

Bardos, Kornél
1975 *Volksmusikartige Variierungstechnik in den ungarischen Passionen (15. bis 18. Jahrhundert)*. Musicologica Hungarica, Neue Folge 5. Kassel: Bärenreiter.

Barnes, Andrew E.
1990 "Religious Reform and the War against Ritual." *Journal of Ritual Studies* 4:127–33.

Baroffio, Giacomo Bonifazio
1980 "Ambrosian [Milanese] Rite, Music of the." *The New Grove Dictionary* 1:314–20.

Baroni, M., and L. Callegari, eds.
1984 *Musical Grammars and Computer Analysis: Atti del Convegno (Modena, 4–6 ottobre 1982)*. Quaderni della Rivista Italiana di Musicologia 8. Florence: Leo S. Olschki.

Barry, Phillips
1914 "The Transmission of Folk-Song." *Journal of American Folklore* 27:67–76.
1933 "Communal Re-Creation." *Bulletin of the Folk-Song Society of the Northeast* 5:4–6.

Bas, Giulio
1909 "Da quando s'è incominciato ad accompagnare il canto gregoriano?" *Rassegna Gregoriana* 8:117–26.

Baud-Bovy, Samuel
1979 "L'ornementation dans le chant de l'église grecque et la chanson populaire grecque moderne." *Studia Musicologica Academiae Scientiarum Hungaricae* 21:281–93.

Bäuml, Franz H.
1980 "Varieties and Consequences of Medieval Literacy and Illiteracy." *Speculum* 55:237–65.

Baumstark, Anton
1958 *Comparative Liturgy*. Rev. Bernard Botte. English ed. F. L. Cross. London: A. R. Mowbray.

Bayard, Samuel P.
1950 "Prolegomena to a Study of the Principal Melodic Families of British-American Folk Song." *Journal of American Folklore* 63:1–44.
1954 "Two Representative Tune Families of British Tradition." *Midwest Folklore* 4:13–34.

Beaton, Roderick
1981 "Was *Digenes Akrites* an Oral Poem?" *Byzantine and Modern Greek Studies* 7:7–27.

Béhague, Gerard, ed.
1984 *Performance Practice: Ethnomusicological Perspectives*. Westport, Connecticut: Greenwood Press.

Benson, Larry D.
1966 "The Literary Character of Anglo-Saxon Formulaic Poetry." *Proceedings of the Modern Language Association* 81:334–41.

Bent, Margaret
1983 "*Resfacta* and *Cantare super Librum*." *Journal of the American Musicological Society* 36:371–91.

Berger, Samuel
1893 *Histoire de la Vulgate pendant les premiers siècles du moyen age*. Paris: Hachette. Reprinted New York: Burt Franklin, n.d.
Bernhard, Michael, Arno Borst, Detlef Illmer, Albrecht Reithmüller, Klaus-Jürgen Sachs
1990 *Rezeption des antiken Fachs im Mittelalter*. Geschichte der Musiktheorie 3. Ed. Friedrich Zaminer. Darmstadt: Wissenschaftliche Buchgesellschaft.
Berry, Mary [Mother Thomas More]
1965–6 "The Performance of Plainsong in the Later Middle Ages and the Sixteenth Century." *Proceedings of the Royal Musical Association* 92: 121–34, Plates I–IV.
1967 "The Practice of Alternatim: Organ-playing and Polyphony in the fifteenth and sixteenth centuries, with special reference to the choir of Notre-Dame de Paris." *Journal of Ecclesiastical History* 18: 15–32.
1980 "Machicotage." *The New Grove Dictionary* 11: 437–8.
Bévenot, Maurice
1961 *The Tradition of Manuscripts: A Study in the Transmission of St. Cyprian's Treatises*. Oxford: Clarendon Press.
Bevil, Jack
1984 "Centonization and concordance in the American Southern Uplands folksong melody: A study of the musical generative and transmittive processes of an oral tradition." Ph.D. diss., North Texas State University.
Biguenet, John, and Rainer Schulte, eds.
1989 *The Craft of Translation*. Chicago: University of Chicago Press.
Binder, Abraham Wolf
1959 *Biblical Chant*. New York: Philosophical Library.
Birlea, Ovidiu
1987 "Folklore: An Overview." *The Encyclopedia of Religion* 5: 363–70.
Bischoff, Bernard
1989 *Latin Palaeography: Antiquity and the Middle Ages*. Transl. Dáibhí Croínin and David Ganz. Cambridge University Press. Originally published as *Paläographie des römischen Altertums und des abendländischen Mittelalters*. 2nd rev. ed. Grundlagen der Germanistik 24. Berlin: E. Schmidt, 1986.
Bleyon, Jean
1910–11 "Vestiges d'un Kyrie 'farci.' " *Revue du chant grégorien* 19: 14–8.
Blin, Jules, ed.
1888 *Chants liturgiques des coptes* 1: *Partie chantée par le peuple et le diacre*. Cairo: Imprimerie Nationale.

Boilès, Charles Lafayette
1973 "Reconstruction of Proto-Melody." *Yearbook for Inter-American Musical Research* 9:45–63.
Bolinger, Dwight
1989 *Intonation and Its Uses: Melody in Grammar and Discourse.* Stanford, California: Stanford University Press.
Borsai, Ilona
1968a "Mélodies traditionnelles des égyptiens et leur importance dans la recherche de l'ancienne musique pharaonique." *Studia Musicologica Academiae Scientiarum Hungaricae* 10:69–90.
1968b "A la recherche de l'ancienne musique pharaonique." *Cahiers d'Histoire Egyptienne* 11:25–42.
1971 "Un type mélodique particulier des hymnes coptes du mois de Kiahk." *Studia Musicologica Academiae Scientiarum Hungaricae* 13:73–85.
1974 "Die musikhistorische Bedeutung der orientalischen christlichen Riten." *Studia Musicologica Academiae Scientiarum Hungariae* 16:3–14.
1980a "Coptic Rite, Music of the." *The New Grove Dictionary* 4:730–4.
1980b "Métrique et mélodie dans les Théotokies coptes." *Studia Musicologica Academiae Scientiarum Hungaricae* 22:15–60.
1982 "Melody-Formulas of Greek Acclamations in Coptic Liturgy." In Raasted, ed. 1982:109–18.
Borsai, Ilona, and Margit Tóth
1969 "Variations ornementales dans l'interprétation d'un hymne copte." *Studia Musicologica Academiae Scientiarum Hungaricae* 11:91–105.
Boyce, Mary
1979 *Zoroastrians: Their Religious Beliefs and Practices.* London: Routledge and Kegan Paul.
Boyle, Leonard E.
1984 *Medieval Latin Palaeography: A Bibliographical Introduction.* Toronto Medieval Bibliographies 8. Toronto: University of Toronto Press.
Brăiloiu, Constantin
1984 "Concerning a Russian Melody." *Problems of Ethnomusicology,* 239–89. Ed. and transl. A. L. Lloyd. Cambridge University Press. Originally published as "Sur une mélodie russe," in *Musique Russe,* ed. Pierre Souvtchinsky (Paris: Presses Universitaires de France, 1953) 2:329–91.
Brandl, Rudolf M.
1985 "Some Aspects of Oral History in Consideration of Musical Traditions from Africa and Levante, based on a Neurosemioti-

cal Approach." *International Review of the Aesthetics and Sociology of Music* 16:3–42.

1989 "Continuity and Change in Oral Music History of a Greek Island (Karpathos) from the Nineteenth Century until 1981." In Philipp, ed. 1989:111–25.

Brenn, Franz

1956 "Zur Frage gregorianischer Lesarten." *Die Musikforschung* 9:442–3.

Brett, Philip

1988 "Text, Context, and the Early Music Editor." *Authenticity and Early Music: A Symposium,* ed. Nicholas Kenyon, 83–114. Oxford University Press.

Breydy, Michael, ed.

1971 *Kult, Dichtung und Musik im Wochenbrevier des Syro-Maroniten* 2: *Texte: Breviarium Diurnale.* Kobayath, Lebanon: no publisher.

1979 *Kult, Dichtung und Musik bei den Syro-Maroniten* 3: *Rishaiqole: Die Leitstrophen der Syro-aramäischen Liturgien: Repertorium und Kommentar.* Kobayath, Lebanon: no publisher.

Bronson, Bertrand H.

1951 "Melodic Stability in Oral Tradition," *Journal of the International Folk Music Council* 3:50–5.

1959–72 *The Traditional Tunes of the Child Ballads.* 5 vols. Princeton: Princeton University Press.

Brown, Gillian, and George Yule

1983 *Discourse Analysis.* Cambridge Textbooks in Linguistics. Cambridge University Press.

Brown, Howard Mayer, and Stanley Sadie, eds.

1990 *Performance Practice: Music before 1600.* The Norton/Grove Handbooks in Music. New York: W. W. Norton.

Brown, Raymond E., Joseph A. Fitzmyer, Roland E. Murphy, eds.

1990 *The New Jerome Biblical Commentary.* Englewood Cliffs: Prentice Hall.

Bugnini, Annibale

1990 *The Reform of the Liturgy (1948–1975).* Transl. Matthew J. O'Connell. Collegeville, Minnesota: The Liturgical Press. Originally published as *La riforma liturgica, 1948–1975.* Bibliotheca "Ephemenides Liturgicae" Subsidia 30. Rome: Edizioni Liturgiche, 1983.

Bukofzer, Manfred

1950 "The Beginnings of Choral Polyphony." In Manfred Bukofzer, *Studies in Medieval and Renaissance Music* 176–89. New York: W. W. Norton.

Burman-Hall, Linda C.
1978 "Tune Identity and Performance Style: The Case of Bonaparte's Retreat." *Selected Reports in Ethnomusicology* 3/1: 77–97.
Busch, Richard von
1971 *Untersuchungen zum byzantinischen Heirmologion: der Echos Deuteros.* Hamburger Beiträge zur Musikwissenschaft 4. Hamburg: K. D. Wagner.
Buzzetti, Carlo
1973 *La Parola tradotta: Aspetti linguistici ermeneutici e teologici della traduzione della sacra scrittura.* Pubblicazioni del Pontificio Seminario Lombardo in Roma: Ricerche di Scienze Teologiche 12. Brescia: Morcelliana.
Bynum, Caroline Walker
1987 *Holy Feast and Holy Fast: The Religious Significance of Food to Medieval Women.* Berkeley and Los Angeles: University of California Press.
Cardine, Eugène
1950 "De l'édition critique du Graduel: nécessité, avantages, méthode." *Revue grégorienne* 29: 202–8. Reprinted in Anglès, ed. 1952: 187–91.
1988 "La notation du chant grégorien aux XVIIe–XIXe siècles." *Anuario musical* 43: 9–33.
Carr, Philip
1990 *Linguistic Realities: An Autonomist Metatheory for the Generative Enterprise.* Cambridge University Studies in Linguistics 53. Cambridge University Press.
Carroll, Catherine A.
1989 *A History of the Pius X School of Liturgical Music: 1916–1969.* St. Louis: Society of the Sacred Heart.
Caspers, Charles, and Marc Schneiders, eds.
1990 *Omnes Circumadstantes: Contributions towards a history of the role of the people in the liturgy, presented to Herman Wegman on the occasion of his retirement from the chair of History of Liturgy and Theology in the Katholieke Theologische Universiteit Utrecht.* Kampen, Netherlands: Uitgeversmaatschappij J. H. Kok.
Cavanagh, Beverly
1987 "Problems in Investigating the History of an Oral Tradition: Reconciling Different Types of Data about Inuit Drum Dance Traditions." *Anuario Musical* 42: 29–52.
Chabrier, Jean-Claude C.
1989 "Le système acoustique arménien d'Hambardzoum au XIXème siècle." In Philipp, ed. 1989: 130–2.

Chailley, Jacques
1980 "Du pentatonisme à l'octoéchos." *Etudes grégoriennes* 19: 165–84.
1982 "La messe polyphonique du village de Rusio." *Revue de musicologie* 68:164–73.

Chambers, E. K.
1903 *The Medieval Stage*. 2 vols. Oxford: Clarendon Press.

Chambers, G. B.
1956 *Folksong—Plainsong: A Study in Origins and Musical Relationships*. London: The Merlin Press. 2nd ed. 1972.

Chandlee, H. Ellsworth
1986 "Liturgical Movement, The." *The New Westminster Dictionary of Liturgy and Worship*, 307–14. Ed. J. G. Davies. Philadelphia: The Westminster Press.

Chartier, Yves
1987 "Musical Treatises." *Dictionary of the Middle Ages* 8:636–49

Chavasse, Antoine
1952 "Les plus anciens types du lectionnaire et de l'antiphonaire romain de la messe." *Revue Bénédictine* 62:1–91.
1984 "Cantatorium et Antiphonale Missarum: Quelques procédés de confection, dimanche après la Pentecôte, graduels de sanctoral." *Ecclesia Orans* 1:15–55.

Chen, Matthew Y.
1983 "Toward a Grammar of Singing: Tune-Text Association in Gregorian Chant." *Music Perception* 1:84–122.

Chiel, Arthur A.
1971 *Guide to Sidrot and Haftarot*. New York: Ktav Publishing House.

Claire, Jean
1962–3 "L'Evolution modale dans les répertoires liturgiques occidentaux." *Revue grégorienne* 40 (1962): 196–211; 41 (1963): 8–29 + 10 tables, 49–62 + 4 tables, 77–102 + 7 tables, 127–51 + 4 tables.
1975 "Les répertoires liturgiques latins avant l'octoéchos, I: L'Office férial romano-franc." *Etudes grégoriennes* 15:5–192.
[1976] "Cantus recitativi." *Conservare et Promovere: VI. Internationaler Kongress für Kirchenmusik, Salzburg, 26. August bis 2. September 1974*, 124–39. Ed. Johannes Overath. Rome: Consociatio Internationalis Musicae Sacrae.
1981 "Les formules centons des *alleluia* anciens." *Etudes grégoriennes* 20:3–4 + 12 pp. of charts.
1986 "La place traditionnelle du mélisme dans la cantillation." *Yuval: Studies of the Jewish Music Research Center* 5:265–91. Jerusalem: Magnes Press of Hebrew University.
n.d. "Le répertoire grégorien de l'office: structure musicale et

formes." International Musicologisch Colloquium, *Het Gregoriaans, Europees Erfgoed: Leuven 25 tot 28 September 1980,* 27–50. Louvain: Seminarie voor Muziekwetenschap van de Katholieke Universiteit te Leuven.

Claire, Jean, and Clément Morin

1977 Review of Haïk Vantoura 1976a, 1976b. *Etudes grégoriennes* 16:216–9.

Cody, Aelred

1982 "The Early History of the Octoechos in Syria." *East of Byzantium: Syria and Armenia in the Formative Period,* ed. Nina Garsoïan et al., 89–113. Dumbarton Oaks Symposium 1980. Washington, D.C.: Dumbarton Oaks Center for Byzantine Studies.

Cohen, Dalia

1971 "The Meaning of the Modal Framework in the Singing of Religious Hymns by Christian Arabs in Israel." *Yuval: Studies of the Jewish Music Research Center* 2:23–57. Jerusalem: Magnes Press of Hebrew University.

1973 "Theory and Practice in Liturgical Music of Christian Arabs in Israel." *Studies in Eastern Chant* 3:1–50. London: Oxford University Press.

Collins, Mary

1987 *Worship: Renewal to Practice.* Washington, D.C.: Pastoral Press.

Collins, Mary, David Power, Mellonee Burnim, eds.

1989 *Music and the Experience of God: Liturgy 1989.* Concilium: International Review of Theology 222. Edinburgh: T. and T. Clark.

Combe, Pierre

1969 *Histoire de la restauration du chant grégorien d'après des documents inédits.* Solesmes: Abbaye de Solesmes.

1987 *Justine Ward and Solesmes.* Washington, D.C.: The Catholic University of America Press.

Connolly, Thomas

1972 "Introits and Archetypes: Some Archaisms of the Old Roman Chant." *Journal of the American Musicological Society* 25:157–74.

Conomos, Dmitri E.

1974 *Byzantine Trisagia and Cheroubika of the Fourteenth and Fifteenth Centuries: A Study of Late Byzantine Liturgical Chant.* Thessaloniki: Patriarchal Institute for Patristic Studies.

1979 "The Iviron Folk-songs—A Re-examination." *Studies in Eastern Chant* 4:28–53. Crestwood, New York: St. Vladimir's Seminary Press.

1980 "Change in Early Christian and Byzantine Liturgical Chant."

Studies in Music from the University of Western Ontario 5:49–63.

Constable, Giles
1976 *Medieval Monasticism: A Select Bibliography.* Toronto Medieval Bibliographies 6. Toronto and Buffalo: University of Toronto Press.

Cook, Nicholas
1990 *Music, Imagination, and Culture.* Oxford: Clarendon.

Coplan, David B.
1991 "Ethnomusicology and the Meaning of Tradition." *Ethnomusicology and Modern Music History,* 35–48. Ed. Stephen Blum, Philip V. Bohlman, Daniel M. Neuman. Urbana and Chicago: University of Illinois Press.

The Coptic Encyclopedia.
1991 Ed. Aziz S. Atiya. 8 vols. New York: Macmillan.

Costa, Eugenio
1971 "La réflexion post conciliaire sur le chant et la musique dans la liturgie." *La Maison-Dieu* 108 (1971, no. 4):21–31.

Courcelle, Pierre
1969 *Late Latin Writers and Their Greek Sources.* Translated by Harry E. Wedeck. Cambridge, Massachusetts: Harvard University Press. Originally published as *Les Lettres grecques en occident de Macrobe à Cassiodore.* 2nd ed. Paris: Editions E. de Boccard, 1948.

Courtenay, William J.
1987 *Schools and Scholars in Fourteenth-Century England.* Princeton: Princeton University Press.

Cowdery, James R.
1984 "A Fresh Look at the Concept of Tune Family." *Ethnomusicology* 28:495–504.
1990 *The Melodic Tradition of Ireland.* Kent, Ohio: The Kent State University Press.

Crochu Lozac'hmeur, Dominique
1985 "Remarques vocales sur un répertoire nouveau." *La Revue Musicale* 379–80:105–27.

Crocker, Richard L.
1977 *The Early Medieval Sequence.* Berkeley and Los Angeles: University of California Press.
1986 "Matins Antiphons at St. Denis." *Journal of the American Musicological Society* 39:441–90.

Culham, Phyllis, and Lowell Edmunds, eds.
1989 *Classics: A Discipline and Profession in Crisis?* Lanham, Maryland: University Press of America.

Cusack, Pearse Aidan
1983 "The International Colloquium on Saint Gregory the Great,

Chantilly, Sept. 15–19, 1982." *Cistercian Studies* 18: 156–66.

Cutter, Paul F.
1967 "The Old Roman Tradition: Oral or Written?" *Journal of the American Musicological Society* 20: 167–81.
1976 "Oral Transmission of the Old-Roman Responsories?" *Musical Quarterly* 62: 182–94.

Czekanowska, Anna
1976 "On the Theory and Definition of the Melodic Type." *Yearbook of the International Folk Music Council* 8: 108–16.

Dauvillier, Jean
1983 *Histoire et institutions des églises orientales au moyen age.* London: Variorum Reprints.

Dayan, Leonzio
1952 "I canti armeni attraverso la tradizione dei secoli." In Anglès, ed. 1952: 152–4.
1957 "La publication des 'Hymnes de l'église arménienne.'" *Actes du troisième congres international de musique sacrée (Paris 1er–8 juillet 1957),* 324–5. Paris: Edition du Congrès.
1960– *Les hymnes de l'église arménienne en notation européenne.* Vols. 2–. San Lazzaro, Venice: Casa Editrice Armena.

De Clerck, Paul, and Eric Palazzo, eds.
1990 *Rituels: Mélanges offerts au Père Gy, O.P.* Paris: Editions du Cerf.

Deiss, Lucien
1976 *Spirit and Song of the New Liturgy.* Rev. ed. Transl. Lyla C. Haggard and Michael L. Mazzarese. Cincinnati, Ohio: World Library Publications. Originally published as *Concile et Chant nouveau.* Paris: Editions du Levain, 1969.

Deshusses, Jean, ed.
1971–82 *Le sacramentaire grégorien: ses principles formes d'après les plus anciens manuscrits.* 3 vols. Spicilegium Friburgense 16, 24, 28. Fribourg: Editions Universitaires, 1971 (2nd ed. 1979), 1979, 1982.

Deusen, Nancy van
1982 "Style, Nationality and the Sequence in the Middle Ages." *Journal of the Plainsong and Medieval Music Society* 5: 44–55.

Deyrieux, Sébastien
1977 "Elements de bibliographie sur la musique." *La Maison-Dieu* 131 (1977, no. 3): 200–6.

Dictionary of the Middle Ages.
1982–9 Ed. Joseph R. Strayer. 13 vols. New York: Charles Scribner's Sons.

Dinges, William D.
1987–8 "Ritual Conflict as Social Conflict: Liturgical Reform in the

Roman Catholic Church." *Sociological Analysis* 48/2: 138–58.

Dobszay, László
1971 "Dies est leticie." *Acta Ethnographica Academiae Scientiarum Hungaricae* 20:387–410.
1988 "Folksong Classification in Hungary: Some Methodological Conclusions." *Studia Musicologica Academiae Scientiarum Hungaricae* 30:235–80.
1990 "Experiences in the Musical Classification of Antiphons." In Dobszay et al., eds. 1990:143–56.

Dobszay, László, and Janka Szendrei, eds.
1988 *Népdaltípusok Katalógusa: Stílusok szerint rendezve* [Catalogue of Folksong-Types: Listed According to their Styles (in Hungarian)] 1. Budapest: Magyar Tudományos Akadémia, Zenetudományi Intézet.

Dobszay, László, Péter Halász, János Mezei, Gábor Prózéky, eds.
1990 *International Musicological Society Study Group Cantus Planus: Papers Read at the Third Meeting, Tihany, Hungary, 19–24 September 1988*. Budapest: Hungarian Academy of Sciences, Institute for Musicology.

Donakowski, Conrad L.
1977 *A Muse for the Masses: Ritual and Music in an Age of Democratic Revolution, 1770–1870*. Chicago and London: University of Chicago Press.

Dragoumis, Markos Ph.
1966 "The Survival of Byzantine Chant in the Monophonic Music of the Modern Greek Church." *Studies in Eastern Chant* 1:9–36. Ed. Miloš Velimirović. London: Oxford University Press 1966.
1971 "Some Remarks on the Traditional Music of the Greeks of Corsica." *Studies in Eastern Chant* 2:28–34. Ed. Miloš Velimirović. London: Oxford University Press.

Duby, Georges
1980 *The Three Orders: Feudal Society Imagined*. Transl. Arthur Goldhammer. Chicago: University of Chicago Press. Originally published as *Les trois ordres: ou, l'imaginaire du féodalisme*. Paris: Gallimard, 1978.

Duft, Johannes, and Rudolf Schnyder
1984 *Die Elfenbein-Einbände der Stiftsbibliothek St. Gallen*. Beuron: Beuroner Kunstverlag.

Dummer, Jürgen, ed.
1987 *Texte und Textkritik: Eine Aufsatzsammlung*. Texte und Untersuchungen 133. Berlin: Akademie-Verlag.

Dyer, Joseph
1981 "Augustine and the 'Hymni ante oblationem': The Earliest Offertory Chants?" *Revue des études augustiniennes* 27:85–99.

Edelman, Marsha Bryan
1978–9 "An Index to Gershon Ephros' *Cantorial Anthology*." *Musica Judaica* 2/2. New York: The American Society for Jewish Music.

Edsman, C.-M.
1962 "Trauerbräuche" 1: "Religiongeschichtlich." *Die Religion in Geschichte und Gegenwart: Handwörterbuch für Theologie und Religionswissenschaft* 6:997–1000. 3rd ed. Tübingen: J. C. B. Mohr.

Edwards, Carol C.
1983 "The Parry-Lord Theory Meets Operational Structuralism." *Journal of American Folklore* 96:151–69.

Edworthy, Judy.
1985 "Melodic Contour and Musical Structure." In Howell et al., eds. 1985: 169–88.

Eggebrecht, Hans Heinrich, ed.
1972– *Handwörterbuch der musikalischen Terminologie*. Wiesbaden: Franz Steiner.

Ehrman, Bart D.
1987 "The Use of Group Profiles for the Classification of New Testament Documentary Evidence." *Journal of Biblical Literature* 106:465–86.

Ellard, Gerald
1948 *The Mass of the Future*. Milwaukee: Bruce.
1956 *The Mass in Transition*. Milwaukee: Bruce.

Ellingson, Ter
1979 "*ʾDon rta dbyangs gsum:* Tibetan Chant and Melodic Categories." *Asian Music* 10/2:112–56.
1986 "Buddhist Musical Notations." In Tokumaru and Yamaguti, eds. 1986:302–41.
1987 "Music and Religion." *The Encyclopedia of Religion* 10:163–72.

Elschek, Oskár
1985 "Die historische Erforschung mündlich, teilschriftlich und schriftlich überlieferter traditioneller Musikkulturen." *Beiträge zur Musikwissenschaft* 27:103–9.

Elschek, Oskár, ed.
1969 *Methoden der Klassifikation von Volksliedweisen*. Bratislava: Verlag der Slowakischen Akademie der Wissenschaften.

Elsner, Jürgen.
1981 "*Maqām* und Modus." In Heartz and Wade, eds. 1981: 517–25; with discussion, 544–9.

Ember, Carol R.
1977 "Cross-Cultural Cognitive Studies." *Annual Review of Anthropology* 6:33–56.

The Encyclopedia of Religion.
1987 Ed. Mircea Eliade. 15 vols. New York: Macmillan.

Engberg, Sysse Gudrun
1982 "Ekphonetic Chant—The Oral Tradition and the Manuscripts." In Raasted, ed. 1982:41–8.

Engels, Odilo
1970 "Religious Orders." *Sacramentum Mundi: An Encyclopedia of Theology* 5:298–314. Ed. Karl Rahner et al. New York: Herder & Herder.

Ephros, Gershon
1957 *Cantorial Anthology of Traditional and Modern Synagogue Music Arranged for Cantor and Choir with Organ Accompaniment.* Rev. ed. 5 vols. New York: Bloch.

Epp, Eldon Jay
1989a "New Testament Textual Criticism Past, Present, and Future: Reflections on the Alands' *Text of the New Testament.*" *Harvard Theological Review* 82:213–29.
1989b "The New Testament Papyrus Manuscripts in Historical Perspective." *To Touch the Text: Biblical and Related Studies in Honor of Joseph A. Fitzmyer, S.J.*, 261–88. Ed. Maurya P. Horgan and Paul J. Kobelski. New York: Crossroad.

Ernetti, Pellegrino, ed.
1978–9 *Canti sacri aquileiesi della tradizione orale raccolti da D. Giuseppe Cargnello.* Jucunda Laudatio 16–7. Venice: San Giorgio Maggiore.

Ertlbauer, Alice
1985 *Geschichte und Theorie der einstimmigen armenischen Kirchenmusik: Eine Kritik der bisherigen Forschung.* Musicae Medievalis Europae Centralis: Dissertationen und Schriften der Universität Wien aus historischer Musikwissenschaft 3. Ed. Christian Hannick and Walter Pass. Vienna: Anton Riegelnik.

Etzion, Judith, and Susanna Weich-Shahak
1988 "The Spanish and the Sephardic Romances: Musical Links." *Ethnomusicology* 32:1–37 (=[73]–[209]).

Falvy, Zoltán
1964 "Über Antiphonvarianten aus dem österreichisch-ungarisch-tschechoslowakischen Raum." *Studien zur Musikwissenschaft* 26:9–24.

Farkas, Ann E.
1985 "Iconostasis." *Dictionary of the Middle Ages* 6:409–10.

al Faruqi, Lois Ibsen
1978 "Accentuation in Qur'ānic Chant: A Study in Musical *Tawāzun.*" *Yearbook of the International Folk Music Council* 10:53–68.

1981 *An Annotated Glossary of Arabic Musical Terms.* Westport, Conn.: Greenwood Press.

1987 "The Cantillation of the Qur'ān." *Asian Music* 19:2–25.

Fassler, Margot E.

1983 "Musical Exegesis in the Sequences of Adam and the Canons of St. Victor." Ph.D. diss., Cornell University.

1984 "Who Was Adam of St. Victor? The Evidence of the Sequence Manuscripts." *Journal of the American Musicological Society* 37:233–69.

1985 "The Office of the Cantor in Early Western Monastic Rules and Customaries: A Preliminary Investigation." *Early Music History* 5:29–51.

forthcoming a "The Feast of Fools and the *Danielis Ludus:* Popular Traditions in a Medieval Cathedral Play." *Plainsong in the Age of Polyphony.* Ed. Thomas Forrest Kelly. Cambridge: Cambridge University Press.

forthcoming b *Gothic Song: Augustinian Ideals of Reform in the Twelfth Century and the Victorine Sequences.* Cambridge: Cambridge University Press.

Feld, Steven

1974 "Linguistic Models in Ethnomusicology." *Ethnomusicology* 18:197–217.

1986 "Orality and Consciousness." In Tokumaru and Yamaguti, eds. 1986:18–28.

Fellerer, Karl Gustav

1970 "Zur Constitutio 'Docta SS. Patrum.' " *Speculum Musicae Artis: Festgabe für Heinrich Husmann,* 125–32. Ed. Heinz Becker and Reinhard Gerlach. Munich: W. Fink.

Fellerer, Karl Gustav, ed.

1972 *Geschichte der katholischen Kirchenmusik* 1: *Von den Anfängen bis zum Tridentinum,* 109–27. Ed. Karl Gustav Fellerer. Kassel: Bärenreiter.

Fenlon, Iain, ed.

1981 *Music in Medieval and Early Modern Europe: Patronage, Sources, and Texts.* Cambridge University Press.

Ferguson, Everett

1983 "Psalm-Singing at the Eucharist: A Liturgical Controversy in the Fourth Century." *Austin Seminary Bulletin* 98:52–77.

Fernandez, Marie-Henriette

1976 "Notes sur les origines du rondeau: Le répons bref—les 'preces' du Graduel de Saint-Yrieix." *Cahiers de civilisation médiévale: X^{e}–XIIe siècles* 19:265–75.

Ferretti, Paolo

1934 *Estetica Gregoriana, ossia Trattato delle forme musicali del canto gregoriano* 1. Rome: Pontificio Istituto di Musica Sacra. Repr. New York: Da Capo Press, 1977.

Ffinch, Michael
1986 *G. K. Chesterton*. San Francisco: Harper & Row.

Figueras, José Romeu
1964 "La canción popular navideña, fuente de un misterio dramático de técnica medieval." *Anuario Musical* 19:167–84.

Finnegan, Ruth
1980 *Oral Poetry: Its Nature, Significance and Social Context*. Cambridge University Press.

Fischer, Kurt von
1971 "Persistence du 'Cantus binatim' au 18e siècle?" *Quadrivium* 12/2:197–209.
1973–4 "The Sacred Polyphony of the Italian Trecento," *Proceedings of the Royal Music Association* 100:143–157.

Fisher, Judith
1976 "Literature Concerning Possible Secular Origins of Sacred Polyphony." In "A Bibliography of Early Organum," ed. Calvin Bower, 37–41. *Current Musicology* 21:16–45.

Fladt, Ellinore
1987 *Die Musikauffassung des Johannes de Grocheo im Kontext der hochmittelalterlichen Aristoteles-Rezeption*. Berliner Musikwissenschaftliche Arbeiten 26. Munich and Salzburg: Emil Katzbichler.

Flannery, Austin, ed.
1975 *Vatican Council II: The Conciliar and Post Conciliar Documents* 1. New revised ed. Collegeville, Minnesota: Liturgical Press.

Fleckenstein, Franz, ed.
1974 *Gloria Deo, Pax Hominibus: Festschrift zum 100-jährigen Bestehen der Kirchenmusikschule Regensburg affiliiert der päpstlichen Hochschule für Kirchenmusik Rom, Fachakademie für katholischen Kirchenmusik und Musikerziehung am 22. November 1974*. Schriftenreihe des Allgemeinen Cäcilien-Verbandes für die Länder der deutschen Sprache 9. Bonn: Sekretariat des ACV.

Foley, Edward
1982 "The Cantor in Historical Perspective." *Worship* 56:194–213.
1989 "When American Roman Catholics Sing." *Worship* 63:98–112.
1990a "Music, Liturgical." *The New Dictionary of Sacramental Worship*, 854–70. Ed. Peter E. Fink, S.J. Collegeville, Minnesota: Liturgical Press.
1990b "Liturgical Musicology Redux." *Worship* 64:264–8.

Foley, Edward, Sue Seid-Martin, Fred R. Anderson, Virgil C. Funk
1989 "Tradition and Enculturation in the Music of the Liturgy: A Symposium." *Proceedings of the Annual Meeting of the North American Academy of Liturgy, Nashville, Tennessee, 2–5 January 1989*, 40–60. Valparaiso, Indiana: North American Academy of Liturgy.

Foley, John Miles
1985 *Oral-Formulaic Theory and Research: An Introduction and Annotated Bibliography*. Garland Folklore Bibliographies 6. New York: Garland.

Foley, John Miles, ed.
1981 *Oral Traditional Literature: A Festschrift for Albert Bates Lord*. Columbus, Ohio: Slavica.
1987 *Comparative Research on Oral Traditions: A Memorial for Milman Parry*. Columbus, Ohio: Slavica.

Fontaine, Jacques, Robert Gillet, Stan Pellistrandi, eds.
1986 *Grégoire le Grand: Chantilly, Centre culturel Les Fontaines, 15–19 septembre 1982*. Colloques internationaux du Centre National de la Recherche Scientifique. Paris: Editions du Centre National de la Recherche Scientifique.

Fox, Anthony
1990 *The Structure of German*. Oxford: Clarendon Press.

Francès, Robert
1988 *The Perception of Music*. Transl. W. Jay Dowling. Hillsdale, New Jersey: Lawrence Erlbaum.

Franklin, Ralph William
1987 *Nineteenth Century Churches: The History of a New Catholicism in Württemberg, England, and France*. Modern European History. New York: Garland.

Franklin, Ralph William, and Robert L. Spaeth
1988 *Virgil Michel: American Catholic*. Collegeville, Minnesota: Liturgical Press.

Frazer, James George
1961 *The New Golden Bough: A New Abridgement of the Classic Work*. Ed. Theodor H. Gaster. Garden City, New York: Doubleday Anchor Books.

Frere, Walter Howard, ed.
1898–1901 *The Use of Sarum*. 2 vols. Cambridge: Cambridge University Press 1898–1901. Repr. Farnborough, Hants.: Gregg Press, 1969.
1901–24 *Antiphonale Sarisburiense*. London: Plainsong and Mediaeval Music Society. Repr. in 6 vols. Farnborough, Hants.: Gregg Press, 1966.

Friedman, Albert B.
1983 "The Oral-Formulaic Theory of Balladry—a Re-rebuttal." *The*

Ballad Image: Essays Presented to Bertrand Harris Bronson, 215–40. Ed. James Porter. Los Angeles: Center for the Study of Comparative Folklore and Mythology.

Frigyesi, Judit Laki
1982–3 "Modulation as an Integral Part of the Modal System in Jewish Music." *Musica Judaica* 5:53–71.

Froger, Jacques
1947–9 "Les chants de la Messe aux VIIIe et IXe siècles." *Revue grégorienne* 26 (1947) 161–72, 218–28; 27 (1948) 56–62, 98–107; 28 (1949) 58–65, 94–102.
1954 "L'Edition critique de l'*Antiphonale Missarum* romain par les moines de Solesmes." *Etudes grégoriennes* 1:151–7.
1978 "The Critical Edition of the Roman Gradual by the Monks of Solesmes." *Journal of the Plainsong and Medieval Music Society* 1:81–97.

Gallo, F. Alberto
1966 "'Cantus planus binatim': Polifonia primitiva in fonti tardive." *Quadrivium* 7:79–89.

Gamber, Klaus
1968 *Codices Liturgici Latini Antiquiores.* 2nd ed. 2 vols. Spicilegii Friburgensis Subsidia 1. Freiburg: Universitätsverlag.
1977 "Das altbairische Petruslied—im Zusammenhang mit dem literarischen Leben in Regensburg während des 9. Jahrhunderts." In Stein, ed. 1977:107–27.

Gamber, Klaus, with B. Baroffio, F. dell'Oro, A. Hänggi, J. Janini, A.M. Triacca
1988 *Codices Liturgici Latini Antiquiores/Supplementum: Ergänzungs- und Registerband.* Spicilegii Friburgensis Subsidia 1A. Freiburg: Universitätsverlag.

Gardner, Johann von, and Erwin Koschmieder, eds.
1963–72 *Ein handschriftliches Lehrbuch der altrussischen Neumenschrift.* Abhandlungen der Bayerische Akademie der Wissenschaften, Philosophisch-Historische Klasse, Neue Folge 57, 62, 68. Munich: Verlag der Bayerischen Akademie der Wissenschaften, in Kommission bei der C. H. Beck'schen Verlagsbuchhandlung, 1963, 1966, 1972.

Gaster, Theodore H.
1987 "Heroes." *The Encyclopedia of Religion* 6:302–5.

Gawron, Jean Mark, and Stanley Peters
1990 *Anaphora and Quantification in Situation Semantics.* CSLI Lecture Note 19. Stanford, California: Center for the Study of Language and Information.

Gelineau, Joseph
1962 *Chant et musique dans le culte chrétien.* Kinnor 1. Paris: Editions Fleurus. [An English translation is Gelineau 1964; see below].

1964 *Voices and Instruments in Christian Worship: Principles, Laws, Applications.* Transl. Clifford Howell. London: Burns & Oates.

1965 "The Role of Sacred Music." Transl. Theodore L. Westow. *The Church and the Liturgy,* 59–65. Concilium: Theology in the Age of Renewal, Liturgy Vol. 2. Ed. Johannes Wagner. Glen Rock, New Jersey: Paulist Press.

1978 "Music and Singing in the Liturgy." In Jones et al., eds. 1978: 440–54.

Gerson-Kiwi, Edith

1965 "The Bards of the Bible." *Studia Musicologica Academiae Scientiarum Hungariae* 7:61–70.

1980 "Cheironomy." *The New Grove Dictionary* 4:191–6.

Giesen, Walter

1977 *Zur Geschichte des buddhistischen Ritualgesangs in Japan: Traktate des 9. bis 14. Jahrhunderts zum Shōmyō der Tendai-Sekte.* Studien zur traditionellen Musik Japans 1. Kassel: Bärenreiter.

Gillespie, John

1978 "Coptic Chant: A Survey of Past Research and a Projection for the Future." *The Future of Coptic Studies,* 227–45. Ed. R. McL. Wilson. Coptic Studies 1. Leiden: E. J. Brill.

Gironés, Gonzalo

1977 "Los origenes del Misterio de Elche." *Marian Library Studies.* New Series 9:19–188.

Gjerdingen, Robert O.

1988 *A Classic Turn of Phrase: Music and the Psychology of Convention.* Studies in the Criticism and Theory of Music. Philadelphia: University of Pennsylvania.

Godard, Marcel

1971 "Musique et chant liturgique dans la presse française (1969–1971)." *La Maison-Dieu* 108 (1971, no. 4):111–6.

Goethals, Gregor

1990 "Ritual and the Representation of Power in High and Popular Art." *Journal of Ritual Studies* 4:149–77.

Goody, Jack

1977 *The Domestication of the Savage Mind.* Themes in the Social Sciences. Cambridge University Press.

Gorman, Frank H.

1990 *The Ideology of Ritual: Space, Time and Status in the Priestly Theology.* Journal for the Study of the Old Testament Supplement Series 91. Sheffield: Sheffield Academic Press.

Gottwald, Clytus

1964 "'In dulci jubilo': Morphogenese eines Weihnachtsliedes." *Jahrbuch für Liturgik und Hymnologie* 9:133–43.

Gould, Richard A.
1990 *Recovering the Past*. Albuquerque: University of New Mexico Press.
Grant, John N., ed.
1989 *Editing Greek and Latin Texts: Papers Given at the Twenty-Third Annual Conference on Editorial Problems, University of Toronto, 6–7 November 1987*. New York: AMS Press.
Green, D. H.
1990 "Orality and Reading: The State of Research in Medieval Studies." *Speculum* 65:267–80.
Grenier, Line, and Jocelyne Guilbault
1990 "'Authority' Revisited: The 'Other' in Anthropology and Popular Music Studies. *Ethnomusicology* 34:381–97.
Grier, James
1988a "The Stemma of the Aquitainian Versaria." *Journal of the American Musicological Society* 41:250–88.
1988b "Lachmann, Bédier and the Bipartite Stemma: Towards a Responsible Application of the Common-Error Method." *Revue d'Histoire des Textes* 18:263–78.
Grimaud, Yvette.
1977 "Musique vocale géorgienne." *Bedi Kartlisa* 35:51–72.
1979a "Sur l'ornementation de certains chants géorgiens d'Europe orientale." *Bedi Kartlisa* 37:180–3.
1979b "Géorgie: Chants religieux." *Bedi Kartlisa* 37:184–93.
Grimes, Ronald L.
1982 *Beginnings in Ritual Studies*. Washington, D.C.: University Press of America.
1985 *Research in Ritual Studies: A Programmatic Essay and Bibliography*. American Theological Library Association Bibliography Series 14. Metuchen, New Jersey: Scarecrow Press.
1990a *Ritual Criticism: Case Studies in Its Practice, Essays on Its Theory*. Columbia: University of South Carolina Press.
1990b "Emerging Ritual." *Proceedings of the North American Academy of Liturgy* 3: *Annual Meeting, Saint Louis, Missouri, 2–5 January 1990,* 15–31. Valparaiso, Indiana: North American Academy of Liturgy.
Guinee, Linda N., and Katharine B. Payne
1988 "Rhyme-like Repetitions in Songs of Humpback Whales." *Ethology* 79:295–306.
Gümpel, Karl-Werner
1981 "Cantus Eugenianus—Cantus melodicus." In Heartz and Wade, eds. 1981:407–13.
Gurevich, Aron
1988 *Medieval Popular Culture: Problems of Belief and Perception.*

Translated by János M. Bak and Paul A. Hollingsworth. Cambridge Studies in Oral and Literate Culture 14. Cambridge University Press.

Gusejnova, Zivar
forthcoming "Russian Znamenny Chant in the First Half of the XVIIth Century." *Cantus Planus 2: Papers Read at the Fourth Meeting, Pécs, Hungary, 3–9 September 1990.* Budapest: Institute for Musicology, Hungarian Academy of Sciences.

Gwacharija, Washa A. (also transliterated as Gvaharia, V.)
1967 "Mehrstimmigkeit in altgrusinischen Handschriften?" *Beiträge zur Musikwissenschaft* 9:284–304, plates IIIb–VI.
1977–8 "La musique en Géorgie au temps de la grande reine Tamar." *Bedi Kartlisa* 35 (1977): 204–35; 36 (1978): 120–48.

Haar, James
1990 "Monophony and the Unwritten Tradition." In Brown and Sadie, eds. 1990:185–200.

Haberl, F. X.
1902 "Geschichte und Wert der offiziellen Choralbücher." *Kirchenmusikalisches Jahrbuch* 17:134–92.

Hage, Louis
1967 "Les mélodies-types dans le chant maronite: recherches musicologiques." *Melto: Recherches Orientales* 3 (= *Mélanges Mgr Pierre Dib*) 326–409.
1972 *Le chant de l'église maronite* 1: *Le chant syro-maronite.* Bibliothèque de l'Université Saint Esprit 4. Beirut, Lebanon: avec le concours du CNRS.
1978 *Maronite Music.* Carreras Arab Lectures 7. London: Longman.
1986 "Le chant du rite maronite." In Honnegger and Prevost, eds. 1986:69–74.

Haïk Vantoura, Suzanne
1976a *La musique de la Bible révélée: Une notation millénaire décryptée.* Paris: Dessain et Tolra. 2nd ed. 1978.
1976b *La musique de la Bible révélée: Une notation millénaire décryptée.* [LP recording]. Harmonia Mundi HMU 989.
1978–81 *La musique de la Bible révélée: Une notation millénaire décryptée.* ["Transcriptions" with "accompaniment for plucked strings"]. Paris: Editions Choudens 1 (1978), 2 (1979). Supplement to 1 (1981).
1981 "La cantillation biblique et ses problèmes: La déchiffrement musical des *Taʿamim:* Communication faite à la Société des Etudes Juives." *Revue des Etudes Juives* 40:283–4.
1985 *Les 150 psaumes dans leurs mélodies antiques: La musique de la Bible révélée, une notation millénaire décryptée.* 2 vols. Paris: Fondation Roi David.

Hall, F. W.
1913 *A Companion to Classical Texts.* Oxford: Clarendon Press. Repr. Hildesheim: Georg Olms, 1968.
Hallinger, Kassius, ed.
1963– *Corpus Consuetudinum Monasticarum.* Siegburg: Franz Schmitt.
Halmo, Joan, and Todd Ridder
1990 "Liturgical Musicology." *Worship* 64:460–2.
Hameline, Jean-Yves
1977 "Le son de l'histoire: Chant et musique dans la restauration catholique." *La Maison-Dieu* 131 (1977, no. 3):5–47.
Handelman, Don
1987 "Clowns." *The Encyclopedia of Religion* 3:547–51.
Hansen, Finn Egeland
1979 *The Grammar of Gregorian Tonality.* 2 vols. Copenhagen: Dan Fog.
Hanssens, Jean Michel, ed.
1948–50 *Amalarii Episcopi Opera Liturgica Omnia.* 3 vols. Studi e Testi 138–40. Vatican City: Bibliotheca Apostolica Vaticana.
Harnoncourt, Philipp
1974 "Katholische Kirchenmusik vom Cäcilianismus bis zur Gegenwart." *Traditionen und Reformen in der Kirchenmusik: Festschrift für Konrad Ameln zum 75. Geburtstag am 6. Juli 1974* 78–133. Ed. Gerhard Schuhmacher. Kassel: Bärenreiter.
Harrán, Don
1989 *In Defense of Music: The Case for Music as Argued by a Singer and Scholar of the Late Fifteenth Century.* Lincoln: University of Nebraska Press.
Harris, Marvin
1976 "History and Significance of the Emic/Etic Distinction." *Annual Review of Anthropology* 5:329–5.
Harrison, Frank Ll.
1972 "Music and Cult: The Functions of Music in Social and Religious Systems." *Perspectives in Musicology,* 307–34. Ed. Barry S. Brook et al. New York: W. W. Norton.
1979 "Tradition and Acculturation: A View of Some Historic Processes." *Essays on Music for Charles Warren Fox,* 114–25. Ed. Jerald C. Graue. Rochester, New York: Eastman School of Music Press.
1980 *Music in Medieval Britain.* 4th ed. Buran, Netherlands: Frits Knuf. (First published London: Routledge & Kegan Paul, 1958.)
Hatch, William Henry Paine
1946 *An Album of Dated Syriac Manuscripts.* Boston: American Academy of Arts and Sciences.

Havnevik, Hanna
[1989] *Tibetan Buddhist Nuns: History, Cultural Norms and Social Reality*. Institutt for sammenlignende Kulturforskning, Serie B: Skrifter 79. Oslo: Norwegian University Press.
Hayburn, Robert F.
1979 *Papal Legislation on Sacred Music, 95 A.D. to 1977 A.D.* Collegeville, Minnesota: Liturgical Press.
Heartz, Daniel, and Bonnie Wade, eds.
1981 *International Musicological Society, Report of the Twelfth Congress, Berkeley 1977*. Basel: Bärenreiter.
Hecker, Wolf, et al., eds.
1953–4 *Out-of-Print Classics of Cantorial Liturgy*. 25 vols. New York: Sacred Music Press, Hebrew Union School of Sacred Music and American Conference of Certified Cantors.
Henrotte, Gayle A.
1980 "Armenian Liturgical Music: An Encounter in Jerusalem." *Miscellanea Musicologica: Adelaide Studies in Musicology* 11:215–25.
Henry, H. T.
1915 "Music-Reform in the Catholic Church." *Musical Quarterly* 1:102–17.
Hermelink, Siegfried
1970 "Eine Kirchenliedweise als Credomelodie." *Die Musikforschung* 23:160–5.
Hervé, L.
1924 "Mélodies bretonnes et théories solesmiennes." *Revue grégorienne* 9:169–71.
Herzog, Avigdor
1963 *The Intonation of the Pentateuch in the Heder of Tunis*. Tel Aviv: Israel Music Institute.
1971 "Masoretic Accents (Musical Rendition)." *Encyclopedia Judaica* 11:1098–1112. Jerusalem: Encyclopedia Judaica; New York: Macmillan.
Hesbert, René-Jean, ed.
1963–79 *Corpus Antiphonalium Officii*. 6 vols. Rerum Ecclesiasticarum Documenta, Series Major, 7–12. Rome: Herder.
Higgins, Jon B.
1965 "Chants in Medieval European Music." *Journal of the Music Academy, Madras* 36:91–8.
Higgins, Paula
1990 "Tracing the Careers of Late Medieval Composers: The Case of Philippe Basiron of Bourges." *Acta Musicologica* 62:1–28.
Hiley, David
1980–1 "The Norman Chant Traditions—Normandy, Britain, Sicily." *Proceedings of the Royal Musical Association* 107:1–33.

1990 "Chant." In Brown and Sadie, eds. 1990:37–54.

Hoffman, Lawrence A.

1987 *Beyond the Text: A Holistic Approach to Liturgy.* Bloomington: Indiana University Press.

Hoffman-Axthelm, Dagmar

1972 "Faburdon / fauxbourdon / falso bordone." In Eggebrecht 1972–.

Honegger, Marc, and Paul Prevost, eds.

1986 *La musique et le rite: sacré et profane Actes du XIIIe Congrès de la Société Internationale de Musicologie, Strasbourg, 29 août – 3 septembre 1982 2: Communications libres.* Strasbourg: Association des Publications près les Universités de Strasbourg.

Honko, Lauri

1987 "Finno-Ugric Religions: An Overview." *The Encyclopedia of Religion* 5:330–5.

Hood, Mantle

1954 *The Nuclear Theme as a Determinant of Patet in Javanese Music.* Groningen: J. B. Wolters. Reprinted New York: Da Capo Press, 1977.

1959 "The Reliability of Oral Tradition," *Journal of the American Musicological Society* 12:201–9.

Hoppin, Richard H.

1978 *Medieval Music.* New York: W. W. Norton.

Horn, Michel

1901–2 "La question du Plain-Chant en Allemagne." *Revue du chant grégorien* 10:25–31, 38–42.

Hourlier, Jacques

1963 "Neumes sur des diptyques." *Etudes grégoriennes* 6:149–52.

1973 "Notes sur l'antiphonie." *Gattungen der Musik in Einzeldarstellungen: Gedenkschrift Leo Schrade* 1: 116–45. Ed. Wulf Arlt et al. Bern and Munich: Francke.

Howard, Wayne

1977 *Sāmavedic Chant.* New Haven: Yale University Press.

Howell, Peter, Ian Cross, Robert West, eds.

1985 *Musical Structure and Cognition.* London: Academic Press.

Hucke, Helmut

1963 "Die Neumierung des althochdeutschen Petruslieds." *Organicae Voces: Festschrift Joseph Smits van Waesberghe,* 71–8. Ed. Pieter Fischer. Amsterdam: Instituut voor Middeleeuwse Muziekwetenschap.

1965 "Church Music." Transl. Theodore L. Westow. *The Church and the Liturgy,* 110–31. Ed. Johannes Wagner. Concilium: Theology in the Age of Renewal, Liturgy Volume 2. Glen Rock, New Jersey: Paulist Press.

1966 "Musical Requirements of Liturgical Reform." Transl. Eileen O'Gorman. *The Church Worships*, 45–73. Ed. Johannes Wagner and Heinrich Rennings. Concilium: Theology in the Age of Renewal 12. New York and Glen Rock, New Jersey: Paulist Press.

1967 "L'evoluzione del concetto di 'musica sacra' nel quadro del rinnovamento liturgico." *Rinnovamento liturgico e musica sacra: Commento alla Istruzione "Musicam Sacram,"* 244–8. Bibliotheca "Ephemerides Liturgicae" Sectio Pastoralis 4. Rome: Edizioni Liturgiche.

1969 "Jazz and Folk Music in the Liturgy." *The Crisis of Liturgical Reform*, 138–72. Transl. John Drury. Concilium: Theology in the Age of Renewal 42. New York and Glen Rock, New Jersey: Paulist Press.

1971 "Towards a New Kind of Church Music." Transl. N. D. Smith. *Liturgy in Transition*, 87–97. Ed. Hermann Schmidt. Concilium: Theology in the Age of Renewal 62. New York: Herder & Herder.

1973 "Das Responsorium." *Gattungen der Musik in Einzeldarstellungen: Gedenkschrift Leo Schrade* 1:144–91. Ed. Wulf Arlt, Ernst Lichtenhahn, Hans Oesch, Max Haas. Bern and Munich: Franke Verlag.

1975 "Karolingische Renaissance und Gregorianischer Gesang." *Die Musikforschung* 28:4–18.

1978 Review of Wagenaar-Nolthenius 1974. *Die Musikforschung* 31:352–3.

1979a "Was ist eigentlich Kirchenmusik? Das Verhältnis von Kirchenmusik und Liturgie." *Musica Sacra: Cäcilien-Verbands Organ* 99/4:193–9.

1979b "Über Herkunft und Abgrenzung des Begriffs 'Kirchenmusik.'" *Renaissance Studien: Helmuth Osthoff zum 80. Geburtstag*, 103–25. Ed. Ludwig Finscher. Frankfurter Beiträge zur Musikwissenschaft 11. Tutzing: Schneider.

1979c "Changing Concepts of Church Music." In Pol-Topis et al., eds. 1979:17–29.

1980a "Gregorian and Old Roman chant." *The New Grove Dictionary* 7:693–7.

1980b "Die Herkunft der Tonarten und die fränkische Überlieferung des gregorianischen Gesangs." *Bericht über den Internationalen Musikwissenschaftlichen Kongress, Berlin 1974*, 257–60. Ed. Hellmut Kühn and Peter Nitsche. Kassel: Bärenreiter.

1980c "Zur Aufzeichnung der altrömischen Offertorien." *Ut mens concordet voci: Festschrift Eugène Cardine*, 296–308. Ed. Johannes Berchmans Göschl. St. Ottilien: EOS Verlag.

1980d "Toward a New Historical View of Gregorian Chant." *Journal of the American Musicological Society* 33:437–67.

1981 "Der Übergang von mündlicher zu schriftlicher Musiküberlieferung im Mittelalter." In Heartz and Wade, eds. 1981:180–91.

[1982] "Die Wiederentdeckung der Kirchenmusik durch die Liturgiereform." *Liturgia opera divina e umana: Studi sulla riforma liturgica offerti a S.E. Mons. Annibale Bugnini in occasione del suo 70° compleanno* 150–70. Ed. Pierre Jounel, Reiner Kaczynski, Gottardo Pasqualetti. Bibliotheca "Ephemerides Liturgicae" 26. Rome: Edizioni Liturgiche.

1983 "Die Anfänge der Bearbeitung." *Schweizer Jahrbuch für Musikwissenschaft,* Neue Folge 3 (1983 [1986]): 15–20.

1984a "Das Dekret 'Docta Sanctorum Patrum' Papst Johannes' XXII." *Musica Disciplina* 38:119–31.

1984b "Die römisch-katholische Kirche." *Religiöse Autoritäten und Musik: Ein Symposium* 24–46. Ed. Dorothea Baumann and Kurt von Fischer. Kassel: Johannes Stauda Verlag.

1985 "Zur melodischen Überlieferung der Tropen." In Silagi, ed. 1985:107–24.

1988a "Gregorianische Fragen." *Musikforschung* 41:304–30.

1988b "Choralforschung und Musikwissenschaft." *Das musikalische Kunstwerk: Geschichte, Ästhetik, Theorie: Festschrift Carl Dahlhaus zum 60. Geburtstag,* 131–4. Ed. H. Danuser, H. de la Motte-Haber, S. Leopold, N. Miller. Laaber: Laaber-Verlag.

1990 "Die Entstehung des gregorianischen Gesangs." *Neue Musik und Tradition: Festschrift Rudolf Stephan zum 65. Geburtstag,* 11–23. Ed. Josef Kuckertz, Helga de la Motte-Haber, Christian Martin Schmidt, and Wilhelm Seidel. Laaber: Laaber-Verlag.

Hucke, Helmut, ed.

1974 *Musik in der feiernden Gemeinde: Hilfen zur Orientierung in der kirchenmusikalischen Theorie und Praxis.* Pastoralliturgische Reihe in Verbindung mit der Zeitschrift *Gottesdienst.* Zurich: Benziger; Freiburg: Herder.

Hucke, Helmut, René Reboud, Erhard Quack, Stephen Mbunga, Wilhelmus van Bekkum, Guilford C. Young

1966 "New Church Music in the Vernacular." Transl. Eileen O'Gorman, et al. *The Church Worships,* 93–130. Ed. Johannes Wagner and Heinrich Rennings. Concilium: Theology in the Age of Renewal 12. New York and Glen Rock, New Jersey: Paulist Press.

Hughes, Andrew

1980 *Medieval Music: The Sixth Liberal Art.* Rev. ed. Toronto Medieval Bibliographies 4. Toronto: University of Toronto Press.

Hughes, David G.
1986 "Variants in Antiphon Families: Notation and Tradition." In Honegger and Prevost, eds. 1986:29–47.
1987 "Evidence for the Traditional View of the Transmission of Gregorian Chant." *Journal of the American Musicological Society* 40:377–404.
Hughes, David W.
1988 "Deep Structure and Surface Structure in Javanese Music: A Grammar of *Gendhing Lampah.*" *Ethnomusicology* 32:23–74.
1989 "The Historical Uses of Nonsense: Vowel-Pitch Solfege from Scotland to Japan." In Philipp 1989:3–18.
Hughes, Kathleen, ed.
1990 *How Firm a Foundation: Voices of the Early Liturgical Movement.* Chicago: Liturgy Training Publications.
Huglo, Michel
1971 *Les tonaires: Inventaire, analyse, comparaison.* Paris: Société Française de Musicologie.
1973 "Tradition orale et tradition écrite dans la transmission des mélodies grégoriennes." *Studien zur Tradition in der Musik: Kurt von Fischer zum 60. Geburtstag,* 31–42. Ed. H. H. Eggebrecht and M. Lütolff. Munich: Musikverlag Katzbichler.
1982 "Le Répons-Graduel de la Messe: Evolution de la forme, Permanence de la fonction." *Schweizer Jahrbuch für Musikwissenschaft,* Neue Folge 2:53–77.
1984 Review of Hansen 1979. *Journal of the American Musicological Society* 37:416–24.
1985 "L'Edition critique de l'antiphonaire grégorien." *Scriptorium* 39:130–8.
1988 *Les livres de chant liturgique.* Typologie des sources du moyen âge occidental 52. Turnhout, Belgium: Brepols.
1990 "The Study of Ancient Sources of Music Theory in the Medieval Universities." Transl. Fabian C. Lochner. *Music Theory and Its Sources: Antiquity and the Middle Ages* 150–72. Ed. André Barbera. Notre Dame, Indiana: University of Notre Dame Press.
Huglo, Michel, ed.
1987 *Musicologie médiévale: Notations et séquences: Actes de la table ronde de C.N.R.S. à l'Institut de Recherche et d'Histoire des Textes, 6–7 septembre 1982.* Paris: Champion.
Huijbers, Bernard
1980 "Liturgical Music after the Second Vatican Council." *Symbol and Art in Worship,* 101–11. Ed. Luis Maldonado and David Power. Concilium: Religion in the Eighties 132 (1980, no. 2). New York: Seabury Press; Edinburgh: T. & T. Clark.

Husmann, Heinrich

1966 "The Practice of Organum in the Liturgical Singing of the Syrian Churches of the Near and Middle East." *Aspects of Medieval and Renaissance Music: A Birthday Offering for Gustave Reese,* 435–9. Ed. Jan LaRue. New York: W. W. Norton; repr. New York: Pendragon, 1978.

1967 *Die Melodien des chaldäischen Breviers, Commune nach den Traditionen Vorderasiens und der Malabarküste.* Orientalia Christiana Analecta 178. Rome: Pontificium Institutum Studiorum Orientalium.

1969 *Die Melodien der Jakobitischen Kirche: Die Melodien des Wochenbreviers (Šḥimtā) gesungen von Qurillāos Jaᶜqub Kas Görgös, Metropolit von Damaskus.* Sitzungsberichte der Osterreichischen Akademie der Wissenschaften, Philosophisch-Historische Klasse 262/1. Vienna: Hermann Böhlaus Nachfolger.

1971 *Die Melodien der Jakobitischen Kirche: Die Qāle gaoānāie des Beit Gazā.* Sitzungsberichte der Osterreichischen Akademie der Wissenschaften, Philosophisch-Historische Klasse 273/4. Vienna: Hermann Böhlaus Nachfolger.

1972 "Die Gesänge der syrischen Liturgien." In Fellerer, ed. 1972:69–98.

1974a "Eine Konkordanztabelle syrischer Kirchentöne und arabischen Maqamen in einem syrischen Musiknotizbuch." *Symposium Syriacum 1972,* 371–85. Orientalia Christiana Analecta 197. Rome: Pontificium Institutum Studiorum Orientalium.

1974b "Ein syrisches Sticherarion mit paläobyzantinischer Notation (Sinai syr. 261)." *Hamburger Jahrbuch für Musikwissenschaft* 1:9–57.

1975–8 *Ein syro-melkitisches Tropologion mit altbyzantinischer Notation, Sinai Syr. 261.* 2 vols. Göttinger Orientforschungen, 1 Reihe: Syriaka 9. Wiesbaden: O. Harrassowitz, 1975, 1978.

1979 "Echos und Makam nach der Handschrift Leningrad, Öffentliche Bibliothek, gr. 127." *Archiv für Musikwissenschaft* 36:237–53.

1980 "Syrian Church Music." *The New Grove Dictionary* 18: 472–81.

Idelsohn, Abraham Zwi

1929 *Jewish Music in Its Historical Development.* New York: Tudor Publishing Co. Reprinted New York: Schocken, 1967.

International Commission on English in the Liturgy

1982 *Documents on the Liturgy, 1963–1979: Conciliar, Papal, and Curial Texts.* Collegeville, Minnesota: The Liturgical Press.

Irwin, Joyce, ed.

1983 *Sacred Sound: Music in Religious Thought and Practice.* Journal of the American Academy of Religion: Thematic Studies 50.1. Chico, California: Scholars Press, 1983.

Isobe, Jiro
1982 "On the Variants of Sticherarion" [in Japanese with an English abstract]. *Ongaku Gaku: Journal of the Japanese Musicological Association* 28 : 1–12.

Iversen, Gunilla, ed.
1983 *Research on Tropes: Proceedings of a Symposium Organized by the Royal Academy of Literature, History and Antiquities and the Corpus Troporum, Stockholm, June 1–3, 1981.* Kungl. Vitterhets Historie och Antikvitets Akademien, Konferenser 8. Stockholm: Almqvist & Wiksell.

Jackson, Roland
1988 *Performance Practice: Medieval to Contemporary: A Bibliographic Guide.* New York: Garland.

Jacobsen, Bent
1986 *Modern Transformational Grammar.* North-Holland Linguistic Series 53. Amsterdam: North-Holland.

Janota, Johannes
1980 "Schola cantorum und Gemeindelied im Spätmittelalter." *Jahrbuch für Liturgik und Hymnologie* 24 : 37–52.

Járdányi, Pál.
1959 "Über Anordnung von Melodien und Formanalyse in der Gregorianik." *Acta Ethnographica Academiae Scientiarum Hungaricae* 8 : 327–37.

Jarrett, Janice Carole
1977 "The Song of Lament: An Artistic Women's Heritage (A Study of the Modern Greek Lamenting Tradition and Its Ancient West Asian and Mediterranean Prototypes)." Ph.D. dissertation, Wesleyan University.

Jeannin, J.
1932–3 "Qu'étaient les 'tabulae' dont portent les liturgistes du moyen âge?" *Revue du Chant Grégorien* 36 (1932): 139–46, 173–7; 37 (1933): 15–21, 50–6.

Jeffery, Peter
1981 "Popular Culture on the Periphery of the Medieval Liturgy." *Worship* 55 : 419–27.

1982 "An Early Cantatorium Fragment Related to MS Laon 239," *Scriptorium* 36 : 245–52, plates 29–30.

1983 "The Oldest Sources of the *Graduale:* A Checklist of Manuscripts Copied before About 900 AD," *Journal of Musicology* 2 : 316–21.

1984a "The Introduction of Psalmody into the Roman Mass by Pope Celestine I (422–432): Reinterpreting a Passage in the *Liber Pontificalis.*" *Archiv für Liturgiewissenschaft* 26 : 147–65.

1984b Review of Irwin, ed. 1983. *Worship* 58:545–7.

1986a "Lost Melodies of the Rite of Jerusalem, and Partial Survivals in the Byzantine and Latin Chant Repertoires." *The Seventeenth International Byzantine Congress 1986: Abstracts of Short Papers,* 154–5. Washington, D.C.: U.S. National Committee for Byzantine Studies.

1986b Review of Tomasello 1983. *Speculum* 61:215–7.

1987 "Werner's *The Sacred Bridge,* Volume 2: A Review Essay," *Jewish Quarterly Review* 77:283–98.

1988a "The Music Sessions at the Seventeenth International Congress of Byzantine Studies, Georgetown University, 3–8 August 1986." *The Journal of Musicology* 6:130–4.

1988b Review of Vogel 1986. *Worship* 62:183–5.

1989a "Chant East and West: Toward a Renewal of the Tradition." In Collins et al., eds. 1989:20–9.

1989b "A Response" to "Tradition and Enculturation in the Music of the Liturgy: A Symposium." *Proceedings of the Annual Meeting of the North American Academy of Liturgy, Nashville, Tennessee, 2–5 January 1989,* 61–71. Valparaiso, Indiana: North American Academy of Liturgy.

1990 "The Formation of the Earliest Christian Chant Traditions: Four Processes That Shaped the Texts." *PRISM: Yale Institute of Sacred Music, Worship and the Arts* 14 (December 1990): 10–3.

1991a "The Sunday Office of Seventh-Century Jerusalem in the Georgian Chantbook (Iadgari): A Preliminary Report." *Studia Liturgica* 21 (1991) 52–75.

1991b "The New Chantbooks from Solesmes," *Notes: The Quarterly Journal of the Music Library Association* 48 (1991), 1039–63.

forthcoming "Rome and Jerusalem: From Oral Tradition to Written Repertory in Two Ancient Liturgical Centers." *From Rome to the Passing of the Gothic: Festschrift for David G. Hughes.* Ed. Graeme Boone. Cambridge, Massachusetts: Harvard University Music Department.

Jeffery, Peter, and Margot E. Fassler

forthcoming "Christian Liturgical Music from the Bible to the Counter-Reformation." *Two Liturgical Traditions* 3: *Sacred Sound and Social Change.* Ed. Janet Walton and Lawrence Hoffman. South Bend, Indiana: University of Notre Dame Press.

Jelič, Luka [Lucas]

1906 *Fontes Historici Liturgiae Glagolito-Romanae a XIII ad XIX Saeculum.* Krk [Veglia], Yugoslavia: Sumptibus Ephemeridis "Slavorum Litterae Theologicae" Pragae. [There are editions of the same date by at least three other publishers with different paginations.]

Jennings, Theodore W., Jr.
1987 "Ritual Studies and Liturgical Theology: An Invitation to Dialogue." *Journal of Ritual Studies* 1: 35–56.

Jones, Cheslyn, Geoffrey Wainwright, Edward Yarnold, eds.
1978 *The Study of Liturgy*. New York: Oxford University Press.

Jonsson [now Jacobsson], Ritva, Gunilla Björkvall, Gunilla Iversen, et al., eds.
1975– *Corpus Troporum* 1–. Studia Latina Stockholmiensia 21–. Stockholm: Almqvist & Wiksell.

Jonsson, Ritva, and Leo Treitler
1983 "Medieval Music and Language: A Reconsideration of the Relationship." *Studies in the History of Music* 1: *Music and Language,* 1–23. New York: Broude Brothers.

Jourdan[-Hemmerdinger], Denise
1970 Review of Hage 1967 in *Revue de Musicologie* 56:230–1.
1986 Review of Haïk Vantoura 1985. *Revue des Etudes Juives* 145:127–31.
1987 "Aspects méconnus des théories et notations antiques et de leur transmission." In Huglo, ed. 1987:67–99.

Kapronyi, Theresia
1982 "First Tone-Troparion Melody-Type in Hungarian Greek-Catholic Chant." In Raasted, ed. 1982:119–28.

Kartsovnik, Viatcheslav, ed.
1988 *Muzykal'naja kul'tura srednevekov'ja: Teorija, praktika, tradicija* [The Musical Culture of the Middle Ages: Theory, Practice, Tradition (in Russian and English)]. Problemy muzykoznanijaz 1. Leningrad: Ministero Kul'tury RSFSR.
1989 *Tradicija v istorii muzykal'noj kul'tury: Antičnost' srednevekov'e, novoe vremja* [Tradition in the History of Musical Culture: Antiquity, Middle Ages, Modern Era (in Russian and English)]. Problemy muzykoznanijaz 2. Leningrad: Ministero Kul'tury RSFSR.

Karwoski, T. F., H. S. Odbert, and C. E. Osgood
1942 "Studies in Synesthetic Thinking II: The Role of Form in Visual Responses to Music." *The Journal of General Psychology* 26:199–222. Reprinted in *Language, Meaning and Culture: The Selected Papers of C. E. Osgood,* 138–57. Ed. Charles E. Osgood and Oliver C. S. Tzeng. Centennial Psychology Series. New York: Praeger, 1990.

Katz, Ruth
1974 "The Reliability of Oral Transmission: The Case of Samaritan Music." *Yuval: Studies of the Jewish Music Research Center* 3:109–35. Jerusalem: Magnes Press of Hebrew University.

Kaufman, Walter
1967 *Musical Notations of the Orient*. Bloomington: Indiana University Press. Reprinted Gloucester Mass.: Peter Smith, 1972.

1975 *Tibetan Buddhist Chant.* Bloomington: Indiana University Press.

Kavanagh, Aidan

1988 "Liturgical and Credal Studies." *A Century of Church History: The Legacy of Philip Schaff,* 216–44. Ed. Henry W. Bowden. Carbondale: Southern Illinois University Press.

Keiler, Allan

1978 "Bernstein's *The Unanswered Question* and the Problem of Musical Competence." *Musical Quarterly* 64 : 195–222.

Kelly, Thomas

1985 "Melisma and Prosula: The Performance of Responsory Tropes." In Silagi, ed. 1985 : 163–80.

1989 *The Beneventan Chant.* Cambridge Studies in Music. Cambridge University Press.

Kim, Seong Nae

1989 "Lamentations of the Dead: The Historical Imagery of Violence on Cheju Island, South Korea." *Journal of Ritual Studies* 3 : 251–85.

Kippen, James

1987 "An Ethnomusicological Approach to the Analysis of Musical Cognition." *Music Perception* 5 : 173–96.

Kirsch, Winfried

1981 "Unterterz- und Leittonklauseln als quellentypische Varianten." *Quellenstudien zur Musik der Renaissance* I: *Formen und Probleme der Überlieferung mehrstimmiger Musik im Zeitalter Josquins Desprez,* 167–79. Ed. Ludwig Finscher. Wolfenbüttler Forschungen 6. Munich: Kraus.

Klammer, Edward W.

1963 "The Quempas Goes 'Round." *The Musical Heritage of the Church* 6 : 55–63. Ed. Theodore Hoelty-Nickel. St. Louis, Missouri: Concordia.

Klauser, Theodor

1979 *A Short History of the Western Liturgy: An Account and Some Reflections.* 2nd ed. Oxford University Press.

Kleeman, Janice E.

1985–6 "The Parameters of Musical Transmission." *The Journal of Musicology* 4 : 1–22.

Klöckner, Stefan

1988 "Analytische Untersuchungen an 16 Introiten im I. Ton des altrömischen und des fränkisch-gregorianischen Repertoires hinsichtlich einer bewussten melodischen Abhängigkeit." *Beiträge zur Gregorianik* 5 : 3–95.

Knowles, David

1969 *Christian Monasticism.* World University Library. New York: McGraw-Hill.

Kodály, Zoltán
1971 *Folk Music of Hungary.* 2nd ed. Rev. Lajos Vargyas, trans. Ronald Tempest and Cynthia Jolly. London: Barrie & Jenkins. Originally published as *A Magyar Népzene.* Budapest: Zeneműkiadó Vállalat, 1952.

Kolinsky, Mieczyslaw
1978 "Malbrough s'en va-t-en guerre: Seven Canadian versions of a French Folksong." *Yearbook of the International Folk Music Council* 10:1–32.

Korolevsky, Cyril
1957 *Living Languages in Catholic Worship: An Historical Inquiry.* Trans. Donald Attwater. London: Longmans, Green.

Kōsaki, Hisao
1982 "Theory of 'Formal Music' as a Formal Language (1)—A Survey of Applications of Generative Grammars to Music and the Definition of Formal Music." *Ongaku Gaku: Journal of the Japanese Musicological Society* 28:89–100. [In Japanese with an English abstract.]
1985 "Theory of 'Formal Music' as a Formal Language (2)—Phrase Structure Grammar and the Fundamental Structure of Music." *Ongaku Gaku: Journal of the Japanese Musicological Society* 30:108–24. [In Japanese with an English abstract.]

Kouyumdjieva, Svetlana, and Todor Todorov, eds.
1989 *Profesionalizm"t v narodnata muzikalna i srednovekovnata pevčeska praktika* [Professionalism in Folk-Musical and Medieval Singing Practice (in Russian with English summaries)]. Informacionen Bjuletin "Muzikalni Chorizonti" 12–13. Sofia: S"juz na Muzikalnite Deyci v B"lgarija.

Kramer, Richard
1975 "Notes to Beethoven's Education." *Journal of the American Musicological Society* 28:72–101.

Kuckertz, Josef
1969 "Die Melodietypen der westsyrischen liturgischen Gesänge." *Kirchenmusikalisches Jahrbuch* 53:61–9 + 14 foldouts.

Kunz, Lucas
1956 "Organum und Choralvortrag." *Kirchenmusikalisches Jahrbuch* 40:12–5.

Lachmann, Robert
1978 *Gesänge der Juden auf der Insel Djerba.* Ed. Edith Gerson-Kiwi. Jerusalem: Magnes Press, Hebrew University.

Lardner, Gerald V.
1989 "'Hoffman's Laws': A Proposal." *Proceedings of the Annual Meeting of the North American Academy of Liturgy, Nashville, Tennessee, 2–5 January 1989,* 142–6, see also 92–4. Valparaiso, Indiana: North American Academy of Liturgy.

Laub, Thomas
1904 "Vore folkevise-melodier og deres fornyelse." *Danske Studier* 177–209.

Lebeuf, Jean
1741 *Traité historique et pratique sur le chant ecclésiastique.* Paris: Herissant. Reprinted Geneva: Minkoff, 1972.

Leclercq, Jean
1982 *The Love of Learning and the Desire for God: A Study of Monastic Culture.* Transl. Catharine Misrahi. 3rd ed. New York: Fordham University Press. Originally published as *L'Amour des lettres et le désir de Dieu: Initiation des auteurs monastiques du moyen âge.* Paris: Editions du Cerf, 1957.

Le Goff, Jacques
1980 *Time, Work, and Culture in the Middle Ages.* Trans. Arthur Goldhammer. Chicago: University of Chicago Press. Originally published as *Pour un autre moyen âge: Temps, travail et culture en occident: 18 essais.* Paris: Gallimard, 1977.

Leiman, Sid Z., ed.
1974 *The Canon and Masorah of the Hebrew Bible: An Introductory Reader.* The Library of Biblical Studies. New York: Ktav Publishing House.

Lerdahl, Fred, and Ray Jackendoff
1983 *A Generative Theory of Tonal Music.* Cambridge, Massachusetts: MIT Press.

Levine, Joseph A.
1980–1 "Toward Defining the Jewish Prayer Modes with Particular Emphasis on the *Adonay Malakh* Mode." *Musica Judaica* 3:13–41.
1982–3 "The Biblical Trope System in Ashkenazic Prophetic Reading." *Musica Judaica* 5:35–52.

Levy, Kenneth
1970 "The Italian Neophytes' Chants." *Journal of the American Musicological Society* 23:181–227.
1978 "The Earliest Slavic Melismatic Chants." *Fundamental Problems of Early Slavic Music and Poetry,* ed. Christian Hannick, 197–210. Studies on the Fragmenta Chiliandarica Palaeoslavica 2. Monumenta Musicae Byzantinae, Subsidia 6. Copenhagen: Munksgaard.
1984 "Toledo, Rome, and the Legacy of Gaul." *Early Music History* 4:49–99.
1987a "Charlemagne's Archetype of Gregorian Chant." *Journal of the American Musicological Society* 40:1–30.
1987b "On the Origin of Neumes." *Early Music History* 7:59–90.
1988 Reply to Treitler 1988. *Journal of the American Musicological Society* 41:575–8.

Ling, Jan, and Märta Ramsten
1985 "The Gärdeby Folk Melody—A Musical Migrant." *Analytica: Studies in the Description and Analysis of Music,* 301–21. Ed. Anders Lönn and Erik Kjellberg. Uppsala: by the authors; Stockholm: Almqvist & Wiksell.

Lipphardt, Walther
1952 "Une source importante pour l'histoire de la tradition grégorienne en Allemagne." *Revue Grégorienne* 31:140–3.
1960 "'Christ ist erstanden': Zur Geschichte des Liedes," *Jahrbuch für Liturgik und Hymnologie* 5:96–114.
1961 "'Laus tibi Christe'—'Ach du armer Judas,' Untersuchungen zum ältesten deutschen Passionslied." *Jahrbuch für Liturgik und Hymnologie* 6:71–100.
1963 "'Mitten wir im Leben sind': Zur Geschichte des Liedes und seiner Weise." *Jahrbuch für Liturgik und Hymnologie* 8: 99–118.
1966 "Die älteste Quelle des deutschen 'Media vita': Eine Salzburger Handschrift vom Jahre 1456." *Jahrbuch für Liturgik und Hymnologie* 11:161–2.
1979 "Leisen und Rufe." *Die Musik in Geschichte und Gegenwart* (Kassel: Bärenreiter) 16:1105–1110.
1983 "Deutsche Antiphonenlieder des Spätmittelalters in einer Salzburger Handschrift (Michaelbeuern Ms. cart. 1)." *Jahrbuch für Liturgik und Hymnologie* 27:39–82.

List, George
1979 "The Distribution of a Melodic Formula: Diffusion or Polygenesis?" *Yearbook of the International Folk Music Council* 10:33–52.
1985 "Hopi Melodic Concepts." *Journal of the American Musicological Society* 38:143–52.

Lloyd, A. L.
1980 "Lament." *The New Grove Dictionary* 10:407–10.

López-Calo, José, ed.
1966 *Presente e futuro della musica sacra: Conferenze pronunciate alla Radio Vaticana.* Rome: Desclée.

Lord, Albert B.
1960 *The Singer of Tales.* Cambridge, Mass.: Harvard University Press. Reprinted New York: Atheneum, 1965, 1974.

Love, Harold
1984 "The Ranking of Variants in the Analysis of Moderately Contaminated Manuscript Traditions." *Studies in Bibliography* 37:39–57.

Luey, Beth
1990 *Editing Texts and Documents: An Annotated Bibliography.* Madison, Wisconsin: Madison House.

Lütolf, Max, ed.
1987 *Das Graduale von Santa Cecilia in Trastevere (1071) (Cod. Bodmer 74)*. 2 vols. Cologny-Geneva: Fondation Martin Bodmer.

Maas, Paul
1958 *Textual Criticism*. Transl. Barbara Flower. Oxford: Clarendon. Originally published as *Textkritik*. 3rd ed. Leipzig: B. G. Teubner, 1957.

Macdowell, Diane
1986 *Theories of Discourse: An Introduction*. Oxford: Basil Blackwell.

Madrignac, André
1986 "Les formules centons des *Alleluia* anciens." *Etudes grégoriennes* 21:27–45.

Mahling, Christoph-Hellmut
1972 "Die Ausführenden der Kirchenmusik im Mittelalter." In Fellerer 1972:409–15.

Mahling, Christoph-Hellmut, and Sigfrid Wiesmann, eds.
1984 *Gesellschaft für Musikforschung: Bericht über der Internationalen Musikwissenschaftlichen Kongress Bayreuth 1981*. Kassel: Bärenreiter.

Mallion, Jean
1964 *Chartres: Le jubé de la cathédrale*. Chartres: Société Archéologique d'Eure-et-Loir.

Mallory, J. P.
1989 *In Search of the Indo-Europeans: Language, Archaeology and Myth*. London: Thames and Hudson.

Mannion, M. Francis
1988 "Liturgy and the Present Crisis of Culture." *Worship* 62: 98–123.
1990 "The Need for an Adequate Liturgical Musicology." *Worship* 64:78–81.

Marcusson, O.
1979 "Comment a-t-on chanté les prosules? Observations sur la technique des tropes de l'alleluia." *Revue de Musicologie* 65:119–59.

Margot, Jean-Claude
1979 *Traduire sans trahir: La théorie de la traduction et son application aux textes bibliques*. Lausanne: L'Age d'Homme.

Markham, Elizabeth J.
1985 "Tunes from Tang China at Court in Temple in 'Medieval' Japan: First Steps toward Reading Early Japanese Neumatic Notations." *Trends and Perspectives in Musicology: Proceedings of the World Music Conference of the International Music Council October 3–5, 1983*, 117–39. Publications Issued by

the Royal Swedish Academy of Music 48. Stockholm: Kungl. Musikaliska Akademien.

Markham, Elizabeth J., L. E. R. Picken, R. F. Wolpert
1988 "Pieces for *biwa* in calendrically correct tunings, from a manuscript in the Heian Museum, Kyōto." *Musica Asiatica* 5: 191–209.

Marrett, Allan
1985 "Tōgaku: Where have the Tang melodies gone, and where have the new melodies come from?" *Ethnomusicology* 29:409–31.
1986 "In search of the lost melodies of Tang China: an account of recent research and its implications for the history and analysis of Tōgaku." *Musicology Australia* 9:29–38.
1988 "An investigation of sources for *Chū Ōga ryūteki yōroku-fu*, a Japanese flute score of the fourteenth century." *Musica Asiatica* 5:210–67.

Martinić, Jerko
1981 *Glagolitische Gesänge Mitteldalmatiens.* 2 vols. Kölner Beiträge zur Musikforschung 103. Regensburg: Bosse.

Mateos, Juan
1962 *Le Typicon de la grande église* 1: *Le cycle des douze mois.* Orientalia Christiana Analecta 165. Rome: Pontificium Institutum Orientalium Studiorum.

Mathews, Thomas F.
1982 "Architecture, Liturgical Aspects." *Dictionary of the Middle Ages* 1:441–5.

Mathiesen, Thomas J.
1990 "Ars Critica and Fata Libellorum: The Significance of Codicology to Text Critical Theory." *Music Theory and Its Sources: Antiquity and the Middle Ages,* 19–37. Ed. André Barbera. Notre Dame, Indiana: University of Notre Dame Press.

McCormick, Michael
1985 "Analyzing Imperial Ceremonies." *Jahrbuch der österreichischen Byzantinistik* 35:1–20.

McGann, Jerome J., ed.
1985 *Textual Criticism and Literary Interpretation.* Chicago: University of Chicago.

McGinn, Bernard, John Meyendorff, and Jean Leclercq, eds.
1985 *Christian Spirituality: Origins to the Twelfth Century.* World Spirituality: An Encyclopedic History of the Religious Quest. New York: Crossroad.

McKinnon, James W.
1983 "Fifteenth-Century Northern Book Painting and the *a cappella* Question: An Essay in Iconographic Method." *Studies in the Performance of Late Medieval Music,* 1–17. Stanley Boorman, ed. New York: Cambridge University Press.

1987 *Music in Early Christian Literature.* Cambridge Readings in the Literature of Music. Cambridge University Press.

1990 "The Emergence of Gregorian Chant in the Carolingian Era." In McKinnon, ed. 1990:88–119.

McKinnon, James, ed.

1990 *Antiquity and the Middle Ages from Ancient Greece to the Fifteenth Century.* Music and Society. Englewood, New Jersey: Prentice Hall.

McKitterick, Rosamond

1989 *The Carolingians and the Written Word.* Cambridge University Press.

McKitterick, Rosamond, ed.

1990 *The Uses of Literacy in Early Medieval Europe.* Cambridge University Press.

McLeod, Norma, and Marcia Herndon, eds.

1980 *The Ethnography of Musical Performance.* Norwood, Penn.: Norwood Editions.

McLuhan, Marshall

1989 *The Global Village: Transformations in World Life and Media in the Twenty-first Century.* New York: Oxford University Press.

Meeûs, Francis de

1960 "Pour l'édition critique du graduel romain." *Scriptorium* 14: 80–97.

Meier, Bernhard

1969 "Modale Korrektur und Wortausdeutung im Choral der Editio Medicaea," *Kirchenmusikalisches Jahrbuch* 53:101–32.

Menard, René.

1952 "Note sur les musiques arabe et copte." *Les Cahiers Coptes* 2:48–54.

1959 "Notes sur la mémorisation et l'improvisation dans le chant copte." *Etudes grégoriennes* 3:135–43.

1972 "Die Gesänge der ägyptischen Liturgien." In Fellerer, ed. 1972: 109–27.

Merriam, Alan P.

1982 "On Objections to Comparison in Ethnomusicology." *Cross Cultural Perspectives on Music: Essays in Memory of Mieczyslaw Kolinski,* 174–89. Ed. Robert Falck and Timothy Rice. Toronto: University of Toronto Press.

Metz, René

1987 "Monasticism, Origins." *Dictionary of the Middle Ages* 8:459–62.

Metzger, Bruce M.

1968 *The Text of the New Testament: Its Transmission, Corruption, and Restoration.* 2nd ed. Oxford: Clarendon.

Meyendorff, John
1983 "Clergy, Byzantine." *Dictionary of the Middle Ages* 3:446–7.
Meyer, Hans Bernard, and Rudolf Pacik, eds.
1981 *Dokumente zur Kirchenmusik unter besonderer Berücksichtigung des deutschen Sprachgebietes.* Regensburg: Pustet.
Mezei, János
1990 "Zur Problematik des 'germanischen' Choraldialekts." In Dobszay et al. 1990:49–60.
Miazga, Tadeusz
1980 *Graduał Jana Olbrachta: Studium muzykologiczne.* [The Gradual of Jan Olbracht: A Musicological Study (in Polish)]. Graz: Akademische Druck.
Mies, Paul
1932 "Stabat mater dolorosa: Probleme und Grundlagen für eine Untersuchung über das Verhältnis von textlicher und musikalischer Struktur." *Kirchenmusikalisches Jahrbuch* 27:146–53.
1933 "Stabat mater dolorosa: Das Verhältnis von textlicher und musikalischer Struktur im Wandel der Zeiten." *Kirchenmusikalisches Jahrbuch* 28:35–76.
Migne, Jacques-Paul, ed.
1844–55 *Patrologiae Cursus Completus . . . Series Latina.* 217 vols. Paris: J.-P. Migne. Numerous reprints.
Milanese, Guido
1987 "Testo e formula: Due saggi d'indagine." *Studi Gregoriani* 3:129–57.
Miller, Terry E.
1984 "Oral Tradition Psalmody Surviving in England and Scotland." *The Hymn* 35:15–22.
Moeller, Hartmut
1984 "Auf dem Weg zur Rekonstruktion des Antiphonale S. Gregorii? Kritisches zu den Klassifizierungen des *Corpus Antiphonalium Officii.*" *Die Musikforschung* 37:207–15.
Moines de Solesmes
1957–62 *Le Graduel romain: Edition critique par les moines de Solesmes.* 2: *Les Sources.* 1957. 4: *Le Texte neumatique.* 2 parts. [1960?], 1962. Solesmes: Abbaye de Saint-Pierre.
Molitor, Raphael
1901–2 *Die Nach-Tridentinische Choral-Reform: Ein Beitrag zur Musikgeschichte des. XVI. und XVII. Jahrhunderts.* 2 vols. Leipzig: F. E. C. Leuckart.
1904 *Our Position: A Word in Reference to the Plainchant Question.* New York: F. Pustet.
Monachi Abbatiae Sancti Hieronymi
1926– *Biblia Sacra iuxta latinam vulgatam versionem ad codicum fidem . . . cura et studio monachorum Abbatiae Pontificiae*

Sancti Hieronymi in Urbe Ordinis Sancti Benedicti edita. Rome: Typis Polyglottis Vaticanis.

Moneta Caglio, Ernesto
1960–3 "Dom André Mocquereau e la restaurazione del Canto Gregoriano." *Musica Sacra: Rivista Bismestrale* (Milan) 84 (2nd ser. 5):2–17, 34–49, 98–117, 130–42, 162–72; 85 (2nd ser. 6):8–20, 34–46, 68–87, 151–9; 86 (2nd ser. 7):70–84, 108–18; 87 (2nd ser. 8):4–16, 38–50, 75–85.

Moran, Neil K.
1980 "The Chant 'Crucem tuam' in the Byzantine, Slavonic, and Latin Recension." *Studies in Music from the University of Western Ontario* 5:35–48.

Murphy, William P.
1978 "Oral Literature." *Annual Review of Anthropology* 7: 113–36.

Murray, Gregory
1977 *Music and the Mass: A Personal History.* Essex, England: Kevin Mayhew.

Musch, Hans, ed.
1975 *Musik im Gottesdienst: ein Handbuch zur Grundausbildung in der katholischen Kirchenmusik, im Auftrag der Konferenz der Leiter katholischer Kirchenmusikalischer Ausbildungsstätten Deutschlands.* Regensburg: Gustav Bosse.

Nagy, Gregory
1989 "Early Greek Views of Poets and Poetry." *The Cambridge History of Literary Criticism* 1: *Classical Criticism,* 1–77. Ed. George A. Kennedy. Cambridge University Press.

Ne'eman, Yehoshua L. [also Joshua L.]
1966–7 *Qera Beta'am* [Read with Cantillation]: *A Textbook for Reading the Biblical Text according to the Traditional Cantillation* [in Hebrew with English title pages]. Vol. 1 in 2 parts. Jerusalem: Israel Institute for Sacred Music.
1968–9 *Nosaḥ laḥazan* [Chant for the Cantor]: *The Traditional Chant of the Synagogue According to the Lithuanian-Jerusalem Musical Tradition* 2: *Sabbath Service* [in Hebrew with English title page]. Jerusalem: Israel Institute for Sacred Music.
1972 *Nosaḥ laḥazan* [Chant for the Cantor]: *The Traditional Chant of the Synagogue According to the Lithuanian-Jerusalem Musical Tradition* 1: *Complete Service for the High Holidays* [in Hebrew with English title page]. Revised ed. Jerusalem: Israel Institute for Sacred Music. First ed. 1963.

Nelson, Janet L.
1986 *Politics and Ritual in Early Medieval Europe.* London: Hambledon Press.

Nelson, Kristina
1982 "Reciter and Listener: Some Factors Shaping the Majawwad Style of Qur'ānic Reciting." *Ethnomusicology* 26:41–7.
1985 *The Art of Reciting the Qur'ān*. University of Texas at Austin Modern Middle East Series 11. Austin: University of Texas Press.

Nelson, Steven G.
1986 *Documentary Sources of Japanese Music*. Tokyo: Research Archives for Japanese Music, Ueno Gakuen College.

Nemmers, Erwin Esser
1949 *Twenty Centuries of Catholic Church Music*. Milwaukee: Bruce.

Nersessian, Vrej, ed.
1978 *Essays on Armenian Music*. London: Institute of Armenian Music.

Nettl, Bruno
1981 "Some Notes on the State of Knowledge about Oral Transmission and Music." In Heartz and Wade 1981: 139–144.
1982 "Types of Tradition and Transmission." *Cross-Cultural Perspectives on Music: Essays in Memory of Mieczyslaw Kolinski*, 3–19. Ed. Robert Falck and Timothy Rice. Toronto: University of Toronto Press.
1983 *The Study of Ethnomusicology: Twenty-Nine Issues and Concepts*. Urbana: University of Illinois Press.

Neunheuser, Burkhard
1987 "Liturgiewissenschaft: Exakte Geschichtsforschung oder (und) Theologie der Liturgie?" *Ecclesia Orans* 4:87–102.
1989 "Handbücher der Liturgiewissenschaft, in den grossen europäischen Sprachen, 25 Jahre nach SC, der Liturgiekonstitution des 2. Vatikanums." *Ecclesia Orans* 6:89–103.

The New Grove Dictionary of Music and Musicians
1980 Ed. Stanley Sadie. 20 vols. 6th ed. London: Macmillan.

Nichols, Stephen G., ed.
1990 "The New Philology." Theme issue of *Speculum* 65/1:1–108.

Nida, Eugene A., and Charles R. Taber, eds.
1969 *The Theory and Practice of Translation*. United Bible Societies Helps for Translators 8. Leiden: E. J. Brill.

Nowacki, Edward
1980 "Studies on the Office Antiphons of the Old Roman Manuscripts." Ph.D. dissertation, Brandeis University, 1980. 2 vols.
1981 "The Syntactical Analysis of Plainchant." In Heartz and Wade 1981:191–201.
1985–6 "The Gregorian Office Antiphons and the Comparative Method." *The Journal of Musicology* 4:243–75.

1986 "Text Declamation as a Determinant of Melodic Form in the Old Roman Eighth-Mode Tracts." *Early Music History* 6: 193–226.

Nulman, Macy
1984–5 "The Shirah Melody in the Ashkenazic and Sephardic Traditions." *Journal of Jewish Music and Liturgy* 7: 12–21. Reprinted in M. Nulman, *Concepts of Jewish Music and Prayer,* 137–45. New York: Cantorial Council of America at Yeshiva University, 1985.

Olsen, Poul Rovsing
1981 "Melodic Structures in Traditional Music." In Heartz and Wade 1981: 145–51.

Oltolina, Carlo
1984 *I salmi di tradizione orale delle valli orsolane.* Musica liturgica tradizionale. Milan: Ricordi.

Omanson, Roger L.
1990 "Dynamic-Equivalence Translations Reconsidered." *Theological Studies* 51: 497–505.

Onasch, Konrad
1981 *Liturgie und Kunst der Ostkirche in Stichworten unter Berücksichtigung der Alten Kirche.* Leipzig: Koehler & Amelang.

Ong, Walter J.
1982 *Orality and Literacy: The Technologizing of the Word.* New Accents. London and New York: Methuen.

d'Ortigue, M. J.
1854 "Machicotage." *Dictionnaire liturgique, historique et théorique de plain-chant et de musique d'église au moyen age et dans les temps modernes,* 765–7. Paris: L. Potier. Reprinted New York: Da Capo Press, 1971.

Ottosen, Knud
1973 "Le problématique de l'édition des textes liturgiques latins." *Classica et mediaevalia Francisco Blatt septuagenario dedicata,* 541–56. Ed. O. S. Due, H. Friis Johansen, and B. Dalsgaard Larsen. Classica et Mediaevalia, Dissertationes 9. Copenhagen: Gyldendal.

1986 *L'antiphonaire latin au moyen-âge: Réorganisation des séries de répons de l'Avent classés par R.-J. Hesbert.* Rerum Ecclesiasticarum Documenta, extra seriem. Rome: Herder.

Oura, Yoko, and Giyoo Hatano
1988 "Memory for Melodies among Subjects Differing in Age and Experience in Music." *Psychology of Music* 16: 91–109.

Outtier, Bernard
1973 "Recherches sur la genèse de l'octoéchos arménien III: Etude critique des documents présentés." *Etudes grégoriennes* 14:

181–211, from which it is cited here. Reprinted in Nersessian, ed. 1978: 102–28.
1985 "Les chants des églises du Caucase: Musiques géorgienne et arménienne," *Le monde de la Bible* 37 (Jan.–Feb. 1985) 46–7.

Overath, Johannes, ed.
1969 *Sacred Music and Liturgy Reform after Vatican II: Proceedings of the Fifth International Church Music Congress, Chicago-Milwaukee, August 21–28, 1966.* Rome: Consociatio Internationalis Musicae Sacrae.

Palikarova Verdeil, R.
1953 *La musique byzantine chez les Bulgares et les Russes (du IXe au XIVe siècle).* Monumenta Musicae Byzantinae, Subsidia 3. Copenhagen: Ejnar Munksgaard; and Boston: Byzantine Institute.

Pandian, Jacob
1991 *Culture, Religion and the Sacred Self: A Critical Introduction to the Anthropological Study of Religion.* Englewood Cliffs, New Jersey: Prentice Hall.

Papp, Štefan, and Nikifor Petraševič.
1970 *Irmologion grekokatolícky liturgicky' spiv eparchiji Mukačevskoji.* [Greek-Catholic Liturgical Irmologion for the Eparchy of Mukachëvo (in Czech and Old Slavonic)]. Prešov, Czechoslovakia: Greko-katolickij Ordinariat.

Paradisi, Bruno, ed.
1971 *La Critica del testo: Atti del Secondo Congresso Internazionale della Società Italiana di Storia del Diritto.* 2 vols. Florence: Leo S. Olschki.

Parry, Milman
1971 *The Making of Homeric Verse: The Collected Papers of Milman Parry.* Ed. Adam Parry. Oxford: Clarendon Press.

Pasquali, Giorgio
1962 *Storia della tradizione e critica del testo.* 2nd ed. Florence: Felice le Monnier.

Patterson, Lee
1987 *Negotiating the Past: The Historical Understanding of Medieval Literature.* Madison: The University of Wisconsin Press, 1987.

Paxton, Frederick S.
1990 *Christianizing Death: The Creation of a Ritual Process in Early Medieval Europe.* Ithaca, New York: Cornell University Press.

Pedrell, Felipe
1905 "La Festa d'Elche ou le drame lyrique liturgique: Le trépas et l'Assomption de la Vierge." *La Tribune de Saint-Gervais* 11: 289–322, 353–68.

Pĕnije
1914 *Pĕnije Rimskago Misala po Izdaniju Vatikanskomu.* [Chants of the Roman Missal according to the Vatican Edition (in Serbo-Croatian, Italian, Old Slavonic)]. Publicationes Academiae Palaeoslavicae Veglensis. Rome: Tipi Vatikanskimi.

Petrescu [Trebici-Marin], Hrisanta
1982 "The Relation Text-Melodical and Rhythmical Formulas, an Element of Continuity in the Romanian Post-Medieval Church Music." In Raasted, ed. 1982:109–18.

Petrobelli, Pierluigi, ed.
1980 *Le Polifonie Primitive in Cividale: Congresso Internazionale Le Polifonie Primitive in Friuli e in Europa, 22–23–24 Agosto 1980.* Cividale del Friuli: Associazione per lo Sviluppo degli Studi Storici ed Artistici di Cividale del Friuli.

Peyrot, J.
1913 "Autour des grands traités: Deux traités d''improvisation chorale' au XVIIIe siècle." *La Tribune de Saint-Gervais* 19:236–8.

Philipp, Margot Lieth, ed.
1989 *Ethnomusicology and the Historical Dimension: Papers Presented at the European Seminar in Ethnomusicology, London, May 20–23 1986.* Ludwigsburg, West Germany: Philipp Verlag.

Phillips, Nancy
1983 Review of Schmid 1981. *Journal of the American Musicological Society* 36:128–42.

Picken, Laurence, et multi al., eds.
1981 *Music from the Tang Court* 1. London: Oxford University Press.
1985– *Music from the Tang Court* 2–. Cambridge University Press.

Pinell i Pons, Jordi
1984 "Repertorio del 'Sacrificium' (canto offertorial del rito hispanico) para el ciclo dominical 'De quotidiano.'" *Ecclesia Orans* 1:57–111.

Pirrotta, Nino
1966 "Music and Cultural Tendencies in Fifteenth-Century Italy." *Journal of the American Musicological Society* 19:127–61. Reprinted in Pirrotta 1984:80–112, 382–91.
1970 "Tradizione orale e tradizione scritta della musica." *L'Ars Nova Italiana del Trecento* 3: *Secondo Convegno Internazionale 17–22 luglio 1969,* 431–41. Ed. F. Alberto Gallo. Certaldo: Centro di Studi sull'Ars Nova Italiana del Trecento. Reprinted in Pirrotta 1984:72–9, 380–2.
1972 "New Glimpses of an Unwritten Tradition." *Words and Music: The Scholar's View: A Medley of Problems and Solutions Compiled in Honor of A. Tillman Merritt,* 271–91. Ed. Laur-

ence Berman. Cambridge, Mass.: Harvard University Department of Music. Reprinted with an appendix in Pirrotta 1984:51–71, 377–80.

1984 *Music and Culture in Italy from the Middle Ages to the Baroque.* Cambridge, Mass.: Harvard University Press.

1985 "Back to Ars Nova Themes." *Music and Context: Essays for John Ward,* 166–79. Ed. Anne Dhu Shapiro. Cambridge, Mass.: Harvard University Music Department.

Pitman, Mary Anne, Rivka A. Eisikovits, Marion Lundy Dobbert, eds.

1989 *Culture Acquisition: A Holistic Approach to Human Learning.* New York: Praeger.

Planchart, Alejandro

1988 "On the Nature of Transmission and Change in Trope Repertories." *Journal of the American Musicological Society* 41:215–49.

Pol-Topis, Margaret, Kevin Donovan, Christopher Willcock, and Paul Inwood, eds. and transl.

1979 *Growing in Church Music: Proceedings of a Meeting on "Why Church Music?" Conducted by the Society of St. Gregory and Universa Laus, Strawberry Hill, London, England.* Washington, D.C.: Universa Laus English Edition; National Association of Pastoral Musicians.

Porter, Lewis

1985 "John Coltrane's *A Love Supreme:* Jazz Improvisation as Composition." *Journal of the American Musicological Society* 38:591–621.

Potier, Francis

1939 "L'Art d'accompagnement du chant grégorien" 10: "Petit essai d'histoire de l'accompagnement." *Revue grégorienne* 24:97–109, 186–91, 214–21.

Powers, Harold S.

1980a "Mode." *The New Grove Dictionary* 12:376–450.

1980b "Language Models and Musical Analysis." *Ethnomusicology* 24:1–60.

1988 "First Meeting of the ICTM Study Group on Maqam." *Yearbook for Traditional Music* 20:199–218.

Pressing, Jeff

1988 "Improvisation: Methods and Models." In Sloboda, ed. 1988: 129–78.

Prim, Jean

1961 "*Chant sur le Livre* in French Churches in the Eighteenth Century." *Journal of the American Musicological Society* 14:37–49.

Quilici, Félix

1971 "Polyphonies vocales traditionnelles en Corse." *Revue de musicologie* 57:3–10.

Quinn, Frank C.
1989 "Music in Catholic Worship: The Effect of Ritual on Music and Music on Ritual." *Proceedings of the Annual Meeting of the North American Academy of Liturgy, Nashville, Tennessee, 2–5 January 1989*, 161–76. Valparaiso, Indiana: North American Academy of Liturgy.

Raasted, Jørgen
1979a "Musical Notation and Quasi Notation in Syro-Melkite Liturgical Manuscripts." *Université de Copenhague, Cahiers de l'Institut du Moyen-âge grec et latin* 31 : 11–37, 53–77.
1979b "Byzantine Chant in Popular Tradition." *Université de Copenhague, Cahiers de l'Institut du Moyen-âge grec et latin* 31 : 39–49, 78–81.
1983 "Troping Techniques in Byzantine Chant." In Iversen, ed. 1983, 89–98.

Raasted, Jørgen, ed.
1982 *Symposion für Musikologie: Byzantinische Musik 1453–1832 als Quelle musikalischer Praxis und Theorie vor 1453*. XVI. Internationaler Byzantinistenkongress, Wien, 4.–9. Oktober 1981: Akten II/7. Jahrbuch der österreichischen Byzantinistik 32/7. Vienna: Verlag der österreichischen Akademie der Wissenschaften.

Raes, Alfonso.
1952 "La Connaissance des liturgies orientales et de leur chant." In Anglès, ed. 1952 : 23–6.

Raghaven, V.
1954 "The Music of the Hebrews: Resemblances to Sama Veda Chant." *Journal of the Music Academy, Madras* 25 : 109–11.

Rainoldi, Felice
1981 "Le document Universa Laus 1980 dans l'histoire de la musique de l'église." *La Maison-Dieu* 145 (1981, no. 1):25–48.

Rajeczky, Benjamin
1956a *Melodiarum Hungariae Medii Aevi* 1: *Hymni et Sequentiae*. 2nd rev. ed. Budapest: Editio Musica, 1976.
1956b "Parallelen spätgregorianischer Verzierungen im ungarischen Volkslied." *Studia Memoriae Belae Bartók Sacra,* ed. Benjamin Rajeczky and Lajos Vargyas, 337–48. Budapest: Akadémiai Kiadó.
1969a "Zur Frage der Verzierung im Choral." *Studia Musicologica Academiae Scientiarum Hungariae* 11 : 349–53.
1969b "Gregorián, Népének, Népdal [Gregorian Chant, Popular Religious Song, Folksong (in Hungarian with English Summary)]." *Magyar Zenetörténeti Tanulmányok: Szabolcsi Bence 70. Születésnapjára,* ed. Ferenc Bónis, 35–64, 405. Budapest: Zenemukiado.

1973 "Europäische Volksmusik und Musik des Mittelalters." *Studia Musicologica Academiae Scientiarum Hungaricae* 15:201–4.

1974 "Choralforschung und Volksmusik des Mittelalters?" *Acta Musicologica* 46:181–92.

1975 "Gregorianik und Volksgesang." *Handbuch des Volksliedes 2: Historisches und Systematisches—Interethnische Beziehungen—Musikethnologie,* ed. Rolf Wilhelm Brednich, Lutz Röhrich, Wolfgang Suppan, 391–405. Munich: Wilhelm Fink.

1982 *Melodiarum Hungariae Medii Aevi* 2: *Supplementband.* Budapest: Editio Musica, 1982.

1984 "Ungarn: Choral im Volksmunde." *Musikalische Volkskunde—Aktuell: Festschrift für Ernst Klusen zum 75. Geburtstag,* 375–90. Ed. Günther Noll and Marianne Bröcker. Bonn am Rhein: Peter Wegener.

1985 "Gregorianische Gesänge in der ungarischen Volkstradition." *Studia Musicologica Academiae Scientarum Hungaricae* 27: 5–22.

1990 "Trends der heutigen Choralforschung." In Dobszay et al., eds. 1990:93–8.

Randel, Don M.

1969 *The Responsorial Psalm Tones for the Mozarabic Office.* Princeton Studies in Music 3. Princeton University Press.

Rankin, Susan

1981 "The Mary Magdalene Scene in the *Visitatio Sepulchri* Ceremonies." *Early Music History* 1:227–55.

1984 "From Memory to Record: Musical Notations in Manuscripts from Exeter." *Anglo-Saxon England* 13:97–112.

1989 *The Music of the Medieval Liturgical Drama in France and England.* 2 vols. Outstanding Dissertations in Music from British Universities. New York and London: Garland.

Rapson, Penelope

1989 *A Technique for Identifying Textual Errors and Its Application to the Sources of Music by Thomas Tallis.* 2 vols. Outstanding Dissertations in Music from British Universities. New York and London: Garland.

Rasmussen, Niels Krogh

1983 "Quelques réflexions sur la théologie des tropes." In Iversen, ed. 1983:77–88.

Ratzinger, Joseph

1986 *The Feast of Faith: Approaches to a Theology of the Liturgy.* Transl. Graham Harrison. San Francisco: Ignatius Press. Originally published as *Das Fest des Glaubens: Versuche zur Theologie des Gottesdienstes.* Einsiedeln, Switzerland: Johannes Verlag, 1981.

Ravina, Menashe
1963 *Organum and the Samaritans.* Tel Aviv: Israel Music Institute.

Reckow, Fritz
1984 "Zur Formung einer europäischen musikalischen Kultur im Mittelalter: Kriterien und Faktoren ihrer Geschichtlichkeit." In Mahling and Wiesmann, eds. 1984: 12–29.

Reimer, Erich
1978 "Musicus—cantor." In Eggebrecht, ed. 1972–.

Renfrew, Colin
1987 *Archaeology and Language: The Puzzle of Indo-European Origins.* New York: Cambridge University Press.

Revell, E. J.
1977 *Biblical Texts with Palestinian Pointing and Their Accents.* Society of Biblical Literature, Masoretic Studies 4. Missoula, Montana: Scholars Press.

1979 "Hebrew Accents and Greek Ekphonetic Neumes." *Studies in Eastern Chant* 4: 140–70. Crestwood, New York: St. Vladimir's Seminary Press.

Reynolds, Christopher
1984 "Musical Careers, Ecclesiastical Benefices, and the Example of Johannes Brunet." *Journal of the American Musicological Society* 37: 49–97.

Reynolds, L. D., and N. G. Wilson
1974 *Scribes and Scholars: A Guide to the Transmission of Greek and Latin Literature.* 2nd edition revised. Oxford: Clarendon Press.

Ribay, Bernard
1988 "Les graduels en IIA." *Etudes grégoriennes* 22: 43–107.

Rice, Timothy, Kay Kaufman Shelemay, Anthony Seeger, Ellen Koskoff, Dane L. Harwood, and Richard Crawford
1987 "Toward the Remodeling of Ethnomusicology." *Ethnomusicology* 31: 469–516

Riché, Pierre
1976 *Education and Culture in the Barbarian West, Sixth through Eighth Centuries.* Transl. John J. Contreni. Columbia: University of South Carolina Press. Originally published as *Education et culture dans l'occidnet barbare VIe–VIIIe siècles.* Patristica Sorbonensia 4. Paris: Editions du Seuil, 1962.

Richter, Ämilius Ludwig, and Friedberg, Emil Albert, eds.
1922 *Corpus Juris Canonici.* 2nd ed. 2 vols. Leipzig: Bernhard Tauchnitz.

Riedel, Johannes
1980 *Leise Settings of the Renaissance and Reformation Era.* Recent Researches in the Music of the Renaissance 35. Madison, Wisconsin: A-R Editions.

Riedinger, Anita
1985 "The Old English Formula in Context." *Speculum* 60:294–317.
Ringer, Alexander L.
1981 "Oral Transmission and Literacy: the Biblical Connection." In Heartz and Wade, eds. 1981:423–5.
Roberts, Colin Henderson
1938 *Catalogue of the Greek and Latin Papyri in the John Rylands Library, Manchester* 3: *Theological and Literary Texts (Nos. 457–551)*. Manchester: University Press.
Robertson, Anne Walters
1988 "*Benedicamus Domino:* The Unwritten Tradition." *Journal of the American Musicological Society* 41:1–62.
Robertson, Marian
1984 "The Reliability of the Oral Tradition in Preserving Coptic Music, Part II: A Comparison of Three Musical Transcriptions of an Extract from the Liturgy of St. Basil." *Bulletin de la Société d'Archéologie Copte* 26:83–93.
1985 "The Reliability of the Oral Tradition in Preserving Coptic Music: A Comparison of Two Recordings of the Hymn *Tenouosht* . . . . " *Bulletin de la Société d'Archéologie Copte* 27:73–85.
1987 "Ernest Newlandsmith's Transcriptions of Coptic Music: A Description and Critique." *Diakonia* 21:190–8.
Roccasalvo, Joan L.
1986 *The Plainchant Tradition of Southwestern Rus'*. East European Monographs 202. Boulder, Colorado: East European Monographs; New York: Columbia University Press.
Rohloff, Ernst, ed.
[1967] *Die Quellenhandschriften zum Musiktraktat des Johannes de Grocheo*. Leipzig: VEB Deutscher Verlag für Musik.
Römer, Markus
1983 *Schriftliche und mündliche Traditionen geistlicher Gesänge auf Korsika*. Wiesbaden: Franz Steiner.
Romita, Fiorenzo
1936 *Ius Musicae Liturgicae: Dissertatio Historico-Iuridica*. Turin: Marietti.
1947 *Ius Musicae Liturgicae: Dissertatio Historico-Iuridica*. 2nd ed. Bibliotheca "Ephemerides Liturgicae" Sectio Practica 2. Rome: Ephemerides Liturgicae.
1952 *Codex Juris Musicae Sacrae*. Rome: Desclée.
Rosowsky, Solomon
1957 *The Cantillation of the Bible: The Five Books of Moses*. New York: Reconstructionist Press.

Ross, Israel J.
1979 "Ritual and Music in South India: Syrian Christian Liturgical Music in Kerala." *Asian Music* 11/1:80–98.

Rubio, Samuel
1965 "La música del 'Misterio' de Elche." *Tesoro Sacro Musicale* 4:61–71.
1968 "Más esclarcimientos entorno a la música del 'Misterio' de Elche." *Tesoro Sacro Musicale* 5:83–4.

Sachs, Curt
1960 "Primitive and Medieval Music: A Parallel." *Journal of the American Musicological Society* 13:43–9.
1962 *The Wellsprings of Music*, ed. Jaap Kunst. The Hague: Martinus Nijhoff; repr. New York: Da Capo Press, 1977.

Sachs, Klaus-Jürgen
1983 "Arten improvisierter Mehrstimmigkeit nach Lehrtexten des 14. bis 16. Jahrhunderts." *Basler Jahrbuch für historische Musikpraxis* 7:166–83.

Sahlins, Marshall David
1981 *Historical Metaphors of Mythical Realities: Structure in the Early History of the Sandwich Islands Kingdom*. A[ssociation for] S[ocial] A[nthropology in] O[ceania] Special Publications 1. Ann Arbor: University of Michigan Press.

Salvo, Bartolomeo Di
1952 "La tradizione orale dei canti liturgici delle colonie Italo-Albanesi di Sicilia comparata con quella dei codici antichi bizantini." In Anglès, ed. 1952:129–30.

Śarana, Gopala
1975 *The Methodology of Anthropological Comparisons: An Analysis of Comparative Methods in Social and Cultural Anthropology*. Viking Fund Publications in Anthropology 53. Tucson: University of Arizona Press.

Sarason, Richard S.
1981 "The Modern Study of Jewish Liturgy" and "Recent Developments in the Study of Jewish Liturgy." *The Study of Ancient Judaism* I: *Mishnah, Midrash, Siddur*, ed. Jacob Neusner, 107–79, 180–7. New York: Ktav.
1983 "Religion and Worship: The Case of Judaism." *Take Judaism, for Example: Studies toward the Comparison of Religions*, ed. Jacob Neusner, 49–65. Chicago: University of Chicago Press.

Sava, Stela
1984 *Die Gesänge des altrussischen Oktoechos samt den Evangelien-Stichiren: Eine Neumenhandschrift des Altgläubigen-Klosters zu Bélaja Kriníca*. 2 vols. Studien zur Volksmusik und aussereuropäischen Kunstmusik 9. Munich and Salzburg: E. Katzbichler.

Sawa, George Dimitri
1987 "Music, Islamic Attitudes Toward." *Dictionary of the Middle Ages* 8:559–61.
1989 *Music Performance in the Early ʿAbbāsid Era, 132–320 AH / 750–932 AD*. Studies and Texts 92. Toronto: Pontifical Institute of Medieval Studies.

Scalia, Giuseppe, ed.
1966 *Salimbene De Adam: Cronica*. 2 vols. Scrittori d'Italia 232–3. Bari: Laterza.

Schalz, Nicolas
1971 "La notion de 'Musique Sacrée': Une tradition récente." *La Maison-Dieu* 108 (1971, no. 4):32–57.
1985 "'Musique sacrée': Naissance et évolution d'un concept." *La Maison-Dieu* 161 (1985, no. 1):87–104.

Schmemann, Alexander
1986 *Introduction to Liturgical Theology*. Transl. Asheleigh E. Moorhouse. Crestwood, New York: St. Vladimir's Seminary Press.

Schmid, Hans
1981 *Musica et Scolica enchiriadis, una cum aliquibus tractatulis adiunctis*. Bayerische Akademie der Wissenschaften: Veröffentlichungen der musikhistorischen Kommission 3. Munich: Verlag der Bayerischen Akademie der Wissenschaften, in Kommission bei der C. H. Beck'schen Verlagsbuchhandlung.

Schmidt, Christopher
1980 "Modus und Melodiegestalt: Untersuchungen zu Offiziumsantiphonen." *Basler Studien zur Interpretation der alten Musik*, 13–43. Forum Musicologicum 2. Winterthur: Amadeus.
1983 "Form in der Organalen Improvisation." *Basler Jahrbuch für historische Musikpraxis* 7:11–22.

Schmidt, Hans
1979 *Zum Formelhaften Aufbau byzantinischer Kanones*. Wiesbaden: Breitkopf & Härtel.
1980 "Gregorianik—Legende oder Wahrheit?" *Ars Musica, Musica Scientia: Festschrift Heinrich Hüschen*, ed. Detlef Altenburg, 400–11. Beiträge zur Rheinischen Musikgeschichte 126. Cologne: Gitarre und Laute Verlagsgesellschaft.

Schmitt, Francis P.
1977 *Church Music Transgressed: Reflections on "Reform."* New York: Seabury Press.

Schneider, Marius
1954 "Le verset 94 de la sourate VI du Coran étudié en une version populaire et en trois nagamât de tradition hispano-musulmane." *Anuario Musical* 9:80–96.

Schreiter, Robert J.
1989 "Faith and Cultures: Challenges to a World Church." *Theological Studies* 50:744–60.

Schütz, Joseph
1963 *Die handschriftliche Missale Illyricum Cyrillicum Lipsiense.* 2 vols. Bibliotheca Slavica. Wiesbaden: Otto Harrasowitz.

Schulz, Hans-Joachim
1986 *The Byzantine Liturgy: Symbolic Structure and Faith Expression.* Transl. Matthew J. O'Connell. New York: Pueblo. Originally published as *Die byzantinische Liturgie: Vom Werden ihrer Symbolgestalt.* Trier: Paulinus-Verlag, 1980.

Sciambra, Matteo
1965–6 "Caratteristiche strutturali dei canti liturgici tradizionali degli albanesi di Sicilia." *Rivista di studi bizantini e neo-ellenici* 12–13 (= n.s. 2–3) 309–20.

Scott, Marcus
1989 "The Periodization of Modern Arab Music Theory: Continuity and Change in the Definition of the Maqāmāt." *Pacific Review of Ethnomusicology* 5:35–49.

Seasoltz, R. Kevin
1966 *The New Liturgy: A Documentation, 1903–1965.* New York: Herder & Herder.
1980 *New Liturgy, New Laws.* Collegeville, Minnesota: Liturgical Press.

Seay, Albert, transl. and ed.
1974 *Johannes de Grocheo: Concerning Music (De Musica).* 2nd ed. Colorado College Music Press Translations 1. Colorado Springs: Colorado College Music Press.

Seeger, Charles
1950 "Oral Tradition in Music." *Funk and Wagnall's Standard Dictionary of Folklore, Mythology, and Legend* 2:825–9. Ed. Maria Leach. New York: Funk and Wagnall's. Reprinted in 1 vol. New York: New English Library, 1972.
1966 "Versions and Variants of 'Barbara Allen' in the Archive of the American Folk Song in the Library of Congress." *Selected Reports in Ethnomusicology* 1/1:120–67. Reprinted as "Versions and Variants of the Tunes of 'Barbara Allen.'" In C. Seeger, *Studies in Musicology 1935–1975,* 273–320. Berkeley and Los Angeles: University of California Press, 1977.

Segal, J. B.
1953 *The Diacritical Point and the Accents in Syriac.* London Oriental Series 2. London: Geoffrey Cumberledge, Oxford University Press.

Serafine, Mary Louise
1988 *Music as Cognition: The Development of Thought in Sound.* New York: Columbia University Press.
Serkoyan, Nishan
1973 "Recherches sur la genèse de l'octoéchos arménien I: Les huit modes de l'hymnaire arménien." *Etudes grégoriennes* 14: 130–60, from which it is cited here. Reprinted in Nersessian 1978: 52–82.
Shapiro, Anne Dhu
1972 "A Short Bibliography on the Tune Family Concept." *Folk Letter* 2/1: 7–8.
1975 "The Tune-Family Concept in British-American Folk-Song Scholarship." 2 vols. Ph.D. diss., Harvard University.
Sharvit, Uri
1980 "The Role of Music in the Yemenite Heder." *Israel Studies in Musicology* 2: 33–49.
1982 "The Musical Realization of Biblical Cantillation Symbols (*Ṭeʿamîm*) in the Jewish Yemenite Tradition." *Yuval: Studies of the Jewish Music Research Center* 4: 179–210. Jerusalem: Magnes Press of Hebrew University.
Shaw, R. Daniel
1988 *Transculturation: The Cultural Factor in Translation and Other Communications Tasks.* Pasadena, Calif.: William Carey Library.
1991 *Kandila: Samo Ceremonialism and Interpersonal Relationships.* Ann Arbor: University of Michigan.
Shelemay, Kay Kaufman
1986a *Music, Ritual, and Falasha History.* Ethiopian Series Monograph No. 17. East Lansing, Michigan: African Studies Center, Michigan State University.
1986b Review of Irwin, ed. 1983. *Ethnomusicology* 30: 176–8.
Shelemay, Kay Kaufman, and Peter Jeffery
forthcoming *Ethiopian Christian Chant: An Anthology.* 3 vols. and cassette tape. Recent Researches in Oral Traditions of Music 1. Madison, Wisconsin: A-R Editions.
Shelemay, Kay Kaufman, Peter Jeffery, and Ingrid Monson
forthcoming "Oral and Written Transmission in Ethiopian Christian Chant."
Shiloah, Amnon
1981 "The Arabic Concept of Mode." *Journal of the American Musicological Society* 34: 19–42.
Silagi, Gabriel, ed.
1985 *Liturgische Tropen: Referate zweier Colloquien des Corpus Troporum in München (1983) und Canterbury (1984).* Mün-

chener Beiträge zur Mediävistik und Renaissance-Forschung 36. Munich: Arbeo-Gesellschaft.

Slobin, Mark
1982 *Tenement Songs: The Popular Music of the Jewish Immigrants.* Urbana: University of Illinois Press.

Sloboda, John A.
1985 *The Musical Mind: The Cognitive Psychology of Music.* Oxford Psychology Series No. 5. Oxford University Press.
1988 "Musique et mémoire: le point de vue du psychologue." *InHarmoniques* 4: *Mémoire et création* 106–19.

Sloboda, John A., ed.
1988 *Generative Processes in Music: The Psychology of Performance, Improvisation, and Composition.* Oxford: Clarendon Press.

Sloboda, John A., and David H. H. Parker
1985 "Immediate Recall of Melodies." In Howell et al., eds. 1985: 143–167.

Smiržík, Stephen
1959 *The Glagolitic or Roman-Slavonic Liturgy.* Series Cyrillomethodiana 2. Cleveland, Ohio and Rome, Italy: Editions Slovak Institute.

Smith, Gregory Eugene
1983 "Homer, Gregory, and Bill Evans? The Theory of Formulaic Composition in the Context of Jazz Piano Improvisation." Ph.D. diss., Musicology, Harvard University.

Smith, Jonathan Z.
1987a "Dying and Rising Gods." *The Encyclopedia of Religion* 4: 521–7.
1987b *To Take Place: Toward Theory in Ritual.* Chicago Studies in the History of Judaism. Chicago: University of Chicago Press.

Smits van Waesberghe, Joseph
1932 "Chant grégorien et castagnettes." *Revue du Chant Grégorien* 36: 39–47, 84–8, 111–4.
1933 "Un dernier mot sur les 'tabulae' du moyen âge." *Revue du Chant Grégorien* 37: 88–91.
n.d. "Gregorian Chant and the Dutch Religious Folksong." In Smits van Waesberghe, *Gregorian Chant and Its Place in the Catholic Liturgy,* 59–63. Stockholm: Continental Book Co., [ca. 1947?].
1962 "Über den Ursprung der Melodie 'Nun siet uns willekommen.'" *Studien zur Musikwissenschaft* 25: 496–503.

Smoldon, William L.
1980 *The Music of the Medieval Church Dramas.* Ed. Cynthia Bourgeault. London: Oxford University Press.

Snell-Hornby, Mary

1988 *Translation Studies: An Integrated Approach.* Amsterdam and Philadelphia: John Benjamins.

Söhngen, Oskar

1967 *Theologie der Musik.* Kassel: Johannes Stauda.

Sorensen, Colin

1989 "Theme Parks and Time Machines." *The New Museology.* Ed. Peter Vergo. London: Reaktion Books.

Spector, Johanna

1965 "The Significance of Samaritan Neumes and Contemporary Practice," *Studia Musicologica Academiae Scientiarum Hungariae* 7:141–53.

1981–2 "The Role of Ethnomusicology in the Study of Jewish Music," *Musica Judaica* 4:20–31.

1984–5 "Yemenite and Babylonian Elements in the Musical Heritage of the Jews of Cochin, India." *Musica Judaica* 7:1–22.

1987 "Chanting." *The Encyclopedia of Religion* 3:204–13.

1986–7 "Chant and Cantillation." *Musica Judaica* 9:1–21.

Spieth-Weissenbacher, Christiane

1980 "Huglo, Michel." *The New Grove Dictionary* 8:768–9.

Spraycar, Rudy S.

1977 "A Reconsideration of the Oral-Formulaic Theory with Special Reference to Serbo-Croatian Oral and Written Traditions and to Medieval Heroic Poetry." Ph.D. diss., Cornell University.

Spraycar, Rudy S., and Lee F. Dunlap

1982 "Formulaic Style in Oral and Literate Epic Poetry." *Perspectives in Computing* 2/4 (December 1982) 24–33.

Stäblein, Bruno

1962 "Die Schwanenklage: Zum Problem Lai—Planctus—Sequenz." *Festschrift Karl Gustav Fellerer zum sechtzigsten Geburtstag,* 491–502. Ed. Heinrich Hüschen. Regensburg: G. Bosse. [Reprinted in Stäblein 1984:259–71.]

1975 *Schriftbild der einstimmigen Musik.* Musikgeschichte in Bildern 3: Musik des Mittelalters und der Renaissance 4. Leipzig: Deutscher Verlag für Musik.

1984 *Musik und Geschichte im Mittelalter: Gesammelte Aufsätze.* Ed. Horst Brunner and Karlheinz Schlager. Göppinger Arbeiten zur Germanistik 344. Göppingen: Kümmerle.

Stathis, Gregorios Th.

1979 "An Analysis of the Sticheron Τὸν ἥλιον κρύψαντα by Germanos, Bishop of New Patras (The Old 'Synoptic' and the New 'Analytical' Method of Byzantine Notation)." *Studies in Eastern Chant* 4:177–227. Crestwood, New York: St. Vladimir's Seminary Press.

1982 "'Δειναί Θέσεις' καί 'ἐξήγνσις'" ['Strange Modulations' and 'Exegesis' (in Greek)]. In Raasted, ed. 1982:49–62.

Stefani, Gino

1967a *L'espressione vocale e musicale nella liturgia: Gesti, riti, repertori.* Turin: Leumann.

1967b *L'acclamation de tout un peuple: Les diverses expressions vocales et chorales de la célébration liturgique.* Kinnor 9. Paris: Fleurus.

1967c "Musica sacra e regía liturgica." *Nuova Rivista Musicale Italiana* 1:744–57.

1969a "Does the Liturgy Still Need Music?" Transl. Anthony M. Buono. *The Crisis of Liturgical Reform,* 71–86. Concilium: Theology in the Age of Renewal 42.

1969b "Musica elettronica e liturgia." *Nuova Rivista Musicale Italiana* 3:934–41.

1970a "L'espressione vocale nella liturgia primitiva." *Ephemerides Liturgicae* 84:97–112.

1970b "Padre Martini e l'Eximeno: bilancio di una celebre polemica sulla musica di chiesa." *Nuova Rivista Musicale Italiana* 4: 463–81.

1971 "Bibliographie de musicologie liturgique." *La Maison-Dieu* 108:175–89.

1974 "Miti barocchi: Palestrina 'Princeps musicae.'" *Nuova Rivista Musicale Italiana* 8:374–55.

1975 "Miti barocchi: l'organo 'rè degl' istrumenti.'" *Nuova Rivista Musicale Italiana* 9:347–57.

1976 "Il mito della 'musica sacra': origini e ideologia." *Nuova Rivista Musicale Italiana* 10:23–40.

1980 "Musica, liturgia, cultura." *Nuova Rivista Musicale Italiana* 14:479–96.

Stein, Franz A., ed.

1977 *Sacerdos et Cantus Gregoriani Magister: Festschrift Ferdinand Haberl zum 70. Geburtstag.* Regensburg: Gustav Bosse Verlag.

Stenzl, Jürg

1976 "Musica sacra / heilige Musik." In Eggebrecht, ed. 1972–.

Stepanov, Stjepan, ed.

1983 *Glagoljaško Pjevanje u Poljicima kod Splita* [Glagolitic Chant in Poljicim near Split (in Serbo-Croatian)]. Spomenici Glagoljaškog Pjevanja 1. Zagreb: Jugoslavenska Akademija Znanosti I Umjetnosti.

Stevens, John

1990 "Medieval Song." *New Oxford History of Music 2: The Early Middle Ages to 1300* 357–451. Rev. ed., ed. Richard Crocker and David Hiley. Oxford University Press.

Stevens, John, ed.
1970 *Mediaeval Carols.* Rev. ed. Musica Britannica 4. London: Stainer and Bell.
1975 *Early Tudor Songs and Carols.* Musica Britannica 36. London: Stainer and Bell.

Stock, Brian
1983 *The Implications of Literacy: Written Language and Models of Interpretation in the Eleventh and Twelfth Centuries.* Princeton University Press.

Stolz, Benjamin A., and Richard S. Shannon, eds.
1976 *Oral Literature and the Formula.* Ann Arbor, Michigan: Center for the Coordination of Ancient and Modern Studies.

Stringer, Martin D.
1989 "Liturgy and Anthropology: The History of a Relationship." *Worship* 63:503–21.

Strunk, Oliver
1955 "St. Gregory Nazianzus and the Proper Hymns for Easter." *Late Classical and Mediaeval Studies in Honor of Albert Mathias Friend, Jr.* 82–7. Ed. Kurt Weitzmann. Princeton, N.J.: Princeton University Press. Repr. in Strunk 1977:55–67.
1977 *Essays on Music in the Byzantine World.* New York: W. W. Norton.

Summers, William John
1986 "The Effect of Monasticism on Fourteenth-Century English Music." In Honegger and Prevost, eds. 1986/2:105–42.

Suppan, Wolfgang, and Alois Mauerhofer, eds.
1978 *Historische Volksmusikforschung: Kongress-Bericht Seggau, 1977.* Musikethnologische Sammelbände 2. Graz: Akademische Druck.

Szigeti, Chilianus
1967 "Les formules dans l'esthétique grégorienne." *Etudes grégoriennes* 7:1–19.

Szövérffy, Josef
1964–5 *Die Annalen der lateinischen Hymnendichtung: Ein Handbuch.* 2 vols. Die lyrische Dichtung des Mittelalters. Berlin: Erich Schmidt.

Tack, Franz
1960 *Gregorian Chant.* Anthology of Music 18. Transl. Everett Helm. Cologne: Arno Volk Verlag. Originally published as *Der gregorianische Choral.* Das Musikwerk 18. Cologne: Arno Volk Verlag, 1960.

Taft, Robert
1984 *Beyond East and West: Problems in Liturgical Understanding.* Washington, D.C.: Pastoral Press.

1985 "Response to the Berakah Award [of the North American Academy of Liturgy]: Anamnesis." *Worship* 59:304–25.

1986 *The Liturgy of the Hours in East and West: The Origins of the Divine Office and Its Meaning for Today.* Collegeville, Minnesota: Liturgical Press.

T'ahmizyan, Nikochios K. [also transliterated Tagmizian, Nikogos]

1970 "Les anciens manuscrits musicaux arméniens et les questions relatives à leur déchiffrement." *Revue des études arméniennes,* n.s. 7:267–80. Reprinted in Nersessian 1978:29–50, from which it is cited here.

1977 *Teorija muzyki v drevnej Armenij* [The Theory of Music in Ancient Armenia (in Russian)]. Yerevan: Izdatl'stvo AN Armyanskoi SSR.

1983 "De l'unité de la parole poétique et de la musique dans le tropologion (saraknoc') arménien." *Revue des études arméniennes,* n.s. 17:553–63.

Tallmadge, William H.

1984 "Folk Organum: A Study in Origins." *American Music* 2/3 (Fall 1984): 47–65.

Tanselle, G. Thomas

1983 "Classical, Biblical, and Medieval Textual Criticism and Modern Editing." *Studies in Bibliography* 36:21–68.

1986 "Historicism and Critical Editing." *Studies in Bibliography* 39:1–46.

Tarchnišvili, Michael, transl. and ed., with Julius Assfalg

1955 *Geschichte der kirchlichen georgischen Literatur auf Grund des ersten Bandes der georgischen Literaturgeschichte von K. Kekelidze.* Studi e Testi 185. Vatican City: Biblioteca Apostolica Vaticana.

Tatar, Elizabeth

1982 *Ninteenth Century Hawaiian Chant.* Pacific Anthropological Records 33. Honolulu: Department of Anthropology, Bernice P. Bishop Museum.

Temperley, Nicholas

1981 "The Old Way of Singing: Its Origins and Development." *Journal of the American Musicological Society* 34:511–44.

Tethong, Rakra

1979 "Conversations on Tibetan Musical Traditions." *Asian Music* 10/2:5–22.

Thomas, Pierre

1947 "Le chant et les chantres dans les monastères bénédictins antérieurs au XVe siècle." *Mélanges bénédictins publiées à l'occasion du XIVe centenaire de la mort de saint Benoît par les moines de l'Abbaye de Saint-Jérôme de Rome,* 405–47. S. Wandrille, Paris: Editions de Fontenelle.

Thomas, Wilhelm
1965 *Der Quempas geht um: Vergangenheit und Zukunft eines deutschen Christnachtbrauches.* Kassel: Bärenreiter.
Thompson, Bard
1989 *A Bibliography of Christian Worship.* American Theological Library Assocation Bibliography Series 25. Metuchen, N.J., and London: The Scarecrow Press.
Thompson, Ewa
1987 *Understanding Russia: The Holy Fool in Russian Culture.* Lanham, Maryland: University Press of America.
Tiersot, Julien
1905 "Des quelques cantiques populaires." *Tribune de Saint-Gervais* 11:369–77.
Timpanaro, Sebastiano
1971 *Die Entstehung der Lachmannschen Methode.* 2nd expanded ed. Hamburg: Helmut Boske.
Tindall, B. Allan
1976 "Theory in the Study of Cultural Transmission." *Annual Review of Anthropology* 5:195–208.
Tiqqun
1946 *Tiqqun laqqorim kolel chamishah chumshey Torah ʿim ha-Haftaroth ʿarukh biktav ashuri lʿumath ktav stam* [Correctorium for Readers, Containing the Five Books of the Torah with the Prophetic Readings, Arranged in Printed Hebrew Letters in Parallel with Scroll Letters (in Hebrew)]. New York: Ktav.
Tischler, Hans
1986 "Trouvère Songs: The Evolution of Their Poetic and Musical Styles." *Musical Quarterly* 72:329–40.
Tokumaru, Yoshihiko
1977 "On the method of comparison in musicology." *Asian Musics in an Asian Perspective: Report of* [*Asian Traditional Performing Arts 1976*] (brackets original), 5–11. Ed. Fumio Koizumi, Yoshihiko Tokumaru, Osamu Yamaguchi. Tokyo: Heibonsha.
Tokumaru, Yoshihiko and Yamaguti, Osamu, eds.
1986 *The Oral and the Literate in Music.* Tokyo: Academia Music.
Tomasello, Andrew
1983 *Music and Ritual at Papal Avignon 1309–1403.* Studies in Musicology 75. Ann Arbor: UMI Research Press.
Topič, Slavko
1986 *Kirchenlieder der bosnischen Katholiken.* Kölner Beiträge zur Musikforschung 147. Regensburg: Gustav Bosse.
Touliatos[-Banker], Diane
1982 "Selected Melodic Formulae of the Standard Nineteenth Century Amomos as Traced from Early Fifteenth Century Thessa-

lonian and Constantinopolitan Sources." In Raasted, ed. 1982:75–84.

1989 "Nonsense Syllables in the Music of the Ancient Greek and Byzantine Tradition." *Journal of Musicology* 7:231–43.

Traub, Andreas

1990 "Zu einigen Melodien der Wolfenbütteler Marienklage." *Neue Musik und Tradition: Festschrift Rudolf Stephan zum 65. Geburtstag,* 55–71. Ed. Josef Kuckertz, Helga de la Motte-Haber, Christian Martin Schmidt, and Wilhelm Seidel. Laaber: Laaber-Verlag.

Treitler, Leo

1974 "Homer and Gregory: The Transmission of Epic Poetry and Plainchant." *Musical Quarterly* 60:333–72.

1975 "Centonate Chant: *Übles Flickwerk* or *E pluribus unus?*" *Journal of the American Musicological Society* 28:1–23.

1981a "Transmission and the Study of Music History." In Heartz and Wade, eds. 1981:202–11.

1981b "Oral, Written, and Literate Process in the Transmission of Medieval Music." *Speculum* 56:471–91.

1982a "Observations on the Transmission of Some Aquitainian Tropes" and "A Short Commentary on 'Zur Interpretationen der Tropen.' " *Aktuelle Fragen der Musikbezogenen Mittelalterforschung: Texte zu einem Basler Kolloquium des Jahres 1975,* 11–60, 91–2. Forum Musicologicum 3. Winterthur, Switzerland: Amadeus.

1982b "The Early History of Music Writing in the West." *Journal of the American Musicological Society* 35:237–79.

1984a "From Ritual through Language to Music." *Schweizer Jahrbuch für Musikwissenschaft,* N.F. 2 (1982 [recte 1984]) 109–23.

1984b "Reading and Singing: On the Genesis of Occidental Music-Writing." *Early Music History* 4:135–208.

1984c "Orality and Literacy in the Music of the Middle Ages." *Parergon: Bulletin of the Australian and New Zealand Association for Medieval and Renaissance Studies,* n.s. 2:143–74.

1985a "Oral and Literate Style in the Regional Transmission of Tropes." *Studia Musicologica Academiae Scientiarum Hungaricae* 27:171–83.

1985b "Speaking of Jesus." In Silagi 1985:125–30.

1986 "Orality and Literacy in the Music of the European Middle Ages." In Tokumaru and Yamaguti, eds. 1986:38–56.

1988 Communication regarding Levy 1987a and D. G. Hughes 1987. *Journal of the American Musicological Society* 41:566–75.

Trend, J. B.
1920 "The Mystery of Elche." *Music and Letters* 1:145–57.
1928 "The First English Songs." *Music and Letters* 9:120–3.

Triacca, Achille M., ed.
1976 *Liturgie de l'église particulière et liturgie de l'église universelle.* Conférences Saint-Serge: XXIIe Semaine d'études liturgiques, Paris, 30 juin – 3 juillet 1975. Bibliotheca "Ephemerides Liturgicae" Subsidia 7. Rome: Edizioni Liturgiche.

Trowell, Brian
1978 "Faburden—New Sources, New Evidence: A Preliminary Survey." *Modern Musical Scholarship* 28–78. Ed. Edward Olleson. Stocksfield, England: Oriel Press.

Tsereteli, E.
1974 "Le chant traditionnel de Géorgie: son passé, son présent." *Bedi Kartlisa* 32:138–46.

Turco, Alberto
1987 "Melodie-tipo e timbri modali nell'*Antiphonale Romanum.*" *Studi Gregoriani* 3:191–241.

Turner, Victor
1976 "Ritual, Tribal and Catholic." *Worship* 50:504–26.

Turner, Victor, and Edith Turner
1978 *Image and Pilgrimage in Christian Culture: Anthropological Perspectives.* New York: Columbia University Press.

Ulff-Møller, Nina Konstantinova
1986 "The Connection between Melodic Formulas and Stereotype Text Phrases in Slavonic Stichera." *Université de Copenhague, Cahiers de l'Institut du Moyen-âge grec et latin* 54:49–60.
1989 *Transcription of the Stichera Idiomela for the Month of April from Russian Manuscripts from the Twelfth Century.* Slavistische Beiträge 236. Munich: Otto Sagner.

Underwood, Peter J.
1982 "Melodic Traditions in Medieval English Antiphoners." *Journal of the Plainsong and Medieval Music Society* 5:1–12.

Universa Laus
1980 "The Music of Christian Ritual: Universa Laus Guidelines 1980." *Universa Laus, An International Study Group for Liturgical Music: Bulletin* 30:4–15. [English translation of 1981.]
1981 "De la musique dans les liturgies chrétiennes (Document)." *La Maison-Dieu* 145 (1981, no. 1):7–23.

Unverricht, Hubert, ed.
1988 *Der Caecilianismus: Anfänge—Grundlagen—Wirkungen: Internationale Symposion zur Kirchenmusik des 19. Jahrhunderts.* Eichstätter Abhandlungen zur Musikwissenschaft 5. Tutzing: Hans Schneider.

Ursprung, Otto
1952 "Das Freisinger Petrus-Lied." *Die Musikforschung* 5:17–21.
Vagaggini, Cipriano
1976 *Theological Dimensions of the Liturgy: A General Treatise on the Theology of the Liturgy.* Transl. L. J. Doyle and W. A. Jurgens. Collegeville, Minnesota: Liturgical Press. Originally published as *Il senso teologico della liturgia.* 4th ed. Rome: Edizioni Padine, 1965.
van den Oudenrijn, M. A.
1960 "Salām laṭenta lāḥeki: Ein äthiopisches Stabat Mater." *Atti del Convegno Internazionale di Studi Etiopici (Roma 2–4 aprile 1959)* 297–322. Accademia Nazionale dei Lincei CCCLVII. Problemi Attuali di Scienza e di Cultura, quaderno 48. Rome: Accademia Nazionale dei Lincei.
Van Dijk, S. J. P.
1960 "Sources of the Roman Gradual." *Scriptorium* 14:98–100.
van Dijk, Teun A., and Walter Kintsch
1983 *Strategies of Discourse Comprehension.* Orlando, Florida: Academic Press.
Vansina, Jan
1965 *Oral Tradition: A Study in Historical Methodology.* Transl. H. M. Wright. Chicago: Aldine Publishing Co. Originally published as *De la tradition orale: Essai de methode historique.* Annales du Musée Royal de l'Afrique centrale, Sciences humaines 36. Tervuren, Belgium: Koninklijk Museum voor Midden-Afrika, 1961.
Vecchi, Giuseppe
n.d. "Teoresi e prassi del canto a due voci in Italia del duecento e nel primo trecento." *L'Ars Nova italiana del trecento* 3: *Secondo convegno internazionale . . . 1969,* 203–14. Certaldo: Edizioni Centro di Studi sull'Ars Nova Italiano del Trecento.
Velimirović, Miloš M.
1960 *Byzantine Elements in Early Slavic Chant: The Hirmologion.* 2 vols. Studies on the Fragmenta Chiliandarica Palaeoslavica 1. Monumenta Musica Byzantinae: Subsidia 4. Copenhagen: Munksgaard.
1973 "The Byzantine Heirmos and Heirmologion." *Gattungen der Musik in Einzeldarstellungen: Gedenkschrift Leo Schrade* 1: 192–244. Ed. Wulf Arlt, Ernst Lichtenhahn, Hans Oesch, and Max Haas. Bern and Munich: Francke.
Vellian, Jacob, ed.
1975 *The Romanization Tendency.* The Syrian Churches Series 8. Kottayam, India: K. P. Press.

Vinquist, Mary, and Neal Zaslaw

1970 *Performance Practice: A Bibliography.* New York: W. W. Norton.

Viret, Jacques

1986 *Le chant grégorien, musique de la parole sacrée.* n.p.: Editions l'Age d'Homme.

Vogel, Cyrille

1986 *Medieval Liturgy: An Introduction to the Sources.* National Association of Pastoral Musicians Studies in Church Music and Liturgy. Rev. and transl. William G. Storey and Niels Krogh Rasmussen. Washington, D.C.: Pastoral Press. Originally published as *Introduction aux sources de l'histoire du culte chrétien au moyen âge.* 2nd ed. Spoleto: Centro Italiano di Studi sull'Alto Medioevo, 1981.

Vogel, Cyrille, and Reinhard Elze, eds.

1963–72 *Le Pontifical romano-germanique du dixième siècle.* 3 vols. Studi e Testi 226, 227, 269. Vatican City: Biblioteca Apostolica Vaticana.

Waard, Jan de, and Eugene A. Nida.

1986 *From One Language to Another: Functional Equivalence in Bible Translating.* Nashville: Nelson.

Wagenaar-Nolthenius, Hélène

1974 *Oud als de Weg naar Rome? Vragen von de herkomst von het Gregoriaans.* [Old as the Road to Rome? Questions on the Origin of Gregorian Chant (in Dutch)]. Medelingen der Koninklijke Nederlandse Akademie van Wetenschappen 37/1. Amsterdam and London: B. V. Hollandsche Uitgevers Maattschappij.

Wagner, Peter

1903 "Histoire d'un livre de plain-chant." *Tribune de Saint-Gervais* 9:341–7, 373–82.

1907 *Der Kampf gegen die Editio Vaticana.* Graz: Styria.

1926 "Germanisches und romanisches im frühmittelalterlichen Kirchengesang." *Bericht über den Internationalen Musikwissenschaftlichen Kongress der deutschen Musikgesellschaft in Leipzig vom 4. bis 8. Juni 1925,* 21–34. Leipzig: Breitkopf & Härtel.

1930–2 *Das Graduale der St. Thomaskirche zu Leipzig (14. Jahrhundert) als Zeuge deutscher Choralüberlieferung.* 2 vols. Publikationen älterer Musik 5, 7. Leipzig: Breitkopf & Härtel. Reprinted Hildesheim: Olms, 1967.

Wagner, Roy

1984 "Ritual as Communication: Order, Meaning, and Secrecy in Melanesian Purification Rites." *Annual Review of Anthropology* 13:143–55.

Walsh, J. P. M.
1989 "Contemporary English Translations of Scripture." *Theological Studies* 50:336–58.
1990 "Dynamic or Formal Equivalence? A Response." *Theological Studies* 51:505–8.

Walter, Karl
1900 "Beiträge zur Geschichte der Choralbegleitung." *Kirchenmusikalisches Jahrbuch* 15:78–87.

Watt, David L. E.
1990 "Rising Pitch Movements in English Intonation Contours." *Word: Journal of the International Linguistic Association* 41:145–59.

Weakland, Rembert
1961–2 Review of: Moines de Solesmes 1957–62. *Notes: The Quarterly Journal of the Music Library Association* 19:62–4.
1967 "Music as Art in Liturgy." *Worship* 41:5–15.

Weber, Robert
1955 "La lettre grecque K employée comme signe de correction dans les manuscrits bibliques latins écrits 'per cola et commata.' " *Scriptorium* 9:57–63.

Wegman, Herman
1985 *Christian Worship in East and West: A Study Guide to Liturgical History*. Transl. Gordon W. Lathrop. New York: Pueblo Press. Originally published as *Geschiedenis van de Christelijke Eredienst in het Westen en in het Oosten*. Hilversum: Gooi en Sticht, 1976.

Weidinger, Joseph
1903 "Zur Choralfrage: Eine ruhige Antwort auf eine unruhige Gegenkritik." *Kirchenmusikalisches Jahrbuch* 18:162–84.

Weissenbäck, Andreas
1937 *Sacra Musica: Lexikon der katholischen Kirchenmusik*. Klosterneuburg: Verlag der Augustinus-Druckerei.

Weitzman, Michael P.
1985 "The Analysis of Open Traditions." *Studies in Bibliography* 38:82–120.
1987 "The Evolution of Manuscript Traditions." *Journal of the Royal Statistical Society*. Series A (General). Vol. 150, pt. 4:287–308.

Wellesz, Egon
1961 *A History of Byzantine Music and Hymnography*. 2nd ed. Oxford University Press; repr. 1971.
1963 "Melody Construction in Byzantine Chant." *Actes du XIIe congrès international d'études byzantines, Ochride 1961*, vol. 1, 135–51. Belgrade: Comité Yougoslave des Etudes Byzantines.

Werner, Eric
1981–2 Review of Haïk Vantoura 1976a. *Notes: The Quarterly Journal of the Music Library Association* 38:923–4.

West, Martin L.
1973 *Textual Criticism and Editorial Technique Applicable to Greek and Latin Texts.* Stuttgart: B. G. Teubner.

West, Robert, Peter Howell, and Ian Cross
1985 "Modelling Perceived Musical Structure." In Howell et al., eds. 1985:21–52.

Whallon, William
1979 "Biblical Poetry and Homeric Epic." *The Bible in its Literary Milieu: Contemporary Essays* 318–25. Ed. Vincent L. Tollers and John R. Maier. Grand Rapids, Mich.: William B. Eerdmans.

Whittington, Gregory
1988 "Screen." *Dictionary of the Middle Ages* 11:117–8.

Widengren, Geo.
1968 "Holy Book and Holy Tradition in Iran: The Problem of the Sassanid Avesta." *Holy Book and Holy Tradition: International Colloquium Held in the Faculty of Theology, University of Manchester,* 36–53. Ed. F. F. Bruce and E. G. Rupp. Grand Rapids, Michigan: William B. Eerdmans.

Williams, Edward
1968 "John Koukouzeles' Reform of Byzantine Chanting." Ph.D. diss., Yale University.

Wilson, Nigel
1987 "Variant Readings with Poor Support in the Manuscript Tradition." *Revue d'Histoire des Textes* 17:1–13.

Winter, Miriam Therese
1984 *Why Sing? Toward a Theology of Catholic Church Music.* Washington, D.C.: The Pastoral Press.

Wiora, Walter
1952 *Europäischer Volksgesang: Gemeinsame Formen in charakteristischen Abwandlungen.* Das Musikwerk 4. Cologne: Arno Volk Verlag. Appeared in translation as: *European Folk Song: Common Forms in Characteristic Modification.* Transl. Robert Kolben. Anthology of Music 4. Cologne: Arno Volk Verlag, 1966.

Wiseman, T. P.
1989 "Roman Legend and Oral Tradition." *The Journal of Roman Studies* 79:129–37.

Wohlberg, Max
1977–8 "The Music of the Synagogue as a Source of the Yiddish Folksong." *Musica Judaica* 2:21–49.

Wooldridge, H. E.
1929 *The Polyphonic Period* 1: *Method of Musical Art 330–1400.*

The Oxford History of Music. 2nd ed., rev. Percy C. Buck. London: Oxford University Press.

Wright, Craig
1989 *Music and Ceremony at Notre Dame of Paris, 500–1550.* Cambridge Studies in Music. Cambridge University Press.

Wright, Stephen K.
1986 "Scribal Errors and Textual Integrity: The Case of Innsbruck Universitätsbibliothek Cod. 960." *Studies in Bibliography* 39:79–92.

Yeivin, Israel
1980 *Introduction to the Tiberian Masorah.* Ed. and transl. E. J. Revell. Society of Biblical Literature Masoretic Studies 5. Missoula, Montana: Scholars Press.

Young, Karl
1933 *The Drama of the Medieval Church.* 2 vols. Oxford: Clarendon Press.

Yudkin, Jeremy
1989 *Music in Medieval Europe.* Englewood Cliffs, New Jersey: Prentice-Hall.

Yung, Bell
1987 "Historical Interdependency of Music: A Case Study of the Chinese Seven-String Zither." *Journal of the American Musicological Society* 40:82–91.

Index